Praise for the First Edition

I like the [book's] uniquely "rhetorical" approach to terrorism. . . . I think Tuman's is the *only* full length book on the subject, with a specific communication focus.

The first edition—but now especially the revised edition—helps my students understand how "terrorists" employ political propaganda, how the governments they oppose respond with their own propagandistic messages, and how both of these message sets are "rhetorical." The book also helps students distinguish between ethical and unethical uses of rhetoric (as propaganda), especially as these occur in the larger context of the "war on terror." The book makes it easier for students to comprehend different definitions of "terrorism," to trace our national conception of what constitutes a "terrorist," and to make critical judgments about propagandistic messages concerning terrorism.

—Kenneth S. Zagacki, *North Carolina State University*

[The text] begins with a solid foundation of theory and definitions and relates these to real world concerns. In addition, students enjoy the text; it is clear, well written, and organized in a manner that helps them understand how foundational theory relates to real world problems.

—Terry Lynn Cornwell, *Liberty University*

In *Communicating Terror*, Joseph Tuman offers a compelling look at one of the more commonly acknowledged, but rarely examined, aspects of terrorism: the perceptual and rhetorical aspects that color the way we interpret and study the phenomenon. Few assessments of terrorism have explored the associated implications the way in which Tuman does. This book examines terrorism as it is constructed and used to frame audience interpretations and responses, either in support of or opposition to the violent group. [T]here is considerable value in his examination of the mechanisms used by terrorists and their opponents to shape and manipulate perceptions of the struggle. In assessing terrorism as a communicative process, Tuman highlights the emotional aspects of fear and uncertainty inherent in terrorism while deconstructing the process of forming and conveying meaning in a way useful for those seeking a fuller understanding of terrorism's dynamics. Tuman does this admirably by incorporating a keen understanding of symbolism, oratory, and mass media's use of verbal and visual cues.

—Daniel S. Gressang IV, *Joint Military Intelligence College*

Professor Tuman has done yeoman's work to give us a concise presentation of these issues from a communication perspective.

—Jonathan David Tankel, *Indiana University Purdue University, Fort Wayne*

Communicating Terror is a tremendously insightful discussion of how terrorists attempt to communicate with multiple target audiences. It begins with a highly useful discussion of the struggle by academic specialists to formulate a consensual definition of terrorism, including how terrorists define themselves. Another valuable contribution to the discipline is Tuman's formulation of a communications model that graphically displays the multiple audiences that terrorists hope will respond to their a[...] [...]ed as a textbook for students and resource for professi[...]

—[...] [...]ter

Communicating
TERROR

edition
2

Communicating
TERROR

The Rhetorical Dimensions of Terrorism

2 edition

Joseph S. Tuman
San Francisco State University

SAGE

Los Angeles | London | New Delhi
Singapore | Washington DC

For information:

SAGE Publications, Inc.
2455 Teller Road
Thousand Oaks,
   California 91320
E-mail: order@sagepub.com

SAGE Publications Ltd.
1 Oliver's Yard
55 City Road
London EC1Y 1SP
United Kingdom

SAGE Publications India Pvt. Ltd.
B 1/I 1 Mohan Cooperative
   Industrial Area
Mathura Road, New Delhi 110 044
India

SAGE Publications Asia-Pacific
   Pte. Ltd.
33 Pekin Street #02-01
Far East Square
Singapore 048763

Printed in the United States of America

Library of Congress Cataloging-in-Publication Data

Tuman, Joseph S.
Communicating terror: the rhetorical dimensions of terrorism/Joseph S. Tuman.—2nd ed.
   p. cm.
Includes bibliographical references and index.
ISBN 978-1-4129-7324-3 (pbk.)
   1. Terrorism. 2. Terrorism and mass media. I. Title.

HV6431.T845 2010
363.32501′4—dc22   2009020521

This book is printed on acid-free paper.

09 10 11 12 13 10 9 8 7 6 5 4 3 2 1

Acquisitions Editor:	Todd R. Armstrong
Editorial Assistant:	Nathan Davidson
Production Editor:	Brittany Bauhaus
Copy Editor:	QuADS Prepress (P) Ltd.
Typesetter:	C&M Digitals (P) Ltd.
Proofreader:	Dennis Webb
Indexer:	Diggs Publication Services, Inc.
Cover Designer:	Bryan Fishman
Marketing Manager:	Jennifer Reed Banando

Contents

Introduction

Humans perceive events through the prism of their own worldview and life experience as these are in turn affected by culture (a loaded, often abused term), education, age, national origin, philosophical or religious underpinnings (or the absence thereof), and the like. All of us have shared the experience of witnessing an event and then reacting with absolute surprise to hear others who had also been present describe that event in totally different ways that were at times even contradictory to our own perception. For example, two partners in a relationship may perceive very differently an issue that divides them, or partisan baseball fans may recall bitterly how they saw a pitch the umpire called as a third strike. In such instances, however, differences in perception will seldom be categorized with academic labels such as *worldview* or *life experience*; more often, they will be described as the product of one's *agenda*. In this way, it is suggested that we construct our perceptions of events according to the personal *agenda* it serves for us. Although this term is overly generalized and is not as useful as a more specific descriptor of human biases and motivations, it may still serve our purposes when we focus on the controversial topic that serves as the subject of this book: terrorism.

What is terrorism? Where does the word come from, and how is it used? For how long has it been a part of our vocabulary? How has it changed throughout the centuries? You may be surprised to know the answers. The word has origins and meanings in many cultures. Those who have studied it in the past four decades have often given contradictory definitions of the word that in turn have fueled controversy about how serious a problem it presents, whatever moral legitimacy it claims or lacks, and how nations and the global community should respond to it. We will address these definitions more fully in the first two chapters of this book. For the time being, it serves to note that the existence of so many definitions raises questions about whose interests or agendas are being served by doing the defining. All of us (myself included) are the products of life experience that informs our own worldview and influences the way we may approach this topic. The reader is cautioned, therefore, to exhibit at least a very healthy curiosity about what any writer asserts about terrorism. In that sense, I encourage you to employ your best critical thinking skills when approaching this topic and those who write about it.

And lest I be accused of preaching one thing and practicing another, let me also encourage the reader to start that critical thinking with me. Who am I? What, if any, is my agenda? Academically, my background is in political science and law—a seemingly good combination for this subject. My research and teaching interests, however, are in communication studies (political and legal communications). When I wrote the first edition of this book about six years ago, there were faculty members in my own university who chafed at the notion that I might examine terrorism as communication, and one professor in my own department (my mentor, no less) who objected to my placing the word *terrorism* in the same sentence with *rhetoric*. As I publish this second edition of *Communicating Terror*, however, I find myself in a world where these associations are not as controversial as they once seemed. Indeed, the central premise of the first edition, associating terrorism and communication, is now more commonly accepted. That acceptance has allowed my own knowledge and awareness of the subject to be assisted by personal experience, which gives one a different sensitivity and insight than what you might ordinarily find in an academic text. In 2004, the success of the first edition resulted in my being invited to participate in an international conference on terrorism and Islam, held in Riyadh, the capital of Saudi Arabia. The conference was attended by theologians and social science scholars from around the world, encompassing a variety of disciplines. Initially, a sizable contingent of scholars from the United States agreed to attend, but that number dwindled to a handful once the State Department issued a warning that a terrorist threat was imminent in Saudi Arabia. Stubbornly, I chose to attend. Less than 24 hours after my arrival, and only 1 hour after my first presentation at the conference, a man drove a truck laden with explosives to the base of a large government building not far from the university where the conference was being hosted. Although blocked by barricades and police officers who shot at his truck and physically tried to restrain him through the driver's window, the man persevered and detonated his bomb. The resulting powerful blast ripped through the apex of the large building, pulling off sections of wall and shattering glass, killing 10 people and severely injuring nearly 150 more. One of the deceased was an 11-year-old girl. The act of terrorism was felt throughout Riyadh, and acutely at our conference; in a matter of hours, what had been an open and candid academic exchange of ideas became something else. Something personal. This was no longer a subject we could write or research about from the luxury of safe academic distance. Every one of us there was aware that the bombing was a direct response to the presence of our conference. Although I had felt a similar kind of involvement and connection during 9/11, it was still something I experienced from a distance and mostly (like the rest of the country) through the medium of television. That day in Riyadh added something to my awareness of terrorism. Partly, it was fear. Maybe, a greater respect for what I write about. At the same time, it reinforced my perspective that this very public act of violence was intended to be communicative. The terrorists involved did not want our public conference to address how Islam condemned terrorism.

My experience drove and in part fueled the writing of this second edition. Although I am well versed in this subject matter, I do not intend to offer you a book that merely restates much of the very good work that has been authored by historians, sociologists, political scientists, criminologists, and international relations experts. Thus, I am not interested in restating historical debates about terrorism as a moral response to imperialism or colonialism or semantic discussion about whether terrorism and guerrilla actions are distinct. I will not attempt psychological profiling of terrorists, nor will I attempt to resolve age-old international disputes, such as those in Northern Ireland or in the Middle East. That ground has already been covered by scholars, thinkers, and politicians who are far better equipped to address these issues. Instead, in this book, I wish to address terrorism by playing to my own particular interests, strengths, and background in political and legal communications. I will approach this subject by delving into its communicative properties and rhetorical dimensions.

To be clear, in the coming chapters I will argue that the meaning of terrorism is socially constructed. By that I mean that what we call terrorism is different and distinct from murder, assault, arson, destruction of property, or the threat of the same, primarily because the impact of terrorist violence and destruction reaches more than the immediate targeted victims. Although this in no way diminishes the pain and suffering of those immediate victims of terror, it does suggest that this violence and destruction becomes terrorism primarily because of its additional capacity to communicate message and meaning to a larger set of audiences.

In Chapter 1, I explore the different origins of terrorism, and in Chapter 2, I offer a new definition of terrorism chiefly as a process of communication between terrorists and multiple target audiences. I will further argue that the way all audiences engage in discourse about terrorism is the manner in which we negotiate the meaning of terrorism. At this level, terrorism may also be seen as rhetorical, for there are several ways that rhetoric envelops the communication process by which we negotiate the meaning of this subject. These rhetorical strands form the rest of the book.

In Chapter 3, we will reexamine the process of defining terrorism as the product of rhetorical choice, distinguishing between defining and labeling, and examining how the act of definition involves empowerment and marginalization. New to this chapter will be material concerning both the conscious and unconscious use of definitions and labels, and within the context of empowerment and marginalization, a treatment of colonialism and Orientalism.

In Chapter 4, we consider a different rhetorical strand by examining how terrorist violence and destruction may be seen as symbolic and once more how the meaning of these symbols is negotiated by and between different target audiences. Here, I review symbolism in terror by considering specific acts of violence, means, and tools of terror.

In Chapter 5, I extend this discussion about symbolism and terror by looking at specific targets, both temporal and spatial, for their rhetorical properties. In this chapter, I will make use of specific rhetorical theories of criticism (both dramatism and postmodernism/ ideological criticism) to examine the symbolism of attacks on intersecting religious holidays, as well as physical locations such as a theater in Moscow or the World Trade Center in New York.

In Chapters 6 and 7, I examine how public rhetoric about terrorism is constructed and in what ways it may affect discourse between targeted audiences. Chapter 6 will introduce the reader to several tools for critically examining public oratory. Readers here will learn to evaluate and understand how this rhetoric works and why it affects social construction of terrorism. Chapter 7 offers three artifacts of speeches for case studies. Although there are many examples of public pronouncements by world leaders to consider here, in this chapter I focus on the American presidency and, for reasons of space and economy, on two influential speeches of President George W. Bush concerning September 11, as well as a significant speech (in response to Bush) by Osama bin Laden on the eve of the 2004 presidential election.

In Chapters 8 and 9, I consider a final rhetorical strand, terrorism and mass media, to explore how mediated imagery also affects and sometimes preconditions our negotiation of the meaning of terrorism.

Specifically, in Chapter 8, I examine mass media as both entertainment and news, broadcast and print media, new and old media, and free and paid media. I also offer an overview of rhetoric and media criticism, before settling on critical media and agenda-setting and framing.

In Chapter 9, I apply these different perspectives of mass media (entertainment and news, broadcast and print, new and old, free and paid) to assess the symbiotic relationship between terrorism and each of these forms of media, *and* to uncover how these forms of media both precondition and eventually contour public discourse about terrorism.

The end product of this second edition should be a more fully developed set of tools with which to understand and see terrorism differently than before. As suggested above, I do not presume that any particular solution to this problem can be immediately found in this approach, although I do believe that giving a different set of tools to understand terrorism is an important first step to developing a response and comprehending why and how it has the capacity to affect us so deeply.

This explains my agenda and intentions in this work. It is also important for the reader, you, to consider your own life experience and worldview when approaching terrorism. What is your agenda here? This will be one of many books on terrorism to emerge post–September 11 *and* since the 2008 presidential election. The tragedy of 9/11, and the resulting *war on terror,* may be the primary reason you are studying this topic in the first place. Consequently, there are three notions I want you to consider in approaching this writing.

First, be aware that this book will include analysis of 9/11 as part of a larger perspective of terrorism and rhetoric but that it is not just a book about 9/11. Indeed, I intend to cover a great many more examples of rhetoric and terror in the United States and around the world. That being said, I do not want to suggest that the events of September 11 and all that has followed play only a small role in this book. It would be foolish, if not impossible, to approach this topic without including this most obvious and contemporary of examples. I do, however, want to stress that 9/11 will be viewed in the context of the larger issues presented by rhetoric and terrorism.

Second, you would be well served to search your own feelings about 9/11 and how "objective" you feel about the topic of terrorism and rhetoric. How has President Bush's "war on terror" in Afghanistan or Iraq changed (if at all) your perceptions about 9/11? How have any of these events made you feel? Have they changed your view of the world or the United States's role in the world? Have they changed or altered the way you define terrorism? Have they affected your perception of who might be a terrorist? Where do these perceptions come from? Some of what you will read may challenge these perceptions or at least add to your knowledge of the subject generally.

Third, and feeding off this last point, remember that this work is intended only to provide analytical tools and ideas for understanding what terrorism is and how its meaning is constructed. Nothing in this writing should ever be construed as an endorsement of violence and destruction or a trivialization of the very real pain and suffering of its victims in any place or at any time. Of necessity, the study of this subject and its examples requires a sense of emotional distance—being able to look at the subject matter as an observer and not as someone affected by it. This is the conceit of much that is social science, and, on occasion, this emotional distance may be seen as implying a lack of compassion and empathy. If my experience in Riyadh taught me anything, it was that you cannot approach a subject such as this without being honest about the fact that we are all to some degree affected and emotionally influenced by it. While I will not ignore my experience, I do not intend to allow it to dominate how I write or what I say about terrorism. My intention is simple: By conceptualizing terrorism as communicative and rhetorical, I seek to broaden our perspective on this complex social issue by applying ideas from the field of communication studies.

No work like this can result without the very significant contributions of other people. Consequently, I would like to offer my thanks for review of the manuscript proposal of this second edition to J. Rocky Colavito of Butler University; Terri Lynn Cornwell of Liberty University; Kevin Douglas Kuswa from The University of Richmond; J. Gregory Payne of Emerson College; Mark A. Pollock of Loyola University Chicago, School of Communication; Bob Schuessler from North Seattle Community College; Jonathan David Tankel of Indiana University, Purdue University, Fort Wayne (IPFW); and Kenneth S. Zagacki of North Carolina State University. I owe additional appreciation for the review of the first edition of this book to Douglas Fraleigh at California State University, Fresno; Nicholas Burnett at California State University, Sacramento; and Gregory Payne at Emerson College, for valuable insights and suggestions in reviewing the complete manuscript, and to Patricia Palmerton at Hamline University, Randall Rogan at Wake Forest University, Ramona Rush at the University of Kentucky, Mehdi Semati at Eastern Illinois University, and Richard Vatz at Towson University for kindly reviewing early drafts of the first edition of the book and providing valuable feedback about the project, as well. I also thank my friend and colleague Hank Plante of KPIX-CBS for asking questions that initially provoked my thinking about this topic, my student assistant Earl Neconie, and UC Berkeley librarian John D. Berry for invaluable assistance in searching for and acquiring photographs used in this second edition. I offer additional thanks to my acquisitions editor Todd Armstrong, his assistant Aja Baker, marketing manager Jennifer Reed Banando, editorial director Michele Sordi, and executive vice president Alison Mudditt at SAGE Publications for their assistance in shepherding this project from a conversation in my office to the finished product you now hold.

Final thanks must go to my children, Helen and Nathaniel, who both gave up parts of their summer to help their father with research concerning the Mollie Maguires and the Ku Klux Klan, as well as to my loving wife, Kirsten, who graciously looked the other way again as I worked on yet another manuscript, joined at the hip with my laptop, when we were supposed to be enjoying the newfound freedom that comes from being empty nesters. A wise person once told me that a writer's family and loved ones can be his or her best resource.

I will argue later in this book that terror succeeds because it creates a sense of fear—a fear and dread of the unknown. Psychologists tell us that we fear and hate that which we do not understand. If such is the case, this book is offered primarily to engender understanding. If we understand how terrorism operates to affect us, we may approach a response to it that is not the product of our own fears but instead the result of reasoned and comprehensive thinking.

—Joseph S. Tuman

1

The Struggle to
Define Terrorism

❖ ❖ ❖

In the past four decades, much has been written about terrorism and terrorists, some of it focused on the psychological profile of who a terrorist is,[1] what his or her motives are for engaging in terrorism,[2] and how governments should respond.[3] A lively debate has also ensued between academics, self-anointed experts, researchers, and many politicians as to what constitutes terrorism. In the time since September 11, 2001, this debate has taken on an extra sense of urgency, as the definition of terrorism has expanded to reflect the modern realities of extremism in religion.[4] This ongoing debate provides a useful starting place for our discussion in this chapter, as it provides a powerful intersection between the rhetoric that defines terrorism and the public discourse that is affected (and affects). To return to an earlier stated question: what exactly is terrorism?

❖ DEFINING TERRORISM

It should come as little or no surprise that the controversy over defining terrorism is long-standing in both the academic and the geopolitical senses. For decades, academicians and theorists have fared no better at defining the word than governments and the experts they employ.

As I shall describe shortly, this has led to a multiplicity of possibilities and has created its own kind of chaos about the word. *Chaos* describes the state of things today concerning definitions; but it does not help us in understanding how the word came to be so complicated.

The Action Without the Label

Terrorism today may seem like a relatively new phenomenon, but in truth, the practice of terrorizing for political, ideological, religious, and/or economic purposes extends back many thousands of years and across many different cultures. Two specific examples suffice to explain how the violent actions of individuals and groups advancing a religious or political agenda could be seen as terrorism, even if the word was not associated with their activities at the time.

In the first century AD, a Jewish group known as the Zealots-Sicarii operated for nearly 25 years in defense of ancient Judea (what is today Israel), with the multiple goals of inciting an uprising against the large Greek population that lived there and violent insurrection against the Romans, who governed both the Greeks and the indigenous Jewish population, and against Jews who had (at least in the eyes of the Zealots-Sicarii) grown too comfortable with Roman rule. Although little is known of the group, the best historical record of its existence was offered by Flavius Josephus, in his work *Jewish Antiquities* and another shorter document titled *Jewish War*. Josephus himself served as an advisor on Jewish affairs for the Roman rulers Vespasian and his son Titus. As described by Josephus, the Zealots-Sicarii were one of the four "philosophical" sects of Judea and among the most strict in their observance of the rules and traditions of their religion. Their impassioned religious outlook earned them the name "zealot"—from the Greek word *zelos*, meaning "strong spirit"—while the name "sicarii" was derived from their weapon of choice—the dagger—also called *sica*. Josephus wrote,

> The Sicarii committed murders in broad daylight in the heart of Jerusalem. The holy days were their special seasons when they would mingle with the crowd carrying short daggers concealed under their clothing with which they stabbed their enemies. Thus, when they fell, the murderers joined in cries of indignation, and through this plausible behavior were never discovered.... The panic created was more alarming than the calamity itself.[5]

Whether aimed at Greeks, Romans, or other Jews, their tactics proved so successful that they did indeed inspire a revolt against

Roman rule—with the unintended result that the swift and brutal Roman response resulted in the destruction of the Temple of David and the mass execution (by crucifixion) of 2,000 people. The remaining members of the Zealot-Sicarii had to retreat to Massada, where they heroically resisted Roman siege for three years, before electing to commit mass suicide rather than surrender and accept defeat.

In later generations, their activities would also inspire two other rebellions against Rome—the combination of which would eventually lead to the complete destruction of Jewish living centers in Egypt and Cyprus and the mass exodus of Jews from Judea—beginning the exile and state of *Diaspora* that Jews endured for nearly 2,000 years.[6]

The activities of the Zealot-Sicarii contrast in an interesting and perhaps ironic way with that of the *Assassins*, also known as the *Ismailis-Nizari*, who operated between 1090 and 1275 AD. Originating as one of the members of the Ismailis—a group that was formed in 765 AD to show allegiance to Isma'il, the older son of the sixth Imam, Ja'far, who had his succession to his father's position taken from him by his younger brother Musa—this group created a schism between those followers of Islam who believed that the firstborn son should be next in succession and others who supported Musa. Spanning the course of some 200 years, the Ismailis-Nizaris operated originally in northern Iran, where they occupied a fortress in Alamat in the Elburz mountains, and later attempted to spread their influence throughout the growing Muslim world, including Egypt and Syria.

Like the Jewish Zealots described before, the Ismailis—who came to be eventually known as the Assassins—became legendary for killing targeted individuals only by using their daggers and for orchestrating their murders in crowded places, usually on religious holidays guaranteed to draw a large amount of public attention. While it was not uncommon for them to dress in disguise for their crimes,[7] it was also the case that many of their assassinations took place in situations where a younger assassin had been placed in a relationship with his target/victim (e.g., as a young man in the service of a high official). Gaining the victim's trust, the assassin would then await an opportunity for murder.

The assassinations of officials and leaders created opportunities to draw attention to a cause,[8] but they were just as easily used to create panic among a leader or official's troops[9] and to sow confusion and panic within the Muslim community.

Although they showed considerable success in maintaining their presence in Iran, and to a lesser extent in Syria, the Assassins eventually disappeared for reasons similar to those that extinguished the Zealot-Sicarii: Their activities provoked a backlash—in the case of the Assassins, a dismantling of the sect by the Maymak Sultan Baybars.

While the choice of a weapon and the willingness to use it in a public place were direct similarities with the Jewish Zealot-Sicariis, key differences for the Assassins could be found in the way they overtook and even built large fortresses,[10] integrated themselves within a local community (typically one in which poorer Muslims would be susceptible to their messages), and spread their own propaganda with the help of missionaries. In many ways, they were more like a political party.[11]

While both of these groups engaged in politically motivated forms of public murder, designed to sow panic and unrest, neither group was ever referred to as a terrorist organization nor were their actions (at least at the time) referred to as terrorism. That word as a label with a definable meaning did not yet exist.

Tracing the Roots of the Word as a Label

Etymology is the study of the origin and evolution of words—in full recognition that language is organic, capable of change depending on the needs of its users over time and place. Where did the word *terrorism* come from? The original use of the word in English is often believed to have derived from the Latin word *terrere*, meaning "to tremble." When combined with the French suffix *isme*, referencing "to practice," it becomes more like "to practice the trembling," or "to cause or create the trembling." *Trembling* here obviously is another word for fear, panic, and anxiety—what we today call terror. A group of revolutionaries in France called the Jacobins used the term when self-reflexively describing and justifying their own actions in a decisive period of the French Revolution. The meaning of this word in French was mentioned in 1798. The French, who for centuries have practiced a kind of cultural introspection and have always been scrupulous about examining their language to purge it of useless words or to provide more precise definitions for words and expressions (they still follow this practice to this day!), in that year published the supplement for the dictionary of the Academie Francaise, in which the term was explained as the "systeme, regime de la terreur."[12]

The Jacobins were revolutionaries who began their existence as members of a political club, formed originally in 1789 by members of the French middle class. Their initial function was political, and their intent was to "support the transition to a constitutional monarchy in a progressive fashion . . . the Jacobins of 1789 believed that discussion and education at the local level would facilitate the acceptance of a new constitution."[13] In this early period, they were known as Societies of the Friends of the Constitution, and they became responsible for advancing the revolution by priming public opinion against the royal family and putting pressure on the government. In 1792, the royal monarchy was overthrown, and the club became known as the Friends of Liberty and Equality—and with that, the membership of the Jacobins was altered to include lower social class members, or the "common people."[14] This expanding base of the Jacobins would now match the traditional membership of the middle class with members of the so-called *sans-culottes*.[15] The *sans-culottes* in these clubs were

> not day-laborers or even wage earners, and they were most assuredly not from the bottom rung of the indigent. The sans-culottes, rather, were master craftsmen, journeymen, artisans, small shopkeepers, minor clerks and functionaries, and common soldiers. These types in growing numbers joined those citizens of the middle class—lawyers, bureaucrats, teachers, merchants, landed proprietors—who were already well installed in the clubs.[16]

The Jacobins were led in their efforts by Maximillian Robespierre, who would later help lead the National Convention (a constitutional and legislative assembly, formed between 1792 and 1794) and the infamous Committee of Public Safety. Of the period of history that would forever be known as The Terror, Robespierre argued,

> If virtue be the spring of a popular government in times of peace, the spring of that government during a revolution is virtue combined with terror: virtue, without which terror is destructive; terror, without which virtue is impotent. Terror is only justice prompt, severe and inflexible; it is then an emanation of virtue; it is less a distinct principle than a natural consequence of the general principle of democracy, applied to the most pressing wants of the country.[17]

With the assistance of his Jacobin followers, Robespierre helped usher in a period wherein terror was the policy of the new French Republic. By the use of the new policy, the public was encouraged to report on anyone who might have been an enemy of the revolution and/or a beneficiary of the previous economic and political system (the latter was assumed to be the cause of the former). Through public trials, denunciations, humiliations, forced confessions, and eventually public executions, The Terror aimed at selectively stamping out any resistance to the revolution while at the same time centralizing the absolute power of the new government. Between September 5, 1793,[18] and July 27, 1794,[19] some 2,625 people were executed by guillotine in Paris and another 16,600 throughout the country. These were only official "legal" figures, however; although estimates differ, the total number of deaths caused by The Terror may have been between 200,000 and 300,000 when all sources are considered.[20]

The English version of this word, *terrorism*, owes to an Englishman's characterization of the bloodshed he had observed from afar in France, where the same revolution was under way. Using an Anglicized version of the same word he had understood the Jacobins to use in describing their own behavior, Sir Edmund Burke wrote of the revolution in France and warned about "thousands of those hell hounds called terrorists" who were creating havoc and panic in the country.[21] Burke's, *Reflections on the Revolution in France*, reads less like a set of reflections and more like a set of criticisms. Beyond the usual cultural, nationalist motivations for his critique (he was, after all, an Englishman describing the French!)—in one instance, he describes the revolutionaries as a "college of armed fanatics" who mean to promote "assassination, robbery, fraud, faction, oppression, and impiety"[22]— Burke's commentary must also be seen in the context of the social class position he occupied. As an aristocrat, Burke may have been concerned over the threat of the example set in France, where a popular, though violent, revolution had thrown out a monarchy and begun the elimination of the ruling class. Many countries with governments based on monarchy, and with aristocratic classes supported by the crown, would in turn feel threatened by this revolution and be forced to usher in popular rule and democracy. Though Burke did not himself define *terrorism* or *terrorist* in his *Reflections*, he as much as provided the definition by operationalizing it in several ways. In Burke's view, a terrorist was a *fanatic*; therefore, it could be inferred that a terrorist does not follow any means of logic or reason to justify his or her actions. Moreover, a terrorist was an *assassin*—a *murderer*—and a *thief* and a *fraud*—not to mention an *oppressor*. None of these labels describes an individual whose characteristics could be admired or sympathized with. Murderers and thieves were and are criminals. Along with frauds and oppressors, they were and are viewed as lacking a moral center. In providing such an implicit comparison, Burke had begun the process of defining terrorism and terrorists and delegitimizing their behavior; but, as the reader may have noticed, the words *terrorism* and *terrorist* as Burke employed them were perhaps more labels than definitions.

As we shall see, more contemporary attempts at defining terrorism have focused on those against whom this violence is practiced. Much has been made in many definitions about terrorism targeting "innocents" or "noncombatants." In this capacity, it is also worth noting that the victims of the French Revolution (the period is often referred to as the Reign of Terror) were many but chiefly those of the ruling aristocratic class. The vast majority were not military officers or law enforcement officials. Indeed, those who lost their heads at the guillotine were often private citizens—what we might describe as civilians today. But, to the revolutionaries, such distinctions would have been frivolous; for them, these individuals were not innocent or guiltless in any sense of the term. Although these victims had never raised armed opposition to the revolution, they had benefited from the previous state of affairs in a system that brutally oppressed the members of the lower classes. Terrorism after that time came to reference a kind of violent, physical intimidation—real or merely threatened—designed to achieve some objective. In modern terms, we often think of such activity in criminal law as extortion—for example, a shop owner being forced to pay "protection money" to a local gang of young criminals in order to protect his business from destruction or molestation. Of course, in every extortion situation, the money is paid to protect the victim from the very individuals offering the protection!

Over time, however, the word *terrorist* was not used synonymously with *extortion*. Although terrorists might indeed be extortionists, it was not assumed that all extortionists were terrorists. The example initially provided by Burke supplied the difference in meaning, for critical in his use of the term that the Jacobins had themselves used was the *context* within which the label applied. The "hell hound" terrorists that he described followed a crude ideology, pursuing political change by revolution. Thus, terrorism was tied to ideology and politics—usually, as in the French example, in a battle waged over power and control.

Throughout the next two centuries, *terrorism* was used often to describe violence in confrontations over power and control around the globe, including labor disputes and violent protest against the management and over ownership of the means of production; revolutions and armed struggles to overthrow or to achieve independence and statehood from foreign occupiers; and violent struggles over supremacy of ideologies, including those of anarchy, syndicalism, socialism, Marxism, communism, fascism, and capitalism. *Terrorism* was used to describe the activities of groups such as the Molly Maguires (coal miners agitating for more rights), the Industrial Workers of the World, Bolsheviks, and many others. Ideological references for *terrorism* also extended to religion and began to include the battles waged between Islam and Judaism, as well as between Hinduism and Islam and between Christianity and all the aforementioned groups. Common to all of these were the elements of violence *or the threat of violence,* often in a revolution or an armed struggle for control. Also critical to the use of the term was the notion that this use or threat of violence was in some manner outside the accepted norms or rules for war or battle. Of course, this last point in turn depended on an additional factor in the evolution of the word—for it assumed that there were norms and standards for combat. Those who might follow such norms were usually thought to be those with organized, disciplined armed forces—soldiers who would play by the rules, according to some system of honor. Those with the means to wield such an armed force were, of course, nation-states, and as the aforementioned armed struggles suggest, it was nation-states who might ultimately become the targets of some kinds of terrorism.

Of course, it was and is possible that these same nation-states might themselves practice terrorism. Although the Jacobins offered an example of terrorism that seemed the product of revolution from the ground up, in point of fact, the terrorism they practiced was the aforementioned policy of the state itself (in the new revolutionary government). In this respect, they were in fact hardly unique. Nearly every era offers examples of governments that terrorize civilians: the Assyrian empire, once the largest in the world, built by brutalizing all the people it conquered; Adolph Hitler's Third Reich, involving the systematic extermination of millions of Jews, Gypsies, gay people, Poles, and others; and the actions of American Lieutenant William Calley in the massacre of an entire village of civilians at My Lai in Vietnam. History is filled with such examples, and over time, many who studied terrorism began to question why the use of this word referenced intimidation practiced by individuals against innocent victims, designed to coerce governments and nation-states, but did not seem to cover the multitude of examples of terror practiced by government on other people.

From this question emerged a school of thought distinguishing terrorism *from below,* meaning terrorism practiced by those outside the dominant group, usually focusing their violence and threats on those above, and terrorism *from above,* referring to coercive intimidation practiced by the state directly or sponsored by the state indirectly and practiced by surrogates.

This kind of division allowed for a broader inclusion of types of terrorism, including individual or group dissent terrorism, criminal enterprise terrorism, and state-sponsored or direct state terrorism. Even with these distinctions, however, there was very little progress toward arriving at a precise and agreed-on meaning for terrorism. Of course, language scholars might point out that many words are polysemic (capable of multiple or contradictory definitions),[23] but here, the variety of possibilities only exacerbated the confusion over the meaning—largely because the meaning of the word depended rather heavily on *who* was providing the definition.

Academic Definitions

Over time, academicians and theorists have suggested literally hundreds of different definitions for terrorism.[24] Though many of these definitions are similar, they are subtly different, often projecting the agenda of the author. For example, Martha Crenshaw has written that

> terrorism is a conspiratorial style of violence calculated to alter the attitudes and behavior of multitude audiences. It targets the few in a way that claims the attention of the many. Terrorism is not mass or collective violence but rather the direct activity of small groups.[25]

Though Crenshaw's definition recognizes that terrorism is directed at certain audiences, she also limits her definition to small-group activity, effectively precluding any discussion of state-based terrorism.

Walter Laqueur, whose book *The Age of Terrorism* is considered by many to be a classic on the history of terrorism, has suggested that

> terrorism is the use or the threat of the use of violence, a method of combat, or a strategy to achieve certain targets. . . . [I]t aims to induce a state of fear in the victim, that is ruthless and does not conform with humanitarian rules. . . . [P]ublicity is an essential factor in the terrorist strategy.[26]

Laqueur's definition is both similar to and different from Crenshaw's. Note that both authors want to stay away from state-sponsored terrorism, although Laqueur acknowledges that states are capable of and have engaged in violence that might indeed be considered terrorist. He distinguishes them, however, by suggesting that they do not employ terror on a systematic basis. Laqueur's definition here also raises the suggestion that there is some normative standard (which he calls "humanitarian rules") against which to judge what is normal and acceptable and what is unacceptable and abnormal—and terrorist.

Brigitte Nacos observed a trend in recent years to define terrorism primarily as bottom-up, while ignoring any role the state may play. She comments,

> It might well be that this latest shift in the definition of terrorism works in favor of violence perpetuated by governments in that they often escape a negative connotation. But short of a wholesale change in the meaning of terrorism, I suggest a solution that can bridge the

definitional controversies. The starting point is the notion of mass-mediated terrorism and its definition as political violence against noncombatants/innocents that is committed *with the intention to publicize the deed, to gain publicity and thereby public and government attention* [italics added].[27]

In contrast, Annamarie Olivero, in her work *The State of Terror*, has argued that terrorism

contains its own rhetoric, which has been transformed throughout history by different states. By claiming to be defining a type of violence, i.e., one that threatened the site of legitimate violence (the state), it is clear that this term is reserved for the art of statecraft.[28]

From Olivero's perspective, the defining of terrorism is something in which states and their agents (including those in the academy) engage to distinguish illegitimate violence and dissent (practiced by those in opposition to the state) from legitimate violence and repression practiced by the state itself. In this way, terrorism is whatever violence is practiced against the state. Olivero, unlike Crenshaw and Laqueur, is quite clear that the defining of terrorism should and does include this kind of state-sponsored or practiced terror.

State Definitions

The state itself has been no more consistent in defining terrorism than have members of the academy. For example, U.S. law defines terrorism as "premeditated, politically motivated violence against non-combatant targets by subnational groups or clandestine agents."[29] Note how the official legal version of this definition focuses on activity that is premeditated (intentional) political violence by *subnational groups or clandestine agents*; this definition focuses on violence that is done intentionally by groups at a substate level.

In contrast, the U.S. Department of Defense (DOD) has defined terrorism as "the calculated use of violence or the threat of violence against individuals or property, to inculcate fear, intended to coerce or to intimidate government or societies in the pursuit of goals that are political, ideological or religious."[30] It might surprise you to see that different parts of the federal government define this term differently. Doubtless, this was one of the reasons encouraging President George W. Bush to urge reorganization of homeland defense in 2002, in order to coordinate the flow of information between departments and agencies. How is this definition different from that provided by federal law? How is it the same?

Both definitions tend to limit terrorism to that directed *from below*—which is hardly surprising. But note how the DOD definition suggests that terrorism is designed to inculcate fear in the public—but with the purpose of intimidating or coercing the state. This definition suggests that terrorism creates political leverage from the frightened public to influence government or state policy. It also suggests that terrorism involves violence and destruction (against people or property) or the threat of the same.

But, as suggested, not all parts of the federal government are in agreement. At the time of this writing (2009), the Federal Bureau of Investigation (FBI) defines terrorism as "the unlawful use of force or violence against persons or property to intimidate or coerce a government, the civilian population, or any segment thereof, in furtherance of political or social objectives."[31] This definition starts out sounding similar to the others, but it concludes differently, for it extends the possible motives for a terrorist's behavior to include "social objectives."

The FBI further describes terrorism as either domestic or international, depending on the origin, base, and objectives of terrorism, and suggests that

> terrorism refers to activities that involve acts dangerous to human life that are a violation of the criminal laws of the United States or of any state; appear to be intended to intimidate or coerce a civilian population; to influence the policy of a government by mass destruction, assassination, or kidnapping; and occur primarily within the territorial jurisdiction of the United States.[32]

U.S. federal law has further provided some definitional conflict with the passage of the Uniting and Strengthening America by Providing Appropriate Tools Required to Intercept and Obstruct Terrorism Act (or USA PATRIOT Act) 2001, which defines "terrorism" as actions that

> (A) involve violent acts or acts dangerous to human life that are a violation of the criminal laws of the United States or of any State, or that would be a criminal violation if committed within the jurisdiction of the United States or of any State;
>
> (B) appear to be intended to—
>
>   (i)   intimidate or coerce a civilian population;
>   (ii) to influence the policy of a government by intimidation or coercion; or
>   (iii) to affect the conduct of a government by mass destruction, assassination, or kidnapping.[33]

International Definitions

Globally, the community of nation-states is no closer to consensus on this definition than we are in the United States. For example, in the United Kingdom, terrorism is defined as

> the use or threat of action that is designed to influence the government or an international governmental organisation or to intimidate the public or a section of the public, and the use or threat (of action) made for the purpose of advancing a political, religious or ideological cause. Action falls within this subsection if it (a) involves serious violence against a person, (b) involves serious damage to property, (c) endangers a person's life, other than that of the person committing the action, (d) creates a serious risk to the health or safety of the public or a section of the public, or (e) is designed seriously to interfere with or seriously to disrupt an electronic system.[34]

In contrast, France—which helped give us the word *terrorism* as described above—has legally defined terrorism as acts that are "intentionally committed by an individual entity or by a collective entity in order to seriously disturb law and order by intimidation or by terror."[35] French law—in contrast to American law—even goes so far as to specify specific acts of terrorism, including (a) attempted murder, assault, kidnapping, and hostage taking on airplanes, ships, and all means of transport; (b) theft, extortion, destruction, and crimes committed during group combat; (c) the production or ownership of weapons of destruction and explosives, including the production, sale, import, and export of explosives; (d) the acquisition, ownership, and transport of illegal explosive substances; (e) the production, ownership, storage, or acquisition of biological or chemical weapons; and (f) money laundering.[36]

Other countries define terrorism even more broadly. For example, Peru (which has dealt with its own version of terror) says that any individual who

> acts against the life, physical integrity, health, freedom or security of individuals or against property . . . or affects the international relations or safety of society or the State . . . shall be deemed to have committed the crime of terrorism.[37]

Some countries try to be broad and specific at the same time, while also trying to find common ground with international organizations such as the United Nations (UN). For example, Canada (a country that both borders and is a strong ally of the United States) under the Anti-Terrorism Act (ATA) of 2001 defines terrorism as

> an action that takes place either within or outside of Canada which is an offence under the United Nations (UN) Conventions and Protocols; or is committed or threatened for political, religious or ideological purposes and intended to intimidate the public or compel a government to do or refrain from doing an act by killing, seriously harming or endangering a person, causing substantial property damage that is likely to seriously harm people or by interfering with or disrupting an essential service, facility or system.[38]

Under the ATA, a terrorist group is defined as an entity that has as one of its purposes or activities the facilitating or carrying out of terrorist activity or that is set out in a list established by regulation.

Canada's attempt to at least incorporate some of the UN's efforts at defining terrorism also raises the question of where international organizations and governing bodies stand with regard to defining terrorism. Unfortunately, experience shows that they have had little more success at achieving a common definition than individual nation-states. For example, the UN has long struggled to define the concept. In 1937, the original League of Nations (the predecessor to the modern UN) drafted a definition of terrorism as "all criminal acts directed against a State and intended or calculated to create a state of terror in the minds of particular persons or a group of persons or the general public."[39] The convention never came into being, however—and to this day, the UN has no single, agreed-on definition of the word, although there has continued to be considerable debate on the topic. An example of the kind of language the international community has considered can be seen in a draft resolution from a 1999 session of the UN. The resolution stated that the UN

1. *strongly condemns* all acts, methods, and practices of terrorism as criminal and unjustifiable, wherever and by whomsoever committed;

2. *reiterates* that criminal acts intended or calculated to provoke a state of terror in the general public, a group of persons, or particular persons for political purposes are in any circumstance unjustifiable, whatever the considerations of a political, ideological, racial, ethnic, religious, or other nature that may be invoked to justify them.[40]

As the large UN body continued to struggle for a definition of terrorism, it cobbled together 12 different piecemeal conventions and protocols. In 1992, a recommendation was made to the UN Crime Branch that terrorism simply be defined as the "peacetime equivalent of war crimes."[41] This also proved extremely controversial, although it might be much simpler to use. The UN body does not follow this definition today.

The European Union (henceforth, EU), which initially seemed to take its cue from a desire to build an economic power to rival the United States, has found that with economic concerns come political questions. The EU, often the target for terrorist attacks in the past, and sometimes the hiding place for groups that practiced terrorism, has itself struggled to find a definition for the word. Recently proposed language for a framework on fighting terrorism defined the term as

> intentional acts, by their nature and context, which may be seriously damaging to a country or to an international organization, as defined under national law, where committed with the aim of (i) seriously intimidating a population, or (ii) unduly compelling a Government or international organization to perform or abstain from performing an act, or (iii) destabilizing or destroying the fundamental political, constitutional, economic or social structures of a country or international organization.[42]

Fulfilling the desire among some EU member nations to be quite clear about what specific activity would qualify under this definition, however, proved more controversial. Additional language suggested that the above destruction or destabilization could be the result of

> causing extensive damage to a Government or public facility, including an information system, a fixed platform located on a continental shelf [or] a public place or private property likely to put in danger human lives or produce considerable economic loss.[43]

The inclusion of extra language, such as the reference to "a fixed platform located on a continental shelf," was a direct reference to environmental groups' occupation protests on oil platforms in the North Sea—such as Greenpeace's occupation of the Brent Spa oil platform. Equally, the earlier references to "intentional acts" that seriously damaged the work of "an international organization" were seen by some as an attempt to prevent trade unionists from demonstrating violently (as they had, e.g., for three days in Genoa) at meetings of organizations such as the G-7 (now the G-20) or even the EU itself.

Critics were quick to point out that this degree of specificity in defining terrorism was nothing more than an overbroad attempt to censor political dissent and free expression of ideas. It proved just as vexing for the EU as the various attempts at defining the term had for the UN.

How "Terrorists" Define Themselves

The perspectives of individuals labeled as terrorists do not provide much clarity on a definition either. Predictably, their perspectives are self-serving and just as controversial as any academic or nation-state/government's attempt at defining the term. Many individual leaders of organizations or movements labeled as terrorist identify themselves differently, using terms such as *revolutionary, guerrilla,* or *freedom fighter.* Consider the following examples of three men in recent history: Nelson Mandela of South Africa, the late Menachem Begin of Israel, and the late Yasser Arafat of Palestine.

Today, Nelson Mandela occupies a unique and hallowed space in world history—respected for his part in ending a government-sanctioned program of racial discrimination in his country, South Africa. His early skirmishes with the South African government earned him an extensive prison sentence and state condemnation. According to Mandela, his movement of liberation consciously elected to use "guerrilla" rather than "terrorist" tactics—he wrote as much in his 1994 memoirs (although he never defined either label—or necessarily provided examples).[44] He did not see himself as anything but the leader of a political movement to end apartheid and to provide liberation for his people. He was imprisoned for his beliefs and activities and branded a terrorist by the South African government.[45] He never saw himself that way. Eventually, he became the leader of his country, and today he is venerated as a world leader and a moral figure.

In comparison, Menachem Begin served in the group known as Irgun—a Jewish group labeled as terrorists by the British for fighting against British forces in an effort to establish an independent Jewish state.[46] Like Mandela, Begin went on to become the leader of his country—and himself led a fight against what he termed Palestinian terrorism before ultimately attempting a peace settlement with his old foe, Yasser Arafat.

For his part, Arafat saw himself as an opponent of colonialism—and Zionism, which in his view was an extension of European colonial policies.[47] In his life, he aligned himself with resistance movements in Africa and Ireland (to name a few) and saw that his major organization would eventually come to have the name "liberation" in its title (The PLO, or Palestinian Liberation Organization). For Israelis and many

Americans, however, Arafat was seen as a terrorist, although he did not self-identify that way.

Ironically, one other fact connects all three men (besides being accused of terrorism): Each man was awarded the Nobel Prize for Peace, Begin in 1978, Mandela in 1993, and Arafat in 1994.

Nation-states and their leaders who practice "top-down" or state terrorism are also often loath to see their activities described that way. As suggested before, either they are at pains to avoid defining terrorism to include the actions of a state, or more often, they rationalize their violence in the context of a larger political challenge. In later chapters, I will address the examples of Hitler, Stalin, and Pol Pot, to name but a few; here, allow me to elaborate on the case presented by Iran during the reign of Shah Reza Pahlavi, from 1953 to 1977.

As a ruler, Shah Reza Pahlavi saw himself as a contemporary Muslim leader who (like his father, Reza Khan) sought to modernize Iran and bring it in line with the Western countries that had been his benefactors. Modernization—which would come to be seen in his program called the *White Revolution*—referred to economic policies such as land reform, business and tax changes, infrastructure investment and development, and the growth of Iran's sizable petroleum industry, as well as to social programs such as education reform and allowing women the right to vote. The Shah did not seek total secularization of his country, merely one that moderated and severely limited the reach of Islam and its leaders—such as Ayatollah Khomeini.

To the outside world, through the 1960s, some of the ways the Shah self-identified as a benevolent and educated leader trying to modernize his country was reflected by the results of his program. Indeed, during this period, it "appeared to many, especially outside Iran, as a great success story, and in support of this contention they could point to large increases in Iran's GNP, impressive industrial, agricultural, and infrastructural projects, and a number of social welfare activities."[48] Inside the country, however, critics charged that his economic programs had only driven large numbers of Iran's peasant class into the big cities, where housing and employment were scarce, and that through fraud and corruption only the wealthier and politically connected members of Iranian society were able to benefit from his changes. These charges fueled the angry rhetoric of Iran's mullahs—chief among them, the aforementioned Ayatollah Khomeini—that the Shah was destroying the traditional Islamic nature of his country and becoming a slave to Western governments and multinational corporations.[49]

The other truth about the Shah that was too often ignored by Western governments such as the United States or Great Britain was that to consolidate his power and control the appeal of non-secular leaders like Khomeini he tolerated little or no dissent within his own country and enforced that policy by the use of his secret police, also known as the SAVAK. Trained by both American and Israeli specialists, the SAVAK became ruthlessly effective at domestic spying on Iranians, and eventually arresting, detaining, and/or imprisoning the same for crimes no worse than disagreement with the Shah. "While the Shah was in power, close to 1500 people were arrested *monthly* [italics in original], and on only one day, June 5, 1963, SAVAK and the Shah's army allegedly killed as many as 6,000 citizens."[50] The SAVAK also developed a reputation for the horrible torture and mistreatment of political prisoners and the incarceration of as many as 100,000 of them each year in Reza Pahlavi's Iran.[51] In the words of Martha Crenshaw, the "primary role of SAVAK was to terrorize the Iranian population into submission to the Shah. State-sponsored terrorism certainly characterized the Pahlavi era."[52]

It is worth remembering that the revolution that drove the Shah out of Iran (he died in exile) was not only a religious, non-secular wave created by the rhetoric of Khomeini, it was also the product of other political forces that had suffered repression and been terrorized during the reign of Pahlavi. Ironically, the government that replaced him only perpetuated and expanded the state terrorism within Iran.

The Shah provides one example of the way in which leaders of nation-states engage in terrorism but do not define their activity that way; a contrasting recent phenomenon finds some organizations we label as terrorist redefining themselves as pseudo-states once the real states have failed.[53] Two classic examples of this may be found in the groups Hamas and Hezbollah.

Hamas was founded in 1987 and eventually became a counterweight to Yasser Arafat's Palestinian Authority—which was viewed by many as corrupt. The Palestinian Authority had been the closest example of a Palestinian State government. Besides being corrupt, however, the authority often proved incapable of providing basic social services for Palestinians.

In the same time period, Hamas was actively engaged in horrific attacks on Israeli civilian targets, with the use of suicide bombers. Hamas views itself, however, as more than just a paramilitary organization dedicated to defeating Israel; it also sees itself as connected to the Palestinian community. To a degree, this latter awareness from Hamas may have been the product of time spent training in Lebanon with Hezbollah. Hezbollah has developed into a pseudo state actor in Lebanese politics—and is at the very least seen as a major political party. Its example on the social and political fronts provided a frame of reference for Hamas, which gradually sought to redefine itself in similar terms. The result of this transformation was a stunning election victory in 2006. As Michael Leavitt noted recently,

> So why did Hamas surprise everyone, including itself, when it won 44.5% of the vote and became the majority party in the election of January 2006? Because Hamas also provides desperately needed social services to needy Palestinians and—until Hamas' stunning electoral victory—served as a de facto Islamist opposition to the secular Palestinian authority.[54]

The breadth of these social services is substantial, and they serve to help recruit new fighters and suicide bombers for Hamas, as well as creating popular support for the organization and creating the appearance of legitimate bases for fund-raising—the money from which may actually be used to employ terrorism. The services Hamas provides include an education network, food distribution for the poor and needy, camps and sports for young people, funding of scholarship and business development, religious services, public safety, and health care.[55]

In contrast, Hezbollah (the name means *Party of God*) has practiced a policy combining social services and activism in Lebanese politics with the militant violence that has earned it a designation as a terrorist organization. Originally founded in Lebanon in 1982 as a response to the invasion by Israel, Hezbollah joined many other militia groups (e.g., those under the control of the Christians, Druze, or other Shiite Amal militia) that initially had to step in and become "mini-public administrations"[56] in their parts of the country, where the national government was incapable of providing basic services. These included infrastructure necessities damaged by years of war, such as providing electricity, telephone contact, road repair, and basic health services. As a Shiite movement, Hezbollah was influenced by the Shiite revolution in Iran and desired to see Lebanon follow a similar path; this created a connection with Iran that led to patronage and financial and military support for Hezbollah's activities. The United States and Israel have often focused on the connection between Hezbollah and Iran as it relates to military support (Hezbollah being characterized as a proxy for Iran in this area), but what this accounting fails to grasp is that this organization self-defines as a movement—with both a political and a social dimension—in addition to its militant character. While the latter aspect (militant violence) has been reflected in some of the charges of terrorism made against the group—including the bombing of the

U.S. Embassy and the U.S. marine barracks in Beirut and the large number of kidnappings of Westerners in Lebanon—what has made Hezbollah palatable to some people in Lebanon is its willingness to act politically and to become a pseudo-government providing those same social services.

> Hezbollah offers an array of social services to its constituents that include construction companies, schools, hospitals, dispensaries, and micro-finance initiatives (notably al-Qard al-Hasan, literally the "good loan," which began making loans in 1984 and now offers about 750 small loans a month). These tend to be located in predominantly Shiite areas, but some serve anyone requesting help. Hezbollah hospital and clinic staff also treat all walk-in patients, regardless of political views or their sect, for only a small fee.[57]

These two organizations mirror the activities of the Irish groups Sinn Fein and the Irish Republican Army (IRA), both of which evolved and transitioned to become political parties, as well as the Basque separatist groups ETA (*Euskadi 'la Askatasuma*, meaning Basque Homeland and Freedom) and Hari Batasuna.

These organizations further this identity of the pseudo-state by careful use of language. For example, the original IRA elected to call itself an "army" partly out of a desire to counter the label *terrorist*—or the idea that their protest was in some way illegitimate. The original document given to every new recruit for the IRA was called the *Green Book*, and it set forth clearly what was expected from new members, as well as an orientation regarding the violent activity of the organization. It began by stressing, "The Irish Republican Army, as the legal representatives of the Irish people, are morally justified in carrying out a campaign of resistance against foreign occupation forces and domestic collaborators."[58]

By calling itself an "army" and "legal representatives," the IRA became more like a government or a nation-state representative. These word choices by such organizations are rhetorical efforts aimed at conferring legitimacy and official status on their actions. The *Green Book* later speaks of the violence these new recruits must be expected to commit:

> Volunteers are expected to wage a military war of liberation against a numerically superior force. This involves the use of arms and explosives.
>
> Firstly, the use of arms. When volunteers are trained in the use of arms, they must fully understand that guns are dangerous, and their

main purpose is to take human life, in other words to kill people, and volunteers are trained to kill people.

It is not an easy thing to take up a gun and go out and kill some person without strong convictions or justification. The Army, its motivating force, is based upon strong convictions which bonds [sic] the Army into one force, and before any potential volunteer decides to join the Army he must have these strong convictions. Convictions that are strong enough to give him confidence to kill someone without hesitation and without regret. The same can be said about a bombing campaign.[59]

Nowhere in this telling passage is the word *terrorism* used. Instead, the violence—in the form of killing—is referenced as a "military war of liberation" against the British. Those who kill are not killers or terrorists. Instead, they are soldiers in an army, told to follow orders and discipline in warfare, in ways that do not allow for individual conscience and second-guessing. Although these words may sound terrible when contrasted with the loss of life caused by IRA violence through the years, they are really no different from the words and ideas a professional armed force of a nation-state uses to indoctrinate its new members.

Another perspective of terrorism offered by the terrorist grows out of a willingness to dehumanize the victims of terror by treating them as objects. The following passage from a Ku Klux Klan member's speech to other Klan members makes reference to the death by bombing of four African American children, comparing them to animals. The speaker says,

It wasn't no shame they was killed. Why? Because when I go out to kill rattle snakes, I don't make no difference between little rattle snakes and big rattle snakes because I know it is in the nature of all rattle snakes to be enemies and to poison me if they can. So, I kill 'em all, and if there's four less little niggers tonight, then I say, good for whoever planted the bomb. We're all better off.[60]

Again, note that the speaker, however shocking his words and sentiments may be to anyone outside the immediate audience, never uses the word *terrorism* but essentially justifies the terrorist act by comparing children to snakes, objects that can and have been killed by humans in self-defense.

In sum, these various perspectives, whether offered by academics, specialists, governments and their agencies, large or regional international organizations, or even terrorists themselves, only provide too many choices for defining terrorism and very little sense of consistency. What terrorism is depends on who you are and why you are bothering to define it.

Such a reality has led some to suggest that even attempting to define the term can only provoke controversy and debate and will not be very useful in helping us understand how to respond to terrorism. Walter Laqueur, cited earlier in this chapter, has stated that no one definition of terrorism will ever suffice to fully explain and describe the activity.

❖ ATTEMPTS TO SYNTHESIZE A CONSENSUS DEFINITION

Jenkins's Definition

In that spirit, some theorists have tried to capture a consensus of the definition by examining all definitions to see what parts they have in common. Brian Jenkins has worked for many years as a consultant on terrorism and counterterrorism security. He proposed what may be the simplest definition of terrorism, synthesizing what he believed were the most basic components of all definitions on the subject. Jenkins suggested that terrorism is the use or the threatened use of force designed to bring about a political change.[61] This definition, popular with many who look at terrorism and security issues, sidesteps the complexities of the many different definitions by simplifying and reducing the term to violence or threats of violence for political gain. Does this definition make more sense than the others?

Some prefer Jenkins's definition because they find comfort and comprehensiveness in its simplicity—for terrorism here is political violence—regardless of other motives and irrespective of the nature of the target of the violence (civilian, law enforcement, or military personnel) or the perpetrator of the terror act (whether an individual, group, criminal enterprise, or state). Of course, many forms and examples of violence could be placed under such a broad definition. There are no wars that do not involve political motivations and gain, and depending on how the words *political* and *violence* themselves are defined and used, virtually any individual act of violence toward the state or toward another individual may be considered as terrorism. This kind of definition is thus overly broad, but surprisingly, it was almost precisely the way the British once defined the term when legislating against violence in England and Northern Ireland.[62]

What constitutes *"political"* in such a definition? Perhaps it references anything involving matters of state—for example, policies and laws of the government or perhaps elections and candidates. Is something political because it is merely controversial? Or perhaps because it has the capacity to affect a great many people? Does being political refer to questions of oppression and domination, struggles for power, and resistance to authority?

Doubtless the reader will have already observed that there is an inherent looseness with the way this word is used today. Any of the ideas suggested above may form the basis for labeling something as political. And most surely, the continued careless use of the term in expressions such as *political correctness* only serves to obscure the meaning even more.

Likewise, there is controversy over the meaning of *violence* as used in the definition of terrorism above. What constitutes violence in such a definition? Any act of physical aggression—or, at the least, the threat of it? Possibly—but what do we then consider as physical aggression? Perhaps we may refer back to our criminal laws and definitions for assistance here. For example, in nearly all countries, there are standards for assault, battery, rape, attempted murder, and murder, any one of which may provide the basis for the physical aggression we call "violence." Though few would likely dispute that shooting or stabbing another individual would meet the standard necessary for violence in defining terrorism, what of the other forms of proscribed acts of (or attempts at) aggression?

Should we consider rape as an example of physical aggression necessary to define terrorism? Rape may be seen as a tool of oppression (of women by men) and power (even men raping or being raped by other men) with an inherent politicality about it. At present, however, terrorism as defined by law does not include rape.

What of the other forms of aggression referenced above? Assault is usually defined as any kind of intentional attempt to inflict corporal injury on another individual.[63] This can range from grabbing someone at the elbow and pulling them to you, all the way to tackling someone, shoving them, pinning them against the wall, or hugging them. Battery, usually a companion of assault, involves an advanced form of aggression that includes physical violence—for example, a punch or a kick.[64]

So much so good: Attacking and hitting someone might be seen as the kind of physical aggression necessary for terrorism. But if so, how should we consider an attack such as hitting someone in the face with a pie? In the past decade, numerous groups have resorted to pie throwing as a means of civil disobedience. In 1998, for example, a group of Belgian protestors attacked Microsoft founder Bill Gates with "a small armada of cream tarts . . . covering him in whipped cream."[65] Gates was reportedly "surprised and disappointed,"[66] although "angry enough to wish them charged with assault and battery" might be a more accurate description of his feelings. For their part, the pie throwers (already notorious for doing this to other celebrities, officials, and politicians) asserted that their act of civil disobedience was also a symbolic political speech, not to mention an attack on "self-important" people. If so, this kind of aggression (both assault and battery) as violence was most definitely also political, thus making it political violence. But would one consider it terrorism?

In truth, the feature of this definition that makes it so appealing— its simplicity—is also its most pronounced weakness. In reducing terrorism to political violence, one expands the field of possibilities for consideration. In such a world, there is little that would not be considered terrorism.

Schmid's Definition

A second, slightly more complex approach to finding a synthesized, consensus definition may be found in the work of A. P. Schmid, whose advisory work for the UN was cited earlier. Schmid reached a conclusion similar to that of Laqueur, suggesting that because of the complexity and diversity of perspectives on terrorism, no single definition can adequately describe what is occurring during this violence or threat of violence. Nevertheless, recognizing that there may be some commonalities in the different perspectives, Schmid conducted a review of the various definitions, finding some 22 components that they had in common to one degree or another. He then produced a synthesized definition, containing the most common of those 22 components. According to Schmid,

> terrorism is an anxiety-inspiring method of repeated violent action, employed by (semi-) clandestine individual, group or state actors, for idiosyncratic, criminal or political reasons, whereby—in contrast to assassination—the direct targets of violence are not the main targets. The immediate human victims of violence are generally chosen randomly (targets of opportunity) or selectively (representative or symbolic targets) from a target population, and serve as message generators. Threat- and violence-based communication processes between terrorist (organization), (imperiled) victims, and main targets are used to manipulate the main target (audience(s)), turning it into a target of terror, a target of demands, or a target of attention, depending on whether intimidation, coercion, or propaganda is primarily sought.[67]

In Schmid's calculus,[68] terrorism is seen more as a method or form of combat and struggle attempted for a variety of reasons more complex than just the "political." Schmid's perspective also acknowledges that a variety of actors—including the state—can perform or at least sponsor terrorism. His definition also more neatly distinguishes between the immediate victims of terror (who may be selected randomly or on purpose) and the main audience for terrorism (the public and/or the state), in whom the immediate victims serve to leverage fear so as to bring about some kind of action or change desired by the terrorist.

Does this definition create any more clarity than the others? At one level, it is more inclusive than the others in that it recognizes that terrorism may be produced *from above* or *from below*. It thus provides some framework for lawmakers who want to find agreement between nations in defining and outlawing terrorism.

Additionally, Schmid's definition is comprehensive and complex, where Jenkins was simple and reductionist. In this definition of terrorism, Schmid very clearly states exactly what he means by terrorism, allowing for objectives including terror, demands, and attention, as well as examining the means by which objectives are accomplished through intimidation, coercion, or propaganda.

Finally, Schmid's definition is, for our purposes in this book, a better fit because it also reinforces the notion that communication is involved with terrorism. Schmid as much as says so directly when he mentions "threat- and violence-based communication processes" in his definition. In my judgment, this provides us with a good starting place for reconceptualizing terrorism. Laqueur, Jenkins, and many others are right:[69] It is almost impossible to find a single definition of terrorism that will satisfy everyone. Even Schmid's definition will be dismissed by those who reject the concept of state terrorism. But unlike those who find a definition of terrorism elusive and difficult, I believe that a different approach may be found if we dispense for the moment with questions of motive and agenda in the defining and instead use this last point about Schmid's definition as a starting place for our discussion.

❖ SUMMARY

In this chapter, we have examined how the definition of terrorism may vary widely among scholars and academics, as well as among nation-states and their agencies, international organizations, and even terrorists themselves. More broadly, we have seen how terrorism may be classified as being *from above* or *from below* and how it has been placed it in the context of political violence. In the end, however, no clear consensus has developed in any of these communities about terrorism, although the definition offered by Schmid does provide us with an opportunity to reconsider terrorism in a new light, as a process of communication.

❖ NOTES

1. See, for example, J. Margolin, "Psychological Perspectives in Terrorism," in *Terrorism: Interdisciplinary Perspectives*, ed. Yonah Alexander and Seymour Maxwell Finger (New York: John Jay Press, 1977).

2. See, for example, Simon Reeve, *The New Jackals: Ramzi Yousef, Osama bin Laden and the Future of Terrorism* (Boston: Northeastern University Press, 1999).

3. See, for example, Strobe Talbott and Nayan Chanda, *The Age of Terror: America and the World After September 11th* (New York: Basic Books, 2001).

4. Indeed, as shall be discussed later in this chapter, there are many who wish to label and define the political violence associated with groups who claim to represent Islam as "new terrorism." See, for example, *The 9/11 Commission Report,* Chapter 2: Sections 2.1 and 2.2, pp. 47–48 (National Commission on Terrorist Attacks Upon the United States, July 27, 2004). As will also be discussed, others choose to identify the new terrorism by characteristics such as "loose, cell-based networks with minimal lines of command and control" and "asymmetrical methods that maximize casualties." See G. Martin, *Understanding Terrorism,* 2nd ed. (Thousand Oaks, CA: Sage, 2006) at p. 10.

5. Flavius Josephus, "The Jewish War," in *Works,* vol. 2, pp. 254–257 (Loeb Classical Library, London: Henemann, 1926).

6. For more details, see David C. Rapoport, "Fear and Trembling: Terrorism in Three Religious Traditions," *American Political Science Review,* 78(3), 1984 at pp. 658–677.

7. For example, for their first assassination in Syria, the Assassins allegedly disguised themselves as Sufis to get close to the local leader of Homs, before stabbing him to death.

8. In the case of the Assassins, this might have been an endorsement of their more orthodox perspective of Shia'ism or an extension of a political allegiance or accommodation they made in Iran, Syria, or any of the other countries within which they operated.

9. See M. G. S. Hodgson, *The Order of Assassins* (The Hague, The Netherlands: Mouton, 1955) at p. 84.

10. Because they never enjoyed the security of a conventional army, the Ismai'ilis often chose or built fortresses that were difficult or impossible for conventional armies to attack.

11. See G. Chaliand and A. Blin (eds), *The History of Terrorism From Antiquity to Al Qaeda* (Berkeley: University of California Press, 2007) at p. 73: "The Assassins' behavior was, above all, that of a political organization—unusual, to be sure, yet ready to abandon its principles for alliances of convenience."

12. *Dictionnaire, Supplément* (Paris, an VII [1798]) at p. 775.

13. Isser Woloch, *Jacobin Legacy: The Democratic Movement Under the Directory* (Princeton, NJ: Princeton University Press, 1970) at p. 3.

14. See M. Reinhard, *La Revolution Democratique* ("Les Cours de Sorbonne," Paris: Centre de Documentation Universitaire, 1959) at p. 244.

15. French for "without knee breaches"—the white stockings and their knee grips often worn by members of the French aristocracy of the period. Describing people as *sans-culottes,* or without knee breeches, was a way of identifying them as lower class.

16. Woloch, *Jacobin Legacy, op. cit.,* at p. 6.

17. From M. Robespierre, *Report Upon the Principles of Political Morality Which Are to Form the Basis of the Administration of the Interior Concerns of the Republic* (Philadelphia, 1794). Retrieved May 25, 2009, from www.fordham.edu/halsall/mod/1794robespierre.html.

18. This is the date when the Convention officially declared the Terror as the "order of the day."

19. This date marks the fall of Robespierre, who himself was executed one day later.

20. See Chaliand and Blin, *The History of Terrorism From Antiquity to Al Qaeda, op. cit.,* at p. 102.

21. Edmund Burke, *Letters on a Regicide Peace, (1795)* iv. Wks. IX. 75.

22. The *Reflections on the War in France* are contained within: Edmund Burke, *The Works of Edmund Burke* (New York: George Dearborn Publisher, 1834) at p. 572.

23. L. Ceccarelli, "Polysemy: Multiple Meanings in Rhetorical Criticism," *Quarterly Journal of Speech* 84, 1998: 395–415.

24. See, for example, Omar Malik, *Enough of the Definition of Terrorism* (Washington, DC: Brookings Institute Press, 2001).

25. Martha Crenshaw (ed), *Terrorism in Context* (University Park: Penn State University Press, 1995); quoted excerpt retrieved December 16, 2002, fromwww.psupress.org/books/terrorismincontextexcerpts.html#what.

26. Walter Laqueur, *The Age of Terrorism,* 2nd ed. (Boston: Little, Brown, 1987) at p. 143.

27. B. Nacos, *Mass Mediated Terrorism: The Central Role of the Media in Terrorism and Counterterrorism* (Lanham, MA: Rowman & Littlefield, 2002) at p. 17.

28. Annamarie Olivero, *The State of Terror* (Albany: State University of New York Press, 1998) at p. 142.

29. 22 U.S.C.A. A7 2656 (d).

30. See U.S. Department of Defense, DOD Directive 2000.12, Protection of DOD Resources Against Terrorist Acts, June 16, 1986, p. 15.

31. The FBI definition flows directly from the Code of Federal Regulations: 28 C.F.R. A7 085.

32. 18 U.S.C. § 2331(5). This can also be retrieved from the FBI Web site at www.fbi.gov/publications/terror/terror2000_2001.htm (accessed May 25, 2009)

33. 28 U.S.C.A. § 2331.

34. Terrorism Act 2000, § 1. A full treatment of this can be obtained in a report for Parliament titled *The Definition of Terrorism: A Report* by Lord Carlile of Berriew Q.C., Independent Reviewer of Terrorism Legislation, March 2007, at www.homeoffice.gov.uk/documents/carlile-terrorism-definition?view=Binary (accessed May 25, 2009).

35. French Criminal Code, Article 421-1 (Loi No. 96–647 du 22 juillet 1996 art. 1 Journal Officiel du 23 juillet 1996) (Loi No. 98–467 du 17 juin 1998 art. 84 Journal Officiel du 18 juin 1998) (Loi No. 2001–1062 du 15 novembre 2001 art. 33 Journal Officiel du 16 novembre 2001). Retrieved from http://222.legifrance.gouv.fr/html/ frame_codes 1.htm.

36. Ibid., at 421-1. For more on this, see Susan Tiefenbrun,, "A Semiotic Approach to a Legal Definition of Terrorism," *ILSA Journal of International and Comparative Law* 9, 2003: 357–402 (accessed in January of 2009).

37. Decree Law No. 25475, Article 2 (1992). For more on this, see the following report (*Peru*) from Interpol at www.interpol.int/Public/BioTerrorism/NationalLaws/Peru.pdf (accessed May 25, 2009).

38. Criminal Code of Canada, as amended by the Anti-Terrorism Act of 2001. For more details, see *Counter-Terrorism Legislation and Practice: A Survey of Selected Countries* at www.fco.gov.uk/resources/en/pdf/4175218/counter-terrorism-Oct05 (accessed May 25, 2009).

39. See Jane Boulden and Thomas George Weiss, *Terrorism and the UN: Before and After September 11* (Bloomington: Indiana University Press: 2004) at p. 178.

40. General Assembly Resolution 51/210, Measures to Eliminate International Terrorism, 1999; quoted in *Definitions of Terrorism*, retrieved December 28, 2002, from the UN Office on Drugs and Crime Web site: www.undcp.org/odccp/terrorism_definitions.html.

41. The recommendation was made by A. P. Schmid in a report to the Crime Branch as an attempt to simplify the definition and avoid the seemingly endless debate about the term. For a full treatment of this see Alex P. Schmid and Ronald D. Crelitsen, *Western Responses to Terrorism*, (Routledge Publishing: 1993), at p. 336.

42. European Union, Article 1 of the Framework Agreement on Combating Terrorism, December 7, 2001; quoted in *EU Definition of "Terrorism" Could Still Embrace Protests*, retrieved December 18, 2002, from the Statewatch Web site: www.statewatch.org/news/2001/dec/07terrdef.htm.

43. Article 1.e of the Framework Agreement on Combating Terrorism (Art. 3.f in the Commission Draft); quoted in ibid.

44. Nelson Mandela, *Long Walk to Freedom: The Autobiography of Nelson Mandela* (Boston: Little, Brown, 1994) at p. 246.

45. Ibid., at p. 458.

46. Keith Suter, *Global Order and Global Disorder: Globalization and the Nation State* (Westport, CT: Greenwood Publishing Group, 2003) at p. 53.

47. According to Arafat, from his speech to the United Nations in 1974, as cited in Aryeh Yodfat and Yuval Arnon-Ohanna, *PLO Strategy and Tactics* (London: Taylor & Francis, 1981) at p. 181, "the roots of the Palestinian

problem reach back to the end of the 19th century, the period of colonialism and settlement. Zionism was born in that era. It aimed at the conquest of Palestine by European immigrants."

48. Nikki Keddie, *Modern Iran: Roots and Results of Revolution* (New Haven, CT: Yale University Press, 2003) at p. 149.

49. P. Demant and A. Engineer, *Islam v. Islamism* (Westport, CT: Greenwood Publishing Group, 2006) at p. 114.

50. Piers Beirne and James Messerschmidt, *Criminology*, 3rd ed. (Boulder, CO: Westview Press, 2000) at p. 417. See also David R. Simon and D. Stanley Eitzen, *Elite Deviance* (Boston: Allyn & Bacon, 1986) at p. 158.

51. Beirne and Messerschmidt, ibid., at p. 417.

52. Martha Crenshaw, *Terrorism in Context, op. cit.*, at p. 576.

53. John Robb, *Brave New War: The Next Stage of Terrorism and the End of Globalization* (New York: Wiley, 2008) at p. 147.

54. Matthew Leavitt, *Hamas: Politics, Charity, and Terrorism in the Service of Jihad* (New Haven, CT: Yale University Press, 2007) at p. 5.

55. John Robb, *Brave New War, op. cit.*, at p. 147.

56. Judith Palmer Harik, *Hezbollah: The Changing Face of Terrorism* (New York: I. B. Taurus, 2005) at p. 82.

57. Augustus Norton, *Hezbollah: A Short History* (Princeton, NJ: Princeton University Press, 2007); excerpted in Ken Silverstein, "Augustus Norton on Hezbollah's Social Service," *Harper's Magazine*, March 14, 2007. Retrieved May 25, 2009, from www.harpers.org/archive/2007/03/sb-augustus-no-1173896326.

58. Irish Republican Army, *The Green Book*; quoted in Tim Pat Coogan, *The IRA*, rev. ed. (New York: Palgrave Press, 2000) at p. 545.

59. Ibid., at p. 547.

60. See A. C. Rapoport, *Assassinations and Terrorism* (Toronto, Ontario, Canada: T. H. Best, 1971); quoted in Maxwell Taylor, *The Terrorist* (London: Brassey's Defence, 1988) at p. 99.

61. Brian Jenkins, *The Who, What, Where, When and Why of Terrorism* (paper presented at the Detroit Police Department Conference on Urban Terrorism, Detroit, MI, November 1984).

62. See, for example, the British Prevention of Terrorism Act of 1974, which defined terrorism as "the use of violence for political ends, and includes any use of violence for the purpose of putting the public or any section of the public in fear."

63. *State v. Stow*, 97 N.J.L. 349 (1922).

64. *Goodrum v. State*, 60 Ga. 511 (1878).

65. Sarah Lyall, "Philosopher of Pie, Craftily Creaming Pomposity," *New York Times*, April 20, 1998. Retrieved May 1998 from www.nytimes.com.

66. Ibid.

67. Alex P. Schmid, *Political Terrorism: A Research Guide to Concepts, Theories, Data Bases and Literature* (New Brunswick, NJ: Transaction Publishers, 1983) at p. 70.

68. The top half of the 22 identified common characteristics (and their percentage of all the definitions) included the following: violence, force—83.5%; political motive or agenda—65%; creating terror or fear—51%; making a threat—47%; associative psychological impact—41.5%; victim-target differentiation—37.5%; purposive, planned, systematic organized action—32%; method of combat, strategy, tactic—30.5%; breach of humanitarian constraints—30%; coercion and extortion—28%; and publicity aspect—21.5%. See Alex P. Schmid, A. J. Jongman, and Michael Stohl, *Political Terrorism: A New Guide to Actors, Authors, Concepts, Data Bases, Theories, and Literature*, 2nd ed. (New Brunswick, NJ: Transaction Publishers, 2005) at pp. 5–6.

69. See, for example, Jonathan R. White, *Terrorism*, 3rd ed. (Belmont, CA: Wadsworth, 2002).

2

Terrorism as a Communication Process With Rhetorical Dimensions

❖ ❖ ❖

The violence and destruction associated with terrorism have always been about something greater than the immediate impact they have on their victims. If lynching sharecroppers, detonating bombs in crowded marketplaces, or crashing jets into buildings in big cities were only about killing the people in those locations *and nothing more,* we would refer to terrorism only as a kind of murder or destruction of public and private property. But we don't think of it that way. We never have—primarily because these acts of violence were not just ends unto themselves; rather, they were and are part of a larger process of communicating a message and generating a desired response. For the moment, therefore, let us rethink terrorism as a communication process, however morbid and offensive the message communicated may be. Understanding what this process is helps us understand how and why we perceive terrorism as we do—literally, how we construct it and how it constructs our reality. What does this process look like?

❖ TERRORISM AS A COMMUNICATION PROCESS

A simple model of communication suggests that human beings are senders and/or receivers of messages. In this most basic of approaches to human communication—relevant whether we consider how humans communicate in conversation, in public speaking, or even with semi-interactive, mass-mediated communication—a sender of a message *encodes* the message just before sending it, usually by reducing it to some form of symbols (such as language—words, after all, are symbols), which is then sent to the person of the receiver, who in turn *decodes* it (translating and interpreting the symbols) and then considers it. If this process is described as *transactional* and *bidirectional*, the sender *sends* and *receives* messages, and the receiver does likewise.

If into this simple model of communication we place a terrorist as the sender of a message and the public, an organization, a nation-state, or a government as the receiver, we find that the definition of terrorism can be more easily understood. This is in no way intended to trivialize the horror of death, pain, and suffering associated with terror violence; rather, here I am simply attempting to define terrorism differently for the sake of explaining how it works to affect us.

A terrorist sends a message to a target audience (the public, a nation-state, an organization, or the government) by engaging in an act of violence or destruction. The message is *not* the violence or destruction itself; rather, it is encoded within such activity. In this way, terrorism as a communication process has a rhetorical dimension that is independent of the simple coercion associated with violence for its own sake. Terrorism may or may not yield concessions. It may well serve to provoke discourse among target audiences. Or it may be a symbolic expression of the terrorist's rage or a demonstration of revenge. The process of encoding may depend on the symbolic nature of the violence and destruction, as well as the potential for using different media to convey such a message.

The target audience decodes this message by relying on the methods and tools it has for constructing its own sense of reality. These methods and tools may refer back to language and word choice, to discourse about the terrorist act—often suggested by official government interpretations of and responses to the message—and to discourse about how receivers of a mass-mediated message are to interpret and/or understand symbols of all kinds. We will explore each of these aspects in the following chapters. In practice, the process might look like what we see in Figure 2.1.

Figure 2.1

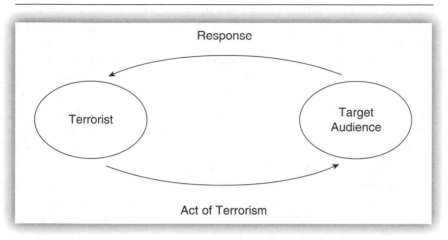

Figure 2.1 diagram showing Terrorist and Target Audience connected by "Response" (top arrow) and "Act of Terrorism" (bottom arrow).

Though it is theoretically possible that a terrorist may operate within a communication process that he or she perceives as being unidirectional—such as one in which the terrorist communicates with violence and an ultimatum demand, threatening worse violence in the case of noncompliance—the reality is that the terrorist message is still transactional and bidirectional because the first message generates some kind of response, which will always be communicated back to the terrorist either directly (in the form of government action, evidence of public discourse, etc.) or indirectly (via interpretation of the response through the media). Other audiences may be involved, adding to the size and complexity of the communication process. If such is the case, there are multiple audiences for the terrorist message, and these audiences may in turn communicate with one another and/or feed back independently or conjointly to the terrorist in the manner described above. This will, of course, alter the way we envision this process diagrammatically (Figure 2.2).

Figure 2.2

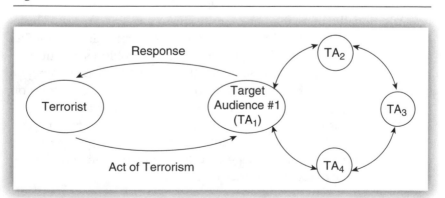

Note that in Figure 2.2, I have delineated four potential target audiences, but this is a random number used only for illustration purposes here. There may be 3 or 5 or 10—the number depends solely on the specific terrorist scenario.

Why do I suggest that multiple audiences may be involved with terrorism as a communication process? The answer to this question takes us back to the definition of terrorism offered by Schmid. Recall that this definition recognized that terrorist violence and destruction may be inflicted against one target with the purpose of influencing another target audience. Schmid is absolutely correct in that assessment. When violence and destruction occur, their recipient is one kind of audience—though most likely not the primary audience. That primary audience will be those who witness and observe the violence and destruction and then engage in discourse about what they have seen. In many situations, that second, more primary target audience may be the public at large.

This occurs if the terrorist seeks a change in policy (e.g., forcing a targeted country to withdraw from occupation—as the Palestinians have long sought from Israel), demands resources (e.g., ransom for hostages), or even seeks revenge (avenging the deaths of colleagues and comrades). In any of these situations, the primary public audience is targeted so that discourse and panic will ensue.

These individuals, in turn, will not constitute the only other audience. Indeed, government officials (if a state policy is implicated in the message) or institutional officials (if an organizational or institutional policy or practice is implicated in the message) will serve as a distinct but potentially overlapping target audience. The public audience will often be used (as suggested before) to leverage pressure against the government or institutional audience to change a policy or practice to comply with the terrorist's demands. The public audience is distinct from the target audience on whom the violence and destruction were inflicted, and both of these audiences will be distinct from the government or institutional audience, which may or may not respond with, for example, a change in policy.

Additionally, there may be other audiences in this process. These may include members and representatives of different kinds of media (broadcast, print, Internet, etc.), or potentially the public as constituted in other countries and cultures, or, for that matter, their governments or institutions. Also, these other countries may be allies or enemies of the nation-state attacked in the terrorist violence. Just as the media (at least in democracies) attempt to act independently of the government of the state, so also the government, institutions, and public of one country or culture will act independently of the government, institutions, and public of other countries or cultures.

To illustrate further, let us reconstitute the terrorism of September 11. Following this diagram, we might say that al Qaeda terrorists launched their deadly attacks on New York and Washington, D.C., communicating a message with their violence and destruction on that fateful day. The first audiences were the recipients of that death and destruction—those who inhabited the Twin Towers (and the immediate surrounding areas in New York) in Manhattan, the employees at the Pentagon, and the unfortunate passengers on all the flights involved in the attacks.

A second primary audience was the American public, all of whom witnessed and were terrified by what they saw of the message played back for them repeatedly over television, on radio, and in print (especially in newspapers and magazines).

A third possible audience would be relevant officials in our federal and even state governments, who were required to respond to these attacks either by contemplating military or law enforcement responses, changes in foreign policy, and changes in domestic security arrangements or by generating messages of calm for the public. This audience could have included anyone from Mayor Rudolph Giuliani (and his staff) of New York City to Governor Gray Davis (and other officials) in faraway California, all the way up to the White House and President Bush, Congress and relevant legislators, the Joint Chiefs of Staff and the military, and so forth.

An additional audience here would have been members of our own media, who operate (at least on the face of it) independently of what they are told by our government, as well as independently of the public to whom they offer news. Their response incorporated coverage and treatment of the terrorist message as well as internal discourse about what to report and how to frame the multiple stories of that tragic day in September.

Other audiences included our allies (e.g., Great Britain), countries that might be neutral with respect to terrorism (e.g., some European countries), and groups that we might consider to be hostile (e.g., the Taliban in Afghanistan). Any and all of them were potential audiences for the violent, destructive message that day because any of them might be targets themselves or might be affected by whatever response the U.S. government eventually chose to make.

This is only a partial list of the potential audiences for that message on that day. Can you think of other audiences for September 11?

As suggested before, these audiences in turn communicate with one another, individually and/or collectively, directly and indirectly, as part of the greater loop that can also feed back to the terrorist. In almost all situations, the connections between the different audiences were already established prior to the communication loop created by the terrorist message. When the various audiences communicate with one another, they will also engage in the encoding and decoding of messages, and any of them may communicate directly or indirectly (as part of the group of audiences) with the terrorist.

For example, this process could describe the ways in which survivors of the violence and destruction in New York communicated with the American public, often via the broadcast and print media; or it could describe the ways President Bush or other representatives of his administration communicated with foreign heads of state and their publics, such as Tony Blair and the public at large in Great Britain; or it could describe the way the reaction of the American public was conveyed to other countries that might have sheltered, sponsored, and assisted in the terrorism of that day. Of course, any of these same messages could have been conveyed back to the terrorists within the same loop. In that way, Osama bin Laden or other members of al Qaeda would have seen and understood the American reaction—or at least a mediated summary of it—via satellite television from CNN or any number of media sources.

This description of the process is useful for discussing what happens with terrorism because it allows for any type of terrorism to be considered, regardless of the ideological or political agendas behind the labels of terrorism. In that way, this conception of terrorism as a communication process could describe state-sponsored terror *from above* as easily as dissent terrorism *from below*. It would be equally relevant for describing William Calley's actions in allowing and participating in the massacre of civilians at My Lai (a direct or indirect—depending on whom you believe in the chain of command—form of state-sponsored terrorism) and the similar tactics of Russian troops in the contemporary battle with Chechnyan fighters (also state-sponsored terror). It could easily describe the actions of groups like the Ku Klux Klan or the Aryan Brotherhood in attacking minorities or threatening violence against gays and lesbians, just as it could describe the efforts of drug cartels in South America and Asia, which employ terror tactics to combat government efforts aimed at diminishing or eliminating the trafficking of drugs.

This much describes the outlines of terrorism as a process of communication, but it does not yet elaborate any details about how the communication occurs and how it is processed and responded to. For this portion of our inquiry, we must begin by going back to the purpose(s) of communicating with terrorism in the first place. At the beginning of the loop sequence, what are the objectives to be achieved from communicating?

Again, Schmid's definition provides some guidance here. At one level, the terrorist may be looking to create terror, panic, and chaos; or possibly to draw attention to an issue or condition that has been given scant or no treatment in the media or in world political forums; or perhaps to make the government or institution attacked or coerced by such action give in to the demands made by the terrorist. In any of these situations, however, we can see that the real goal of the communicated message in terrorism may be persuasion: to persuade audience members that chaos and fear will be their lot in life, to persuade them to pay attention to an issue they have ignored, or to persuade them to do something they might not otherwise do—such as persuading our government to rethink its support for Israel in the Middle East. Terrorism at this level becomes the business of persuading. Some would differ with this last point, seeing terrorism as coercion and suggesting that persuasion and coercion are different and distinct concepts.[1] But these distinctions ignore the fact that coercive terrorism is really just a different form of persuasion. If persuasion involves using rational arguments and logic to enable someone to reach a decision of his or her own free will, terrorism meets this standard as well. Those targeted can still use rational choice to decide whether they will give in, fight back, or simply suffer their punishment. When targets of terror make these decisions based on the discourse that results from the communication about a terrorist act, they are making rational choices, no differently than if they were listening to competing arguments before reaching a conclusion. In this way, at this level, terrorism is persuasion.

Consequently, to understand how the communication process operates and constructs terrorism for us (and by us), we must examine terrorism as persuasion—and assess its rhetorical dimensions.

❖ TERRORISM AND RHETORIC

As you have perhaps already observed, definitions of words can prove very controversial and contentious. This much was already seen in the myriad different and sometimes similar definitions of the word *terrorism*; this is also true of the word *rhetoric*. What does the word *rhetoric* mean, and more important, how am I using it when I suggest that there are rhetorical dimensions to terrorism?

Exploring the Meaning of *Rhetoric*

The term *rhetoric* as used in everyday language and discourse has a fairly simple meaning. When someone references a "politician's campaign rhetoric" or suggests that a statement was "only rhetoric and not substantive," he or she is suggesting a meaning for *rhetoric* that associates it with words that have little purpose other than to persuade or manipulate. As a starting point, that is not necessarily accurate, although it does give us a position from which to build a working definition for our study of terrorism.

In my judgment, *rhetoric* refers to the manner in which symbols (including, but not limited to, words) are used to affect, influence, and persuade people. Any definition of rhetoric, however, will have its detractors and critics. Mine is no exception, and in the spirit of encouraging the reader to discover some other meanings of this term, we will very briefly review the development of rhetoric to modern times to see how I am using the word today.

Rhetoric was studied and practiced in ancient Greece, initially as a component of the practice of democracy by the citizens of Athens, who were encouraged to gather and speak at public assemblies on issues facing the community. Public speaking in this realm involved more than delivery mechanics such as fluency, vocal volume, eye contact with the audience, or expressive gestures. Effective speaking at such assemblies also required mastery of issues, the ability to be articulate, and a sense of sophistication about mustering arguments to advocate one's position on these issues. Not coincidentally, today when we think of the word *sophisticated*, we think of something that is clever, elaborate, and detailed. But this word derives from the word *sophistry*, which described the practices of a group of Athenians known as Sophists, who believed and taught that public speaking was an art form and a virtue unto itself. The Sophists became traveling teachers at this time, teaching others public speaking and how to contrive arguments for persuasion. They were eventually criticized by many, including the philosopher Plato, who charged that the Sophists believed in making arguments only for the sake of arguing and not because (to put it in terms we might understand today) there was anything of merit in the arguments themselves. Sophistry was thus ridiculed as empty rhetoric—making arguments that sounded clever and logical but were, in reality, specious. This initial assessment of sophistry created a belief that rhetoric itself was really empty and perhaps only an attempt to appear clever for the sake of being argumentative.

Plato's view of rhetoric, however, was refined by his pupil Aristotle, who felt that the practice of rhetoric was something worthy of inquiry, investigation, and understanding, as much for those who would practice rhetoric as for those who might be subjected to rhetoric. In a book written nearly 2,400 years ago,[2] Aristotle introduced readers to concepts of rhetoric—admittedly for public-speaking purposes— that are still applicable today and are actually useful in assessing other forms of persuasive communication. Chief among these concepts were his suggestions that effective arguments typically contained one or more of three "species" of proofs: (1) *ethos,* or the credibility of the speaker; (2) *logos,* or the appeal of logic and reason; and (3) *pathos,* or the appeal of emotion.

In the 1st century BCE, in Rome, members of the governing Senate would often vehemently debate and argue about the issues of the day. A Roman politician and thinker named Cicero was a renowned and prolific writer on rhetoric. Like the Greeks, Cicero believed that rhetoric was best seen in the form of persuasive public speaking known as oratory.

This tradition of rhetoric and public speaking was not limited to Greece and Rome. From the time of K'ung-Fu-Tze (Confucius) in the 5th century BCE until the end of the 3rd century BCE, China experienced an intellectual climate that rivaled that of ancient Greece.[3] Scholars traveling among the states rhetorically advocated a variety of systems of political and economic philosophy.

Likewise, in 15th-century western Africa, traveling storytellers recited parables and humorous narratives, and in northeastern Africa, Islamic scholars went on lecture tours and spoke to very large crowds at a single time.[4] On feast days in one African kingdom (near present-day Mali), it was traditional for a bard to dress in a bird's head mask and deliver a speech to persuade the king to live up to the high standards of his predecessors.[5] Indeed, rhetorical oratory skills were highly valued by Native Americans as well; oratorical ability was often deemed to be a better indication of leadership quality than just bravery in battle.[6]

The common thread in all these references is the practice and spread of rhetoric as persuasion in a communication form mostly as public speaking and nearly always with an application to self-governance and participation, or to governing, or perhaps to the significance of religious beliefs. This was a tradition that also played well in the New World—in colonial America. During the Great Awakening of the 1730s and 1740s, preachers sought to revive religious zeal, which had been waning in the colonies. George Whitefield, for example, traveled through the colonies and drew large crowds for his dynamic, oratorical sermons.[7] He preached in fields because churches were not large enough to accommodate the listeners.[8]

Passionate political oratory helped inspire the American Revolution against the British. Patrick Henry, well known for his oratorical skills, concluded before the Virginia House of Burgesses in 1765 that if changes were not made King George III could lose his head, like other tyrants. Subsequently, colonists began gathering in churches, schools, town squares, and taverns to express their dissatisfaction with the British.[9] In December 1773, approximately 5,000 colonists crowded into Boston's Old South Church to hear Samuel Adams and others denounce the British tea tax.[10]

In this same period of time, also referred to as the Age of Reason, those who studied rhetoric began to rethink the original interpretations of what the word meant—and what it could mean. Whereas some extended the original Greek and Roman ideas of rhetoric, others added to and expanded the possibilities for the term. For example, Richard Whately, writing about rhetoric and argumentation, suggested the legal concepts of *presumption* and *burden of proof.* These concepts, which will be explored in greater detail in the next chapter, helped define the ground rules by which rhetoric could be used by competing *rhetors* (advocates using rhetoric in opposition to one another). This empowered the individuals practicing rhetoric as much as it widened the playing field for those who wished to use rhetoric. Whately wrote mostly assuming a legal context (the courts and the law) in Great Britain for this form of rhetoric, but over time, his expansion of rhetoric would come to be used by anyone engaged in formal debate.[11]

In this same period, Giambattista Vico of Italy offered a new and more expansive construct of rhetoric. Vico's vision of rhetoric explored the relationship between human perceptions of reality and the signs we find in everyday life that affect those perceptions. Unique in Vico's contributions about rhetoric was that human reality was constructed and that this construction could be rhetorical.[12] At a critical level, persuasion might still occur—just as it resulted from a public speech in any of the aforementioned examples—but here the persuasion might occur as we are persuaded by our sense of reality to feel one way or another about our life experiences.

The British rhetorical theorist George Campbell built on this widening construct of rhetoric by further suggesting that rhetorical *signs* or *symbols* were not limited to traditional texts of writing or public speaking. In point of fact, Campbell argued, human beings were capable of being affected and persuaded by everyday types of artifacts—not only traditional texts.[13]

Into the 20th century, the concept of rhetoric continued to change and evolve. Key to this change was the development of *rhetorical criticism*—the means by which observers of rhetoric might observe, analyze, and deconstruct traditional texts or other artifacts for their rhetorical possibilities. Among the many contributions here was that offered by rhetorical scholars who desired a return to *neoclassical theory*[14] (a more contemporary version of Aristotle's original ideas about rhetoric, especially as to persuasion and oratory) as well as that offered by those who advocated *dramatistic criticism*[15] (dramatism is concerned with what rhetoric reveals about human motivation, action, and linguistic reality; it derives from the analysis of drama); *cluster analysis*[16] (observing how rhetorical artifacts reveal the worldview or "terministic screens" of the rhetors who create them); *feminist criticism*[17] (to quote Sonja Foss, "Rhetorical criticism done from a feminist perspective . . . is designed to analyze and evaluate the use of rhetoric to construct and maintain particular gender definitions for men and women"[18]); *fantasy theme criticism*[19] (based on the assumptions that communication shapes perceptions of reality and that shared meanings for symbols can converge to create shared reality or communal consciousness); *generic criticism*[20] (uncovering the similarities in rhetorical situations and their artifacts to discover how "people create individual instances of meaning and value within structured discursive fields"[21]); *metaphor criticism*[22] (analyzing the use of metaphors—non-literal comparisons in which one word or term from one context is applied to another context—within an artifact to determine how they advance the rhetoric of the artifact); *ideological criticism*[23] (analysis of a rhetorical artifact to uncover whatever dominant ideologies—a system of beliefs, identity, and values shared by a group that inform its worldview—may be embedded within the artifact); *narrative criticism*[24] (analysis of an artifact as a narrative form—a way of shaping and presenting a worldview by describing a situation or an event according to elements such as characters, actions, settings, narrator, audience, theme, temporal relations, and causal relations); and *media-centered criticism*[25] (this argues that the rhetorical symbols we use to construct our perception of reality should be analyzed in the context of the medium within which they occur—both entertainment and news media).

Connecting Terrorism and Rhetoric

Although the above brief history is *not* intended as a comprehensive treatment of rhetoric, it is intended to demonstrate that rhetoric, though still fundamentally communication as persuasion, is today seen as more than just the construction we find in public address as oratory. It can be found in any kind of text (both verbal and nonverbal) with symbols that give meaning to our reality. Central to understanding rhetoric for our purposes, therefore, is the identification of symbols in communication.

In the chapters that follow, we will examine rhetoric in terrorism by first returning to our discussion of *definition*, but this time focusing not on what terrorism is but on the purpose or motivation behind defining terrorism in the first place. Thereafter, we will examine the *act of terrorism*, treating the action as *symbolic* in its own right. How are the violence and destruction in terrorism symbolic—and ultimately discursive? Next, we will consider how the meaning of terrorism is negotiated through official *discourse,* with particular emphasis on the public address of government leaders or even that of terrorists. Finally, we will explore how our own preconceptions and discourse about terrorism are in turn primed by the symbols embedded within the *media (both news and entertainment) depiction and interpretation of terrorism.*

In examining these areas where rhetoric and terrorism intersect, I will be drawing from some of the more relevant theories of rhetoric enumerated above. These include using theories of rhetorical presumption to help understand how defining terrorism privileges a specific meaning for terrorism and how labeling and defining implicate the distribution of power and create a sense of "otherness," the rhetorical criticism known as dramatism to examine acts of violence as texts with embedded symbolic meaning, a more modern version of neoclassical criticism to understand the public discourse about terror, and, later, media criticism to examine how the media prime public discourse regarding terrorism. Throughout our discussion of these, we will refer back to the various typologies of terrorism enumerated in the first chapter, including terrorism both *from above* and *from below*—dissent terrorism and state-sponsored terrorism.

These components form what I have previously referenced as rhetorical strands, enveloping each connection in the communication process, as shown in Figure 2.3.

Figure 2.3

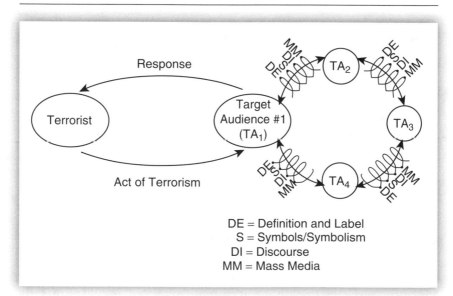

DE = Definition and Label
S = Symbols/Symbolism
DI = Discourse
MM = Mass Media

❖ SUMMARY

In this chapter, we have considered how terrorism may be constructed to have meaning beyond the immediate impact of its violence and/or destruction. To that end, we have examined how terrorism may be seen as a process of communication with messages for multiple target audiences. Seen in this light, terrorism involves persuasion directed at any of these target audiences, and this in turn suggests that there are rhetorical dimensions to the communication process involving terrorism. The concept of rhetoric has developed steadily over the past many centuries, and in this chapter, I have briefly reviewed some of this development, not to condense so much theory and history into a few pages but rather to provide a context for applying this term to terrorism and what I have labeled "rhetorical strands." In the coming chapters, we will examine how each of these strands contributes to the social construction of terrorism for any of its target audiences.

❖ NOTES

1. Some would prefer to define *coercion* as deterrence or compulsion but *persuasion* as the use of logic and reasoning to reach a decision with one's free will. See, for example, Thomas Schelling, *Arms and Influence* (New Haven, CT: Yale University Press, 1966).

2. Aristotle, *On Rhetoric*, trans. George A. Kennedy (New York: Oxford University Press, 1991) at p. 1356a.

3. D. Bodde, *China's First Unifier* (Hong Kong: Hong Kong University Press, 1967) at p. 181.

4. A. A. Boahen, "Kingdoms of West Africa," in *From Freedom to Freedom*, ed. M. Bain and E. Lewis (New York: Random House, 1977) at p. 69.

5. G. Welch, "The Authors Who Talked," in *From Freedom to Freedom*, p. 39, ed. M. Bain and E. Lewis (New York: Random House, 1977).

6. C. Brooks, R. W. B. Lewis, and R. P. Warren, *American Literature: The Makers and the Making* (New York: St. Martin's Press, 1973) at p. 1179.

7. A. Brinkley, *American History: A Survey*, vol. 1, 10th ed. (Burr Ridge, IL: McGraw-Hill, 1999).

8. N. Gabler, "Culture Wars: A Victim of the Third Great Awakening," *Los Angeles Times*, January 14, 2001, p. M1.

9. Brooks et al., *American Literature, op. cit.*, p. 1184.

10. P. Lewis, *The Grand Incendiary: A Biography of Samuel Adams* (New York: Dial Press, 1973) at p. 180.

11. For a fuller description, see R. D. Rieke and M. O. Sillars, *Argumentation and Critical Decision Making*, 3rd ed. (New York: HarperCollins, 1993) at p. 23.

12. See, for example, John D. Schaeffer, *Sensus Communis: Vico, Rhetoric, and the Limits of Relativism* (Durham, NC: Duke University Press, 1990) at p. 114: "Vico describes the way the human mind created human society in his account

of the imaginative universals. These images are 'made true' because the social reality they reflect is called into being precisely when the imaginative universals themselves are created. These imaginative universals are 'true' because they reflect the situation that created them. For Vico, the imaginative universals, not prejudice, form the content of the *sensus communis*."

13. For more, see, for example, Barry Brummett, *Rhetoric in Popular Culture* (Thousand Oaks, CA: Sage, 2006) at p. 62: "Campbell developed a rhetorical theory that explained how human understanding and imagination were addressed by others. Although Campbell also restricted his focus in practice to traditional texts, he and his colleagues opened up the possibility of thinking about ways in which people might be influenced through things other than verbal, expositional, and discrete texts. Because they were concerned with the whole operation of the human mind, these rhetorical psychologists introduced the possibility of thinking about how the mind might be influenced by signs and artifacts found throughout everyday experience, not just during the moment of reading essays or listening to speeches."

14. Much of this was based on H. A. Wichelins, "The Literary Criticism of Oratory," in *Readings in Rhetorical Criticism*, p. 3, ed. Carl Burghardt (State College, PA: Strata, 1995). First published in 1925. For examples of essays employing this method of analysis, see W. N. Brigance (ed), *A History and Criticism of American Public Address*, vols. 1 and 2 (New York: Russell & Russell, 1943) and M. K. Hochmuth (ed), *A History and Criticism of American Public Address*, vol. 3 (New York: Russell & Russell, 1955).

15. See, for example, Kenneth Burke, *The Philosophy of Literary Form: Studies in Symbolic Action*, 3rd ed. (Berkeley: University of California Press, 1973).

16. Kenneth Burke, *Language as Symbolic Action: Essays on Life, Literature and Method* (Berkeley: University of California Press, 1966).

17. See, for example, Karlyn Kohrs Campbell, "The Rhetoric of Women's Liberation: An Oxymoron," *Quarterly Journal of Speech*, 59, 1973: 74–86.

18. Sonja Foss, *Rhetorical Criticism: Exploration and Practice* (Prospect Heights, IL: Waveland Press, 1988), at p. 151.

19. Ernest G. Bormann, "Fantasy and Rhetorical Vision: The Rhetorical Criticism of Social Reality," *Quarterly Journal of Speech*, 58, 1972: 396–407.

20. For more on the development of genre criticism, see Charles Bazerman, "Systems of Genres and the Enactment of Social Intentions," in *Genre and the New Rhetoric*, pp. 79–104, ed. Avia Freedman and Peter Medway (London: Taylor & Francis, 1994).

21. Ibid., at p. 79.

22. For more on metaphor criticism, see Jim Kuypers, *The Art of Rhetorical Criticism* (Boston: Pearson, Allyn & Bacon, 2005) at p. 116.

23. For a fuller treatment of this, see A. Teun van Dijk, *Ideology: A Multidisciplinary Approach* (Thousand Oaks, CA: Sage, 1998).

24. For more on narrative criticism, see Walter R. Fisher, *Human Communication as Narration: Toward a Philosophy of Reason, Value and Action* (Columbia: University of South Carolina Press, 1987).

25. See, for example, W. L. Bennett, *News: The Politics of Illusion*, 2nd ed. (New York: Longman Press, 1988).

3

Labeling and Defining
Terrorism as Rhetoric

❖ ❖ ❖

In the previous chapters, I have on occasion referenced the idea of our reality "being constructed," partially because the "meaning" of symbols has been "negotiated" through our discourse with one another. This concept of ongoing communication sees the process involved as transactional, and to the extent that meaning is negotiated, the process is also to some extent competitive. In some ways, it becomes a game.

Competitive games usually involve winning and losing and are governed by the rules of play. For example, a game may involve rules about boundaries, time limits, the number of players allowable, or the players' conduct. By limiting and refining what players can do, these rules shape what the game will become. This notion of limiting, refining, and shaping a game applies equally well to the process of negotiating meaning in discourse through rhetoric. One very obvious application can be seen in the way definitions are created for discourse.

What is a *definition?* Why does it matter to discourse? In this chapter, we will attempt to answer this question, first by reviewing what a definition is and then by understanding how it is different from a *label.*

❖ DEFINITIONS AND LABELS

Definitions are (according to the definition of the word *definition*) nothing more than the precise, agreed-on formal statements of the meaning of symbols. To define is to make the meaning of something clear. In Chapter 1, I presented numerous definitions of the word *terrorism*. Some (if not all) of these were summarized by Schmid's synthesized definition, which was to see terrorism as "an anxiety-inspiring method of repeated violent action, employed by (semi-) clandestine individual, group or state actors, for idiosyncratic, criminal or political reasons."[1] Defining terrorism in this way allegedly gives meaning to the word by beginning to shape the parameters of the term. According to this synthesized definition, terrorism inspires anxiety but does so with repeated acts of violence (as opposed to singular or random acts of violence). It is "employed" suggesting an intentional, strategic use, as opposed to a serendipitous, unintentional, or mistaken use. In this way, *terrorism* applies to the action of targeting civilians or even military bases purposely but does not apply to accidental violence, such as the United States's accidental bombing of 30 Afghan civilians by a stray shelling of a wedding party.[2] Within Schmid's definition, however, *terrorism* might refer to the actions of a state (thus expanding the possibilities) but only when used systematically and intentionally. Definitions can expand possible meanings and/or contract them. This much describes definition. To define, however, is not necessarily to label. How are the two actions related, and why are they different?

In political communication, to label is to call something or someone by a name. *Terrorism* itself is, after all, a label. In this way, it is a name given to the meaning we associate from the definition above. Labels are distinct from definitions, however; although they give rise to definitions, they also play different roles in the process of discourse. In discourse, labeling provides quick, shorthand identification for whatever is labeled. Using the word *terrorism* to identify a violent attack on civilians in a marketplace gives this violence a quick and easily understood name. Definition, correspondingly, gives shape and narrows or broadens the application of that label and the way it is employed. The negotiation over what labels we should use and how we define their meaning produces different effects, especially when applied to political issues such as terrorism. First, negotiation creates possibilities for both empowering and marginalizing groups who are affected by labels and their definitions. Second, negotiation gives rise to flexible meanings, capable of both inclusiveness and exclusiveness for its users. Third, the end product of a negotiated meaning—the actual meaning or definition of the label—creates a contrast between what is normal/acceptable and what is abnormal/unacceptable. As this negotiated meaning becomes operationalized by common practice and institutionalized by government laws and policy, a presumption of the correctness of the meaning settles in, effectively limiting further negotiation and debate.

In this chapter, I will discuss each of these effects, initially by considering parallel examples of similarly charged labels like *terrorism*; here, I will examine the labels *hate* (as in *hate crime*) and *color* (as in *person of color*), as well as labels that have been reclaimed, such as *queer* and *dyke*, or those—such as *Middle East*—whose unconscious use continues to demonstrate the effects described above. Next, I will apply the same analysis to *terrorism* and will describe how the negotiated meaning of this label is part of a rhetorical process that has the ability to limit its debate and application. In this latter portion of analysis, we will consider how labels and definitions such as those for terrorism may become frames, entrenched by institutionalization and tradition, all of which make changing their meanings more difficult.

Definitions and Labels Can Empower and Marginalize: The Example of *Hate*

In political communication, definitions and labels create possibilities for empowering people, causes, issues, and movements or taking power away from the same. One example of this can be found in the word *hate*. Dictionaries define *hate* as "an intense hostility and aversion usually deriving from fear, anger, or sense of injury,"[3] a descendant of the Old English word *hete*, akin to the Old High German word *haz*. Calling something an "intense hostility" or "aversion," however, is really no different from labeling it an emotion in the generic sense.

In modern parlance, we have come to see *hate* as much greater than a generic reference to hostility or aversion. Contextually, *hate* today refers to bigotry and prejudice and, specifically, to bigotry in the presence of action; hence, the use of terms such as *hate speech* and *hate crime*. In contemporary practice, this bigotry is directed at individuals on the basis of characteristics such as race, ethnicity, sexual preference, gender, and religion and now can also include disability status or even Vietnam-era veteran's status. Of course, this is much different from the original use of the word *hate* as described above. To refer back to our discussion about labels and definitions, this word became a label with a changing and expanding meaning. How and why did that happen?

Though etymology of the word *hate* traces it back to Old English, as well as Old High German, the modern usage of the term in the United States appears to have changed in the early 1970s. Research of various media sources shows that one of the earliest references to the term *hate* as bigotry or prejudice was probably made because of the terminology introduced into public consciousness by the Anti-Defamation League (ADL).

This initial use of the label *hate* appears to have been more in reference to religious bigotry and, more specifically, anti-Semitism. Although he could credit no specific individual for the label *hate* as in *hate crime*, Ira Kaufman, then assistant director of the Central Pacific Region of the ADL, once told me that he believed that the term had originated with the ADL, possibly in connection with anti-Semitic acts about which the ADL had been collecting data for many years.[4] The then ADL board member and practicing attorney Brian Levin, a national expert on hate crimes, concurred in the hypothesis that originally this label was used in reference to anti-Semitism.

> A lot of this came about because of the reporting (of these acts as crimes) . . . and to be honest, Jews in this country would be more likely to report these anti-Semitic crimes for two reasons. First, many of these hate crimes were property crimes, and you couldn't really do anything about it if you didn't report it. Second, Jews in this country didn't have the same distrust of law enforcement that other groups might have, so they wouldn't be reluctant to report.[5]

Levin's point was that American Jewish groups would be more likely to use the label *hate* in this way because they were one of the first groups to formally organize and track data about hate crimes.

By no coincidence, it was through the dogged persistent lobbying efforts of groups such as the ADL that the U.S. Congress began addressing the issue of hate generally, and hate crimes specifically, culminating in the passage of legislation such as the Hate Crimes Statistics Act, enacted in 1990, which required the Department of Justice to acquire data on crimes that "manifest prejudice based upon race, religion, sexual orientation and ethnicity."[6]

The label *hate*, although not paired with the words *crime* or *speech*, could be found in references to anti-Semitism dating back to the early 1970s. For example, a 1973 article in the *New York Times* referred to "hate slogans" when discussing graffiti and vandalism on the walls of Temple Shalom in Brick Town, New Jersey.[7] References in this context were considerably less frequent in this period of time than they are now, although it was more common to see bigotry and prejudice labeled as "bias" or "community disorders"—the latter, a marvelously vacuous if not altogether empty euphemism.

The New York City Police Department, for example, created a Bias Incident Investigation Unit (BIIU) in 1981, charged with investigation of bias-motivated crimes, from incidents such as those occurring at Howard Beach and Bensonhurst. The city of Boston, in comparison, created a special unit in its police department called the "Community Disorders Unit," ostensibly for the same purposes. In the words of the ex–New York Mayor Ed Koch, units such as these were created to ensure that crimes such as "vandalism that consists of a swastika on a synagogue door . . . are treated differently than mere graffiti."[8]

Referring to bigotry and prejudice as "bias" continued to be common in the early part of the 1980s, but by the midpoint of that decade, it became more common to use the label *hate* to describe the same thing. For example, by 1985, even a comparatively conservative mainstream media publication such as the *U.S. News and World Report* embraced this use of the label as it noted the following:

> At a time when Americans are recalling the deadly prejudices of World War II, a new wave of *hatred* [italics added] is building in their own back yard. Jews are targets, as they were in Germany four decades ago, but Blacks, Asians and Hispanics are also being hit.[9]

From roughly this point forward, as the above example illustrates, the label *hate* began to encompass other forms of bigotry and prejudice, including those that are directed at individuals on the basis of their race and ethnicity. Today, we know that the list of those targeted by hate has grown and expanded, even to the point of including groups that might not otherwise be associated with one another.

It is possible to explain the public shift in the use of the label *hate* by looking back at the way an official or institutional embrace of the label *bias* at one time contributed to the official understanding of "bias motivation" as prejudice. It may be that federal laws such as those that authorized data collection officially sanctioned and institutionalized the use of the *hate* label in public discourse. This would be a part of the process of negotiating the use and meaning of labels. There is no doubting the potential of the law to act as a teacher for people in culture and society—but in this instance, such an explanation would be circular. What we label as hate today—bigotry and prejudice—did not begin in 1973, 1985, 1990, or 2010. Unfortunately, bigotry and prejudice are practices that precede these times by thousands of years of human history. So what else explains the use of this label to describe so many forms of bigotry?

One explanation might be that such labels can engage a sort of *umbrella effect* as more and more groups become empowered by and embrace the use of labels originally intended for a more limited group. As more people embrace the term as their own, the label increasingly gains public acceptance and currency in discourse, or if the comparison is not too clumsy, as the umbrella spreads out, more people try to come under it for protection from the elements.

Negotiating Definitions and Labels Creates Flexible Meaning: The Examples of *Color, Queer,* and *Dyke*

On occasion, definitions for labels such as *terrorism* may contract or expand, depending on how their meaning is negotiated. When the meaning expands, the label becomes more inclusive and accessible to different users. When it contracts, the label becomes exclusive, effectively limiting those who may claim it. To illustrate this point, consider the label *color* as used in terms such as *people of color.* The earliest possible references to the label *color* were almost exclusively reserved for race and, specifically, for blacks of African descent. Indeed, the early use of *color,* as in calling a black American *colored* or *a colored person,* referenced the term this way in the pejorative. So common was the use of this label, however, that groups sensitive to the negative meaning in its definition nevertheless used the word in titles such as NAACP (National Association for the Advancement of Colored People).

In our society, labels such as *colored person* and *Negro* were quickly replaced by *black* and later by *African American,* the latter still possessing currency today, although some groups have dropped any reference to *American,* preferring the label *person of African descent.* By the end of the 1980s and into the past decade, a new label had crept into public discourse when referencing members of this community: *people of color.*

Although the early context for this applied to African Americans, the sheer ambiguity in the label *color*—which in many ways meant something darker or different from white—meant that this label could be expanded to include nonblack groups that might otherwise be in positions of minority status relative to the dominant white majority. The list could then grow to include American Indians (Native or Indigenous Americans, as many now prefer to be called), Asian Americans, Hispanic or Latino Americans, Middle Eastern (as in Arab) Americans, Eskimo Americans, Pacific Islander or Samoan Americans, and so forth. In the end, *person of color* came to mean every kind of color—or, in reality, racial grouping (the term *color* is awfully imprecise)—except white European.

The expansiveness of the label pulled many groups into a kind of inclusive solidarity with one another that they might not otherwise— owing to their cultural and political differences—enjoy. The label has empowered these groups by drawing them to one another, as individual minority groups have become a larger collective minority group. In many respects, that is its attractiveness.

A similar result may be observed with the labels *queer* and *dyke*, both of which in common usage were originally intended as pejorative references (respectively) to gay men and lesbians. Although the word *queer* may have seemed less overtly hostile an epithet than the more pejorative label *faggot*, it was surely a hurtful and insulting term, since its definition suggested oddness or something not usual, or out of the ordinary. To be queer was to deviate from the norm. Labeling a gay man "queer" was to imply that his sexuality deviated from the norm or acceptable standard of heterosexuality. Similarly, when used by heterosexuals, the label *dyke* was intended as a vicious kind of insult on lesbians. In use, it may have been intended to label a woman whom a heterosexual man did not find attractive or one who did not appear "feminine" or show interest in men.[10] The origins of this word are not certain, although some have suggested that the label came from its similarity to the word *dick* (as in male penis)[11] or the old English slang *dike*, referring to male clothing; the latter might then imply a sense of masculinity, and hence, women who were labeled "dykes" would be regarded as masculine.[12]

Today, it is clear that labels like these have shifted in their meaning because the communities they once helped marginalize have in turn reclaimed them as their own rhetoric.[13] Emerging from such reclamation is the tendency for the word *queer* to be now used with pride (although this may be more for young people than for older generations of gays and lesbians, who see the word as hateful). Rather than shying away from its meaning of deviating from the norm, they instead claim this meaning as a way of announcing their collective difference. As with the pejorative meaning of "colored" referenced before, embracing the label *queer* has allowed this (mostly younger gay and lesbian) community to dilute this word's capacity to insult or belittle them, and instead it has become a vehicle for empowerment. Again, in a way parallel to the word *color*, some have come to use the word *queer* as an umbrella term, encompassing not only gays and lesbians but also those who are transgendered, transvestites, and bisexuals, as well as people who enjoy the use of leather, bondage and discipline, sadomasochism, and fetishism.[14]

What the examples of *hate, people of color, queer,* and *dyke* demonstrate is that the labels we employ may change over time as their definable meaning becomes negotiated by discourse and normal use. Part of that negotiation involves the inclusiveness or exclusiveness of the intended meaning. Can the definition behind a label be expanded, or is it inherently limited? In the cases of *hate, people of color, queer,* and *dyke,* the definitions were capable of expansion. With *terrorism,* the meaning is still being negotiated, although at this point, it is safe to say that most legal definitions (especially in this country) are not inclusive of terrorism *from above* and thus limit the meaning of the label.

Conscious and Unconscious Use of Labels and Definitions

The previous sections dealt with labels and definitions that were used in ways intentionally to distribute or redistribute power. For rhetorical purposes, this required some intent on the part of rhetors. Interestingly enough, the distributive and redistributive power of labels and definitions can also occur when words are used unconsciously, which is to say, without respect to an intentional impact on their power in any way described before.

As an example, consider the term *Middle East,* which is today a label used to describe a stretch of land, even if there isn't always agreement as to what land qualifies for the term. What exactly is the Middle East? Is it a label for all the land from North Africa to Iran? Does it extend to Central Asia, including Pakistan? Should Afghanistan factor in the equation? Or, possibly, is it more a description of all the Arab and mostly Muslim countries in the area?

The term *Middle East* is believed to have been coined by an American—U.S. Naval Admiral Alfred Thayer Mahan. The author of a well-received book on naval history titled *The Influence of Sea Power Upon History, 1660–1783* (published in 1890), Mahan would later author a significant article for the British *National Review,* in which he argued that Great Britain had a unique opportunity and responsibility to patrol the Persian Gulf region with its powerful navy as a way of fulfilling its colonial protection of India. In making this claim, Mahan wrote,

> The Middle East, if I may adopt a term which I have not seen, will some day need its Malta as well as its Gibraltar. . . . Naval force has the quality of mobility which carries with it the privilege of temporary absences; but it needs to find on every scene of operation

established bases of refit, of supply, and in cases of disaster, of security. The British Navy should have the facility to concentrate in force, if occasion rise, about Aden, India, and the Gulf.[15]

In Mahan's vision, the British Navy would control access to India by controlling the Persian Gulf. Enamored of his ideas, British newspapers such as *The Times* adopted his term *Middle East* and ran a series of articles (20 in all) dealing with the "Middle Eastern Question" and authored by Valentine Chirol. *The Times* reinvented the definition for Mahan's label, expanding the term *Middle East* to now include all coasts and land entrances to India as well.[16] According to Roger Addison, Mahan himself was treated like a hero and even compared with Copernicus: "Just as he had been the first to teach that the earth and other

Photo 3.1   U.S. Admiral Alfred Thayer Mahan is credited with coining the term *Middle East*.

planets revolved around the sun, so Mahan was the first to show that history was determined by the powers that controlled the seas."[17] The definition of the Middle East would become a moving target, continually expanding in ways parallel with the emerging British Empire, which by the end of the First World War sought to fold in the former Ottoman territories in Palestine, Jordan, and Iraq. By this time, Britain was more interested in a natural resource of the area: oil.

By the time of the Second World War, Britain's emphasis in the area would shift from protection of India to defending its interests in Egypt, thus expanding the definition of Middle East again. The United States's growing involvement there would expand this further, over time, bringing us to the point today where there seems to be a "broad consensus that the Middle East extends from the western border of Egypt to the eastern border of Iran and from the Black Sea to the Arabian Sea."[18]

Today, so common is the term *Middle East*—and so accepted is its defining geography—that even residents of the area refer to themselves somewhat unconsciously as "Middle Easterners."[19] But this common acceptance, ne resignation, begs a question, Why is the label *Middle East* called the Middle East?

The answer to this question has less to do with what constitutes the Middle East and its location and more to do with how the word *east* situates its presence relative to somewhere else. To be clear, what is it east of? Following in a tradition begun with the labeling of Asia as "the East," western European countries with economic and strategic interests—and eventually with colonial ambitions—labeled all the land in Asia as "the East" because it was quite literally to the east of Europe and, specifically, to the east of the European countries, such as Great Britain, France, Spain, and Portugal. When Admiral Mahan coined the term *Middle East* in making his argument for the projection of British naval might into the Persian Gulf, he was also extending this form of hegemony. To identify land in a country such as Iran as part of the Middle East was to represent it as something less than itself and more as an object whose geographic existence depended on its latitudinal and longitudinal plotting relative to Great Britain. Doing so, of course, did more than just reduce this land and its inhabitants to mere objects; it also made the referent source (Great Britain) the place of origin. In this latter respect, it privileged and even justified the British position. Placing that in the context of what Mahan was talking about (a projection of British naval might to "protect" its interests in India and check the spread of Russian imperialism) meant that he was in fact suggesting a method for expansion of the British Empire. Is it any wonder then that the American Admiral was compared to Copernicus, the latter having posited the idea of a sun that had planets orbiting around it? In a very real way, the term *Middle East* made Great Britain the equivalent of the sun around which its empire would orbit.

We use this term quite unconsciously today, without considering its origins or its role in helping support not just British but also Western hegemony in the area. It is of little consequence that Britain's empire status has declined in the modern era; that people in this region unconsciously refer to themselves as "Middle Eastern" continues at a very subtle level the practice of marginalizing and subjugating them by those with modern strategic interests in their land and the most precious natural resource: oil.

Definitions, Labels, and the "Opposite of Normal"

An additional feature of labels and the definitions that supply their meaning in the political context is that they provide us with a point of reference for comparison. As suggested with the example of *queer*, labels give meaning to what is abnormal and unacceptable by providing an implicit comparison with what is normal and acceptable, thus reinforcing a preference for the latter over the former. How does this work? Before looking at terrorism, let me return for the moment to a different example: the label *hate.*

An additional appeal of this label (instead of *bigotry* or *prejudice*) owes more to the psychological understanding of hate and its manifestation in human behavior. Unlike political scientists or rhetoricians, psychologists often define hate simply in the context of emotion. For example, hate has been defined as a "hostile emotion, combining feelings of detestation, anger, and a desire to retaliate for real or fancied harm."[20] As an emotion, it has also been defined as "a state of arousal or excitation in humans, in which anger, negative judgments, and impulses of destruction predominate."[21]

Though hate is not itself viewed as innate to the human constitution, it is nevertheless thought to be "indirectly innate"[22] through its association with the emotion of anger and the impulse to aggression, both of which have been described as innate human characteristics. These have been observed in the ancient practice of hunting and gathering by primitive humans, the territorial separation of groups and individuals, strife and conflict between the same, and the creation of hierarchies by social order, class, and division.

Biologists might explain this by associating hate and aggression with the "fight or flight" syndrome, a response arousing the sympathetic nervous system and the endocrine system. With fight or flight, the person manifesting those biological reactions now has an emotional reaction, with the option of engaging the source of the stress or fleeing from it. In the words of Gerald Schoenewolf,

> Hate is the cognitive component of the fight or flight arousal state. The state of aggressive arousal differs from other states of excitement such as anxiety or nervous anticipation. . . . We hate that which frightens, frustrates or unsettles us.[23]

If, as Schoenewolf suggests, we hate that which frightens, frustrates, or unsettles us, and hate is a hostile emotion combining anger and aggression and hostility and detestation, then we can perhaps explain the use of this as a label when seeing hate in the context of bigotry and prejudice. Although it is surely an overstatement of the psychological definition to say that all prejudice and bigotry is hate, we may safely assert that within the confines of bigotry or prejudice rest the potential for anger, negative judgment, and the impulse to aggression or destructive action. The popularization of the term *hate* for bigotry and prejudice may then be explained as an extension of the public willingness to control emotion, to subjugate that which is nonrational to that which is reasoned and rational.

In our society, we teach our children from the time they are young that temper tantrums and uncontrolled outbursts of rage are improper behavior. We reinforce our parental teaching with social rules—in our schools—about civility and orderly conduct. In the curriculum that we offer students, and later in the rules that we follow in life, we emphasize reasoned discourse in decision making. We are critical of emotional responses, even if, by emphasizing what is rational, we go against our own biological tendencies. When adults act in anger or frustration, we may empathize, but we are critical of their failure to control these emotions. If their action is successful, we do not praise the emotion that motivated it; rather, we characterize it as risky and label them "lucky" in the circumstances.

Thus, it is possible that we have labeled this form of bigotry and prejudice as hate because we think of hate as emotion, and emotion is something we can and want to control. It is, after all, far easier to rationalize laws that regulate hate-motivated conduct or expression if we conceptualize hate as an emotion and not as an individual belief or idea. The end result of this defined meaning for the label *hate* is that it also succeeds by providing an implicit comparison between that which is normal, desirable, and acceptable (reasoned discourse, control, rational decision making) and that which is abnormal, unacceptable, and undesirable (hate as emotion, giving rise to anger, aggression, detestation, and possible destructive action). The labels and the definitions that give them meaning provide those contrasts. The same applies as we now look back at the definition and label of terrorism.

❖ RECONSIDERING THE DEFINITION OF TERRORISM

Placing Schmid's synthesized definition of terrorism in the context of the above discussion, we can see that the actual definition is not as important as the purposes for defining and labeling terrorism in the first place. Definitions have several effects: They empower and marginalize at the same time; they create a contrast between us and what I will term *the Other*; and finally, they become legitimized rhetorically by the theory of presumption.

Definitions, Labels, and Empowerment/Marginalization

As indicated above, one effect of providing a definition for a label involves the role of power: how it is rhetorically given and how it can be taken away. The labels *hate* and *color* both had meanings with the inherent capacity to empower audiences. When the word *hate* grew to include many minority groups (on the basis of race, ethnicity, religion, sexuality, disability status, etc.), every one of these groups became stronger by becoming part of a larger, collective whole. Politically, this larger body became empowered to the point where today Congress and all state legislatures have been forced to seriously reconsider hate crime, and to a lesser degree hate speech, and the role that laws might play in eradicating the problem they cause. Likewise, expanding the definition of *color* in *people of color* to mean "groups of other than white European descent" dramatically increased the number and political power of people within that category, again forging alliances (or the perception of them, anyway) between groups that might not otherwise have had a reason or opportunity to combine forces.

In the definition of terrorism, there is also an effect on power, although this time, the redistributive effect of power occurs between the groups of the victims and the terrorists/aggressors. In many situations (if we are referencing dissent/bottom-up terrorism), the terrorists/ aggressors begin in the role of those who are already oppressed or who have the self-perception of being in such a condition. When engaging in terror as a means of fighting back against a perceived oppression, the terrorists reverse the power relationship in that moment, for they now control life and death, destruction or tranquility. The victims, formerly perceived by the terrorists to be in a position benefiting from oppression or the like, are now in the position of becoming the oppressed. Being able to define the act of aggression (violence and/or destruction), however, empowers the victims of terrorism. Why? Because being able to define the violence and/or destruction allows the victim to label it—and the label itself delegitimizes the action.

In the same breath, the act of defining and labeling the action as terrorism also marginalizes the terrorists/aggressors, for it precludes any possibility of legitimacy for their cause or sympathy for their actions. Terrorists are seen as playing outside the rules, without honor, attacking the innocent and weak, who cannot defend themselves. At least, that is the inference drawn from the characterization once the process of defining and labeling has begun.

Terrorism and the Other

In a previous chapter, I briefly described the evolution of *rhetoric*, including discussion of many different forms of rhetorical criticism that have evolved in more recent times. Among these was *ideological criticism*. Ideology refers to a collection of beliefs and values that inform and unify a group's worldview. These can include social, religious, political, cultural, and economic interests, to name but a few. When connected with one another, they help define and identify what a group stands for and/or how it self-conceives. Ideological criticism, in turn, deals with rhetoric that may influence those same beliefs and values. While this rhetorical criticism has been influenced by many different perspectives historically,[24] one influencing factor that has particular resonance in our examination of labeling and defining of terrorism is the concept of hegemony—the idea that some ideologies (values and beliefs) become privileged and prioritized over others and in turn dominate within a culture and between cultures. To paraphrase Antonio Gramsci, hegemony becomes a means of social control, a vehicle for one group or culture to dominate other groups or cultures.[25] Ideological hegemony and privileging of one culture over another can certainly be observed where people within a dominant culture create a sense of shared identity dependent on the construction of a counterpoint—an outsider group or culture that becomes a point of comparison and a rationalizing mechanism for hegemony. We call this outgroup *the Other.*

This is not necessarily a new perspective, and rhetoricians are not the only ones to have studied the concept of the Other. For example, while one of the fathers of modern rhetoric, Aristotle, believed that anyone who did not speak or understand Greek was an excluded Other (presenting a point of comparison with those privileged Greeks who did speak and understand the language),[26] centuries later the German philosopher Georg Wilhelm Friedrich Hegel would employ the same concept to develop a theory of self-consciousness. Hegel argued that "self-consciousness exists in and for itself when, and by the fact that, it so exists for another; that is, it exists only in being acknowledged."[27] By Hegel's reckoning, self-awareness could only exist when there was an awareness of another self. The reality of one's self, therefore, required the recognition of another self-consciousness.[28] This last point became a chief virtue and feature of the Other, creating a context for more than just self-consciousness; indeed, this became a mechanism for self-identity. As Vilo Harle would argue, "just as one cannot know what large means without a sense of the small, one cannot comprehend oneself fully if one has no appreciation of who and what one is not."[29]

In time, this would play out in a variety of methods. The French historian and renowned philosopher René Girard, for example, suggested that societies and cultures needed a sense of the Other to promote those social systems that helped contain and control humankind's more basic instincts to compete and do violence.[30] Knowing how one group of people was different from other groups was what created the necessity for these systems—shared values, traditions, religion, and even laws—that bound one group together and protected them from their more basic instincts.[31]

Another French historian and philosopher named Michel Foucault also employed the sense of the Other to suggest a new ontology that would explain sanity and madness. To paraphrase Foucault, we only know and understand what is sane behavior by observing its counterpart: insanity or madness.[32]

In more recent times, this idea of the Other has also been used to critique power and colonization. In his groundbreaking book *Orientalism*, the late Columbia University professor Edward Said argued that Western (by which he meant western European and, later, American) historical accounts and literary narratives of the Orient generally, and Arabs and Muslims specifically, helped promote a sense of Otherness, which would be contrasted with western European norms. Using a method that would later enrage his critics, Professor Said all too often conflated both those areas now referenced as the Middle East (recalling our earlier discussion in this chapter) with what might be called Central and Far East Asia, assuming that all were under the umbrella label known as the *Orient*. These areas and their peoples were different, to be sure, but pulling them all under the *Orient* label was less carelessness and more deliberate on Said's part. He did not see them as the same; rather, his point was that western Europe saw and treated them the same, for their own purposes at colonization and empire building. The Orient, Said argued, was created for the purpose of contrasting with the *Occident*—the West.

As a Palestinian born in Jerusalem, raised in Egypt, educated in the West, and eventually an American citizen, Said focused his study in *Orientalism* on the Arab and Muslim world and the manner in which it had been depicted in various texts. His account revealed a pattern of representation, not just of Arabs and Muslims in the Orient but as a construction of what it meant to be Oriental. Their representation in historical texts, for example, such as those from Arthur James Balfour or Lord Cromer, based on their personal experiences in the Middle East, were usually used to express the relationship of the self (the Occident) and the Other (Orient) as that between strength and weakness. In Said's words, according to writers like Balfour and Cromer, "The Oriental is irrational, depraved (fallen), childlike, 'different;' thus the European is rational, mature, 'normal.'"[33] Arabs in particular were historically depicted as gullible, lacking initiative, possessed by intrigue, hopelessly unkind to animals, lethargic, and being generally known to be inveterate liars.[34]

Said's larger point was that this construction of Otherness—by academics and government officials—created a base of knowledge of the

Orient in the West, and by those means, they helped rationalize invasion, occupation, and colonization for countries such as Great Britain.

Kenneth Burke suggested that language conveys action and content, reflecting a rhetor's attitudes, values, and worldviews.[35] Burke
also recognized, quite accurately, that all political movements and con-
flicts inevitably require lines to be drawn, sides to be defined, and alle-
giances (or their absence) declared. In analyzing Adolph Hitler's *Mein
Kampf*, he noted the following:

> If a movement must have its Rome, it must also have its devil. For as
> Russell pointed out years ago, an important ingredient of unity in the
> Middle Ages (an ingredient that long did its unifying work despite
> the many factors driving towards disunity) was the symbol of a
> *common enemy*, the Prince of Evil himself. Men who can unite on
> nothing else can unite on the basis of a foe shared by all.[36]

Burke then cited directly from the writing of a younger Hitler, who
had written in *Mein Kampf*,

> As a whole, and at all times, the efficiency of the truly national leader
> consists primarily in preventing the division of the people, and
> always in concentrating it on a single enemy. The more uniformly the
> fighting will of a people is put into action, the greater will be the
> magnetic force of the movement and the more powerful the impetus
> of the blow. It is part of the genius of a great leader to make
> adversaries of different field appear as belonging to one category
> only, because to weak and unstable characters the knowledge that
> there are various enemies will lead only too easily to incipient doubts
> as to their own cause.
>
> As soon as the wavering masses find themselves confronted with
> too many enemies, objectivity steps in, and the question is raised
> whether actually all the others are wrong and their own nation or
> their own movement alone is right.
>
> Also with this comes the first paralysis of their own strength.
> Therefore, a number of essentially different enemies must always be
> regarded as one in such a way that in the opinion of the mass of one's
> own adherents the war is being waged against one enemy alone. This
> strengthens the belief in one's own cause and increases one's
> bitterness against the attacker.[37]

Tragically, history teaches us that Hitler's *one enemy* was the "international Jew," as scapegoating and eventually murdering millions of
Jews became the powerful, horrific "blow" he alluded to in this earlier
phase of his life. Burke's larger point in studying Hitler's words is that
this single focus on a common foe—what Burke refers to as a rhetorical

"unification device"—is a powerful tool for galvanizing the masses and keeping one's own people from questioning or second-guessing a leader. Burke concludes his analysis with a warning for all people to more critically evaluate the rhetoric our leaders use in constructing such enemies.

An important feature of definitions and the labels to which they supply meaning, as suggested earlier, is to create an implicit contrast and comparison between what is normal, acceptable, and desirable and what is abnormal, unacceptable, and undesirable. This allows the audience for such rhetoric to distinguish between the in-group and the outsider—the Other.

The act of defining terrorism, if considered in this light, provides an opportunity for a contrast between us and our enemies, or enemy: the outsider, the Other. In many respects, the drawing of this contrast is more important than the definition of terrorism itself. Furthermore, the definition is not the only place this contrast is made; rather, it is a starting place. To give the contrast more impact, we must also negotiate the meaning of terrorism through our own discourse, which includes the other rhetorical strands that we will explore in the coming chapters. For now, it is enough to point out that the first purpose of defining terrorism is to suggest a distinction between us and the Other—the terrorist. Government definitions for the label of terrorism that limit this concept only to the bottom-up terror also have the effect of creating the Other; in the modern era (post-9/11), the Other has a face and a look that Edward Said would recognize only too well.

Definition of Terrorism and the Theory of Presumption

A third purpose served by defining and labeling terrorism has to do with the theory of presumption. As stated earlier in this book, presumption is shorthand for a theory of rhetoric developed by Richard Whately, asserting that the status quo (the way things are) would be preserved and presumed correct if an initiator of a claim for change could not meet his or her burden of proof in showing that change must occur.

Whately's original argument, used to place stress on the need for evidencing claims made in argument, was initially used in places where people practiced rhetoric in his day—in the legal system. As a legal theory, it can still be found in use today. For example, in a case involving *criminal law,* the accused will be presumed innocent until proven guilty. In a civil law dispute, the plaintiff bears the burden of proof in a claim of liability against the defendant; without such, we presume the innocence of the defendant.

Over time, people have continued using this theory (about presumption) in argument and discourse about government and politics, as well as other aspects of law. In the teaching of traditional forms of debate for students, the concept of presumption is still very much in play, whether students debate propositions of policy or propositions of value.[38] By defining an act as terrorism, we as much limit the debate and negotiation we can have about this subject in discourse because the range of possible acts and motives that constitute this definition has been limited as well. Our tradition in Western culture of using the concept of presumption then rhetorically supports and reinforces the correctness of this definition in practice, effectively limiting discourse and making it very difficult for those who would challenge or seek to expand the definition. In the course of affairs, we become aware of the inconsistencies and contradictions in terrorism. What Basque separatists do to the Spanish government is terrorism, but a French government–sponsored attack on a boat belonging to Greenpeace environmentalists is only a tragic mistake. What the Chechens do to Russians is terrorism, but what Russian troops do in the war with Chechnya is the tragic consequence of a legitimate war. What Palestinians do to Israel is terrorism, but what the Israeli army does in shooting a rock-throwing Palestinian child or an innocent woman answering the door to an apartment suspected (incorrectly) of housing Hamas sympathizers is an unfortunate mistake.

The act of discourse allows us to recognize these as contradictions, but the notion of presumption prevents the discourse from doing more than recognizing. This occurs because the legal definition of terrorism is institutionalized by law and government practice, and presumption recognizes and supports it as the status quo.

A central tenet of the perspective I offer in this book is to suggest that terrorism is also discursive, meaning that it promotes discourse between different audience groups. Their (our) discourse promotes more discourse, and at some point they may bring about policy enactments (e.g., a decision to go to war) and/or changes in the law, including, possibly, a change in the way we label and define terrorism itself. These changes, too, reinforce a sense of rhetorical presumption. As an example, consider the PATRIOT Act, passed in the aftermath of the attacks on September 11, 2001. As suggested in Chapter 1, the act not only introduced sweeping changes to the different ways our law enforcement agencies police against and share information about terrorism, it also reinforced an existing definition of the label terrorism, all of which sees this as primarily bottom-up, practiced against governments and *not by governments.* Note that in this example, the definition of terrorism (privileging a bottom-up perspective) was wrapped inside a sweeping law with a clever name. This was not called an antiterrorism law, nor was it a response to the 9/11 law; rather, it was called the PATRIOT Act. Words have meaning; here, of course, PATRIOT was simply an acronym for "Providing Appropriate Tools Required to Intercept and Obstruct Terrorism." Supporting the act politically thus became literally supporting something identified as PATRIOTic, which is to say that opposing it implied exactly the opposite. Supporting the government position by defining terrorism as bottom-up thus also became synonymous with patriotism, while questioning or challenging the definition was unpatriotic. Even with political opposition to some parts of the PATRIOT Act,[39] there have been few or no questions raised about the definition of terrorism it supports.

In the end, the label *terrorism* becomes synonymous with only certain kinds of illegitimate acts practiced mostly by certain kinds of people. To paraphrase linguist George Lakoff's well-known challenge and warning about words as frames,[40] if I challenged you not to think of a terrorist, you would likely have to force a specific image of a terrorist from your mind. That would be difficult, if not impossible; labeling and defining terrorism as bottom-up means you will have a very limited range of images in your mind, and given the perspective (at least in Western culture) of the Other as different from us, most likely that image will today incorporate a certain ethnicity made plain by its appearance. Perhaps a man with a beard and a turban. How rarely (if ever) would we consider a soldier with a helmet?

❖ SUMMARY

Defining a concept such as terrorism is an important first step in seeing how terrorism is fundamentally a communicative process with rhetorical possibilities. Defining is related to but different from labeling. When we label something, such as an action of some kind, we give a name to it. When we define it, we supply meaning for that label. Defining can be crucial in political communication because the definition of an act or concept can expand or contract (depending on its final form), and such an end result can dramatically limit and shape the amount and nature of discourse about the same. For various reasons, definitions may be very expansive or extremely narrow. Definitions also provide a contrast between what is normal and acceptable and what is abnormal and unacceptable.

The current definitions of terrorism—even that offered by Schmid—are similarly rhetorical. Schmid's definition, for example, provides an implicit contrast between what is normal or acceptable action and what is abnormal and unacceptable. The definition also allows a victim of terror to become empowered by the act of defining, and while it does this, it similarly acts to marginalize or rhetorically take power back from the terrorist. Presumption, as a rhetorical theory, then supports and reinforces the correctness of such a definition, effectively limiting further discourse about terrorism.

As suggested earlier, the reasons and purposes served by defining terrorism have a tremendous significance in our beginning to understand how this concept is communicative and rhetorical. In the next chapter, we will explore how an action that is violent and/or destructive—fitting within the definitions for terrorism—can itself be communicative and rhetorical.

❖ NOTES

1. Alex P. Schmid, *Political Terrorism: A Research Guide to Concepts, Theories, Data Bases and Literature* (New Brunswick, NJ: Transaction Press, 1983) at p. 70.

2. "Villagers Recount Terror of US Air Raid," *New York Times*, July 4, 2002, p. A6.

3. See, for example, *Merriam-Webster's Collegiate Dictionary*, 10th ed. (Springfield, MA: Merriam-Webster, 1993) at p. 532.

4. In a telephone interview with Ira Kaufman in September 1994, Mr.Kaufman reported having spoken with more senior members of ADL, including Mike Lieberman, who noted that the ADL had started using the term in its publications at least "back into the mid-eighties," by which point the context for hate and anti-Semitism was already established and accepted.

5. Interview with Brian Levin, September 1994.

6. Federal Bureau of Investigation, *Summary Reporting System, National Incident Based Reporting System: Hate Crime Data Collection Guidelines* (Washington, DC: U.S. Department of Justice, 1991) at p. 1.

7. "Metropolitan Briefs; From the Police Blotter: Arrests in State Rose in 1972," *New York Times*, May 22, 1973, p. 45

8. Edward Koch, "Toward One Nation, Indivisible," *New York Times*, June 26, 1987, p. A27.

9. Ted Gest, "Sudden Rise of Hate Groups Spurs Federal Crackdown," *U.S. News & World Report*, May 6, 1985, p. 68.

10. See Philip Herbst, *Wimmin, Wimps and Wallflowers: An Encyclopaedic Dictionary of Gender, Sexual Orientation Bias in the United States* (Boston: Intercultural Press, 2001) at p. 79: "Among heterosexuals, *dyke* may be applied to any lesbian, the generalization all the more a term of contempt. In fact, some men find the *dyke* label convenient for putting down women who are seen as unattractive, who do not act "feminine," or who show no interest in men."

11. For more on this, see Robert L. Chapman, *The Dictionary of American Slang*, 2nd ed., abridged (New York: HarperCollins, 1998).

12. For more on this, see Stuart Berg Flexner and Ann Hnov, *Speaking Freely: A Guided Tour of American English* (New York: Oxford University Press, 1997).

13. See Belinda Brooks-Jordan, Andrew Bainham, and Loraine Gelsthorpe, *Sexuality Repositioned: Diversity and the Law* (Oxford, UK: Hart, 2004) at p. 134.

14. See Anna Livia and Kira Hall, *Queerly Phrased: Language, Gender and Sexuality* (New York: Oxford Press, 1997) at p. 23. Livia and Hall note, however, that some in the queer community decry this expansive use of the term, arguing that this "devalues gay people and their interests by burying them in a loose collection of sexually transgressive types."

15. Alfred Thayer Mahan, "The Persian Gulf and International Relations," in the British *National Review,* (September, 1902) at p. 39.

16. See Pinar Bilgin, *Regional Security in the Middle East: A Critical Perspective* (New York: Routledge Curzon, Taylor & Francis, 2005) at p. 72.

17. Roger Adelson, *London and the Invention of the Middle East: Money, Power, and War, 1902–1922* (New Haven, CT: Yale University Press, 1995) at p. 22.

18. Colbert C. Held and Mildred McDonald Held, *Middle East Patterns: Places, Peoples and Politics* (Boulder, CO: Westview Press, 2000) at p. 7.

19. Hamid Dabashi, *Post Orientalism: Knowledge and Power in Time of Terror* (New Brunswick, NJ: Transaction Books, 2008) at pp. 211–212.

20. Robert Goldenson (ed), *Longman Dictionary of Psychology and Psychiatry* (New York: Longman Press, 1984) at p. 335.

21. Gerald Schoenewolf, "Hate," in *The Encyclopedia of Human Behavior,* vol. 2, p. 501 (New York: Academic Press, 1994).

22. Ibid.

23. Ibid., p. 502. See also Sigmund Freud, *Civilization and Its Discontents* (London: Hogarth Press, 1930); I. Eibl-Eibesfeldt, *Love and Hate: The Natural History of Behavior Patterns* (New York: Shocken, 1974); Gerald Schoenewolf, *The Art of Hating* (Northvale, NJ: Jason Aronson Press, 1991).

24. For example, structuralism, poststructuralism, and postmodernism.

25. See Antonio Gramsci, *Selections From the Prison Notebooks,* trans. and ed. Quintin Hoare and Geoffrey Smith (1971; Reprinted, New York: International, 1987).

26. Vilo Harle, *The Enemy With a Thousand Faces: The Tradition of the Other in Western Political Thought and History* (Santa Barbara, CA: Greenwood, 2000) at p. 10.

27. See G. W. F. Hegel, *Phenomenology of Spirit,* trans. A. V. Miller (Oxford, UK: Clarendon Press, 1977) p. 105 and, for the German, Gesammelte Werke, ed. Rheinisch-Westfalischen Akademie der Wissenschaften (Hamburg, Germany: Felix Meiner, 1968 ff.), Vol. IX, p. 104.

28. Philip J. Kain, "Self-consciousness, the Other and Hegel's Dialectic of Recognition: Alternative to a Postmodern Subterfuge" *Philosophy and Social Criticism* 24, 1998: 105–126.

29. Vilo Harle, *The Enemy With a Thousand Faces* (Westport, CT: Praeger 2000) at pp. 10–11.

30. René Girard, *Violence and the Sacred* (Baltimore: Johns Hopkins University Press, 1977) at p. 49: "Order, peace and fecundity depend on

cultural distinctions; it is not these distinctions but the loss of them that gives birth to fierce rivalries and sets members of the same family or social group at one another's throats."

31. David P. Haney, *William Wadsworth and the Hermeneutics of Incarnation* (University Park, IL: Penn State University Press, 1989) at p. 59: "Girard's basic argument is that human society is founded on relationships of rivalry and acts of collective violence. Culture provides systems of differentiation, from sacrificial rituals to judicial systems, in order to contain that violence and to hide the violent nature of culture's origins. To see unity of self and other as a goal and difference as an impediment to that unity is a romantic illusion. The truth of the matter is that difference is the safety mechanism that keeps us from seeing the other as the Same; if self and other are identical, rivalry results and society is reduced to its original state of reciprocal violence."

32. Michel Foucault, Richard Howard, and David Cooper, *Madness and Civilization: A History of Insanity in the Age of Reason* (New York: Routledge, 2001) at p. xi: "We must describe from the start of its trajectory that 'other form,' which relegates Reason and Madness to one side or the other of its action as things henceforth external, deaf to all exchange, and as though dead to one another.

33. Edward Said, *Orientalism* (New York: Vintage Books, 1978) at p. 40.

34. Ibid.

35. Kenneth Burke, *A Grammar of Motives* (1945; Berkeley: University of California Press, 1969) at p. xxii.

36. Kenneth Burke, "The Rhetoric of Hitler's 'Battle'," in *The Philosophy of Literary Form: Studies in Symbolic Action,* 3rd ed., rev. (Berkeley: University of California Press, 1973) at p. 122.

37. Adolph Hitler, *Mein Kampf,* quoted in Burke, "The Rhetoric of Hitler's 'Battle'," *op. cit.*, at p. 122.

38. Joseph Tuman, "Natural Value Hierarchies and Presumption: Merging Stipulated Artificial Presumption With Natural/Psychological Presumption," in *CEDA Yearbook,* vol. 13, p. 10, ed. Ann Gill (Dubuque, IA: Kendall Hunt, 1992).

39. See, for example, Philip P. Purpura, *Terrorism and Homeland Security: An Introduction with Applications* (Oxford, UK: Butterworth-Heinemann, 2007) at p. 176. Concerns have been raised, for example, about the use of roving wire taps, expanded power for search warrants to areas outside a warrant's jurisdiction, so-called delayed notice or sneak and peak investigations, and expanded government power to spy on Internet communications.

40. See George Lakoff, Howard Dean, and Don Hazen, *Don't Think of an Elephant: Know Your Values and Frame the Debate. The Essential Guide for Progressives* (White River Junction, VA: Chelsea-Green, 2004). Using an example of elephants to illustrate his point about how labels become frames for our consciousness, Lakoff challenges the reader to not think of an elephant— and correctly observes that the command is not manageable because the word instantly serves as a frame for a specific acquired image. As a label, there is no other visual image associated with the word.

4

Symbols, Symbolism, and Terrorism

Means and Implements

❖ ❖ ❖

The U.S. Supreme Court long ago correctly recognized that almost any form of nonverbal behavior or action can be potentially expressive,[1] even if not always protected in the United States as a form of free expression. Although the Court's focus here was on distinguishing protected expression from unprotected expression, its point was relevant for our discussion about terrorism because conduct and action can be expressive—most commonly as symbolism.

In this chapter, we will examine how the actual acts of terror violence and destruction are themselves communication with a rhetorical dimension. We will also explore how symbols can be found in the tools and implements of terror, as well as in the targets of terrorism. The word *symbol* derives from the Latin *symbolism,* referring to a token of identity. In modern use, when we describe something as a symbol or declare that it possesses symbolic value, we are suggesting that this thing—whether an object, a word, a sound, or conduct—may be interpreted to mean something more than itself. How is it, then, that terrorism as violence and destruction means more than violence and destruction?

❖ SYMBOLS, SYMBOLISM, AND VIOLENCE/DESTRUCTION

Though a seemingly limitless range of objects, actions, words, and signs may be construed as symbolic, three criteria help us know when a symbol is in play. The first of these is *intent of the communicator/rhetor.* Here we would ask, Does the individual who employs a symbol intend for it to be interpreted in a particular way? Where there is evidence of such intent, the case for treating the act or object (or threat of the same) as symbolic and expressive will be stronger. Does the absence of intent suggest that there is no symbolic meaning? Suppose an individual employs a symbol without intending to do so. For example, in a nonterrorism setting, suppose that you merely wish to engage in the nonverbal behavior of walking on a sidewalk from one end of a block to the other. In this scenario, further suppose that the sidewalk cuts across an area that is police-restricted for security purposes but that you are unaware of this. If you cross this line in ignorance of the restriction, can your walk still be construed as a form of symbolic protest and civil disobedience against the police? Or must you know that your act is unlawful and intend that observers will consider it as a protest, for your conduct to be considered symbolic? Some speech communication theorists distinguish message behavior from nonmessage behavior on the basis of intent,[2] whereas others believe that all behavior is communication if it is interpreted by someone in a meaningful way.[3] The latter of these perspectives makes better sense when we apply the question of intent to determining symbols in actions such as terrorism. Clearly, expressed intent of the communicator/rhetor terrorist, such as a call to "take credit" for a bombing, in which the caller explains the reasoning and meaning of the attack, will be clear evidence that the explosion is intended as symbolic. But the lack of such intent does not mean that an act or object is not symbolic. As will be seen, an action or object may become symbolic for the audience depending on how the meaning of such a symbol is interpreted and negotiated by those who receive it.

A second criterion we may employ in considering a symbol is *context of the communication.* Here we would ask, What is the context for this symbol? Regardless of intent, objects and actions may have different consequences for symbolic value when considered in different contexts. For our purposes, *context* refers to the situation within which the symbol occurs. This can include the surrounding environment, the timing, the audience and its background, and so forth. To extend the earlier example, if you are accompanied on the sidewalk by many other pedestrians, the symbolic value of the action may be very different from the symbolic value of your action if you walk the street with others who are carrying signs and placards protesting the cruel treatment of animals at a business housed in the building on the street. And if you walk with these people, although never carrying a sign yourself, your actions may still have symbolic significance just by your presence at that particular moment. Context, therefore, is a significant consideration for determining the symbolic worth of nonverbal communication. When we apply this to terrorism, we look to the context within which the terror violence and destruction—or even just the threat of it—occurs. Where does the act or threat of terror occur? Who is the target audience? Within this environment, what are the means by which the terrorism takes place? What is the timing for the attack or threat, and how may that affect the way the intended audience perceives the terror?

A third criterion for examining symbolic value is *relativity of the symbolic message.* Here we ask, What are the relative effects of the message on different audience members? It may be argued that regardless of intent and context, symbolic meaning is at best an amorphous concept because of its relative effects. Different people may see and interpret the same action in entirely different ways. The way we, as receivers, interpret messages we receive is a relative consideration. Each of us may indeed look at the same act or object and see it entirely differently. Of relevance here for terrorism is whether those in one of the audiences for the terror (and there will often be more than one audience) will perceive and interpret the symbolic meaning in the same way.

At one level, terrorism may be seen as violent action and destructive consequences on a small or large scale, with loss of life, personal injury, or destruction of property. Some may wonder, Where is the symbolic message in such activity? Indeed, why isn't a punch just a punch? A kick, just a kick? A shooting or an explosion, just a shooting or explosion? Freud once suggested that thoughts and fantasies were symbolic representations of actions, such that they could precede actions and substitute for them as well. Dr. James Gilligan, a director of the Center for the Study of Violence at Harvard Medical School, has argued in response to Freud that

> the opposite is also true. Actions are symbolic representations of thoughts. That is, actions can precede and serve as substitutes for conscious thoughts. They can take the place of thinking in words, if the behavior is never interpreted or translated into words and ideas. . . . Burke wrote that . . . we must learn to interpret language as symbolic action. I am suggesting that in order to understand violence we must reverse that procedure and learn to interpret *action as symbolic language*—with a symbolic logic of its own.[4]

If so, what is the symbolic language of terrorism?

Timothy McVeigh and the Oklahoma City Bombing

Possibly, we might explore the acts of violence as demonstrations of the feelings and emotions of those who commit them. With dissent terrorism (terrorism *from below*), the act of violence and destruction may be seen as the symbolic expression of rage. For example, the explosion that destroyed a federal building and killed 168 innocent people, including children, at Oklahoma City was eventually linked to an American named Timothy McVeigh. With the help of Terry Nichols (McVeigh's accomplice turned state witness); McVeigh was convicted in 1997 and executed for the heinous deed in 2001. His was an act, incidentally, that was first blamed on terrorist groups from other countries and then attributed to someone from the United States in what was labeled "domestic terrorism."

Photos 4.1 and 4.2   The federal building in Oklahoma City after the act of terrorism. Timothy McVeigh was charged with and convicted of the crime, which resulted in the deaths of 168 people.

Source: U.S. Department of Justice.

At the trial, McVeigh's attorneys did not attempt to contest the physical evidence (McVeigh and the truck, the explosive material, etc.) or the mostly circumstantial evidence (there were no eyewitnesses who could place McVeigh at the scene of the crime but plenty who could describe McVeigh's motives and role in the affair), but instead they chose to try and paint a sympathetic portrait of the man with testimony from family and friends in an attempt to humanize him. They then explained his actions as symbolic of the rage he felt against the federal government in general, and the Bureau of Alcohol, Tobacco and Firearms (BATF) specifically, for its role in the deaths of some 70 American members of the Branch Davidian compound at Waco, Texas, during a long assault by FBI and BATF agents. In his own mind, McVeigh's act was symbolic of his rage over the suffering inflicted by his own government. At the trial, prosecutors made much of the T-shirt McVeigh had worn on the day he drove the truck to the Murrah Federal Building in Oklahoma City. On the shirt were written Thomas Paine's famous words: "The tree of liberty must be refreshed from time to time with the blood of patriots and tyrants."

The Japanese Red Army

Another possible way to interpret the language of terrorism as an act of violence and/or destruction is to consider its threat potential—the terror act as a symbol of future threat. When terrorists strike in a public place or in a fashion with potential for publicity, the message for those who witness the terror is often that this can happen to you too—next time. Whereas some targets are chosen purposely for this effect, at times, the random selection of targets makes this message all the more terrifying, creating the impression that terrorism can strike anywhere, any time.

This can occur when the terrorist strikes the public or even when terrorists turn on their own. For example, the Japanese Red Army, a terror group that emerged from the period of student unrest at universities around the world in the 1960s, was initially created to follow the example of a West German terrorist group with the same name (Red Army), hence the reason that the Japanese version required the word *Japanese* in the title. The Japanese Red Army initially engaged in successfully hijacking a plane bound for North Korea but eventually branched out to street violence, armed robbery, bombing, and assassinations.

Later, the group fractured into two smaller groups: One of them (led by Shigenobu Fusako) wanted to expand the international concern and reach of the group, especially in the Middle East, whereas the other (led by Moro Tsuneo) wanted to stay focused on Japan and Asia. Tsuneo later decided to conduct an internal terror campaign, kidnapping Red Army terrorists and beating some to death while leaving others to die, bound and gagged, in the wilderness. This terrorism—a type of internal purging—was meant not only to punish and visit retribution on those Army members out of step with the group's leadership but also to serve as a symbol of future terror, representing what would happen to other Red Army members who deviated from group leadership in this endeavor.[5] In many respects, the deaths of some Red Army members or the image of others left beaten, bound, and gagged in the wilderness served as a particularly potent threat.

The Tupamaros

In Uruguay, a terrorist group known as the Tupamaros[6] practiced an effective decentralized terror campaign against government and foreign targets within the country.[7] According to the economist Arturo Porzecanski,[8] the Tupamaros felt that they could not force a successful revolution unless there was a unique intersection of political, social, and economic factors. This intersection, called the *coyuntura*, would provide a clarifying moment for all Uruguayans to see that revolution was necessary and that support for the Tupamaros was required. Terrorism was seen as a means of bringing on the *coyuntura*. The revolution, also known as the *salto*, against the government would come after this and would be waged by an army of the people. The acts of violence and destruction practiced by this group, which included arson, assassination, kidnapping, hijacking, and bank robbery, were, to some extent, engaged in for their symbolic worth. For example, spectacular daytime robberies of some of the country's largest banks (including one in which the Tupamaros took approximately $6 million) were meant to be symbolic of the image they wanted to create for themselves—that of Robin Hoods who would redistribute wealth to the people. Ultimately, however, this money was used only to finance their own operations, and the Tupamaros faced a public relations disaster with the Uruguayans, who perceived them as little more than common thieves. To counter this impression, they later staged hijacking of food shipments, including one on Christmas Eve, with the food being redistributed to the poor and needy. The hijacking became a symbol of the public image they wanted, although by that point, many in the public were already skeptical about this as empty rhetoric.

❖ SYMBOLISM IN THE IMPLEMENTS
   AND TOOLS OF TERRORISM

Another productive source for study of symbolism and the act of terrorism can be found in the implements and tools of terror. Here I refer not as much to the act of violence and destruction as to the means by which the violence and destruction are enabled. What are the implements and tools of terror? These can include the specific kinds of weapons used, as well as the uniforms and propaganda tactics employed in a terrorist campaign.

The Molly Maguires

Although there is some historical dispute as to how the group known as the Molly Maguires acquired their moniker, there is little disagreement about their contributions in providing a kind of agrarian resistance to English control of rural Irish land. In the 1700s, many Irish were forced under a feudal system to work and farm on land that belonged to an aristocratic class—either by the English or their designates. Under the original agreements, the Irish were allowed to lease small plots of land known as *conacres* where they could grow seasonal crops such as potatoes—often for their own consumption. By the 1760s, many of the landowners had decided to cancel these leases, fencing off land for grazing and raising of livestock, and effectively limiting any space available for the indigenous population to raise food for themselves. As part of a resistance, groups of mostly young men arose, forming secret alliances to subvert the landowners. They went by different names, including the *Whiteboys*, the *Ribbonmen*, and eventually the *Molly Maguires.*

Their forms of resistance initially included tearing down fences, replowing pasture lands (often during the night) for crop growing, and the occasional killing of livestock. Eventually, this was also accompanied by acts of violence on the landowners or their designates. In time, their activities included beatings, burnings, and murders. Another tradition of the period included what was called "coffin notices," as warnings and threats made to potential victims. The original Molly Maguires came into existence near the end of this period of resistance.[9] As suggested above, there are different views about how the Molly Maguires acquired their name. One theory suggests that they were named after a real woman who had been victimized by the new land policy, while another possibility was that the name referenced a woman who led the group during its nighttime raids. In either capacity, the Molly Maguires distinguished themselves from their forerunners by dressing in women's clothes for their raids and also using powder or burnt cork to rub on and blacken their faces.

In this respect, the original Molly Maguires used symbolic implements for their terror that were in some ways parallel to what the Ku Klux Klan would later use: a means of dress to conceal their identity. This made it harder to catch or prosecute them while at the same time allowing their threat to linger; a day after one of their attacks, one would never know if the men one saw then in the village were in fact the same people who had committed violence the night before. The historian Kevin Kenny has suggested that an additional symbolic purpose to dressing in women's clothing was to make an intentional social transgression, itself symbolizing the absurdity of the conditions facing the Irish.[10]

The same difficult and inhumane conditions facing the Irish (most if not all of whom were Catholic) encouraged many of them to seek their fortunes in the New World. Following a wave of Irish immigration to the United States, many of these individuals took up trade working with their Welsh and German immigrant counterparts in the rich anthracite coal fields of northeastern Pennsylvania, for example, in Schuylkill County. Work in these mines, however, was extremely dangerous, and in this period (following the end of the American Civil War), there was tremendous demand for more coal, driving the mine owners and operators to demand more production, even at great risk to their workers. Led by the German miners who brought with them a tradition of organized labor, the miners eventually formed a union called the Workingmen's Benevolent Association (or WBA), which aggressively demanded concessions from mine owners for worker safety and hospital care. A struggle between the union and coal mine owners led to the great strike of 1875, after which time the union was all but broken, and many of these same Irish miners were forced to return to work with diminished wages. It was during this period that a wave of violence against coal mine operators (and managers) and owners swept the area, both in the form of destructive violence such as arson or bombings to close the mines, along with personal attacks from shooting and stabbing. It was suggested that many of these Irish immigrants had brought with them the tradition of the Molly Maguires—now turning what had been an agrarian resistance effort in Ireland to one which targeted the wealthy owners of the mines; the latter were accused of exploiting their workers—a charge which was no doubt accurate, given the hazardous nature of the work and the very low rate of compensation for the risk.[11] Over time, the Molly Maguires were implicated in numerous murders of mine operators, along with episodes of arson and bombings.[12] Although it is not believed that the Irish American version of the Molly Maguires wore dresses to do their work,[13] they did still employ the use of blackface, along with the practice of coffin notices.

Photo 4.3   Example of a coffin notice alleged to have been left by the Molly Maguires.

Source: Franklin B. Gowen's *Argument Before the Joint Committee of the Legislature of Pennsylvania* (1875).

The coffin notices would be sent anonymously to "mine bosses they didn't like. The coffin notices were written threats that promised death if certain grievances weren't put right. If the bosses ignored the threats, the Mollies followed through on their promises."[14] One alleged example of such a coffin notice featured a drawing of a coffin with drawings of pistols on each side. Beneath it were written the words "Notice you have carried this as far as you can by cheating the men you three Bosses be careful if the above don't be you'r hous in a short time." Beneath these words was a drawing of a third pistol, along with the words "From a stranger he nowes you."[15] In this respect, similar to the burning cross or the hangman's noose from the Klan, the Maguires are alleged to have left a threatening calling card as a precursor to death if their demands were not met.

An additional symbolic element for terror attributed to the Maguires owes to their practice of bombing, ostensibly with dynamite. Consider the irony in this kind of terror. Dynamite was also the means by which the mines were opened or enlarged. In this sense, these explosives too were symbolic of that which oppressed the miners. By using this same means to visit retribution on the mine operators and owners, the Molly Maguires were in fact transforming this to a symbol of their revenge.

It is important to remember that much of the historical record about the alleged activities of the American version of the Molly Maguires was in fact supplied initially by a man who owned both railroad and coal interests (his name was Franklin B. Gowen) and collected by a private detective (James McParland) he had hired from the Pinkerton National Detective Agency. Their evidence fueled charges that led to the arrests of more than 50 alleged Maguires, and for many, their conviction and execution by hanging. As we shall explore in a later chapter on mass media, the lasting

Photo 4.4 Franklin B. Gowen was responsible for amassing information that led to the charges against members of the Molly Maguires, and was instrumental in sensationalizing their trial, conviction, and public executions.

image of the Maguires as real terrorists was in part generated by sensationalized news coverage of their activities, along with their depictions in entertainment media such as novels. Worse, in a manner eerily similar to what Edward Said complained of when he accused Western historians of merely reinforcing stereotypes of Middle Easterners and Muslims, it may well have been the case that American historians merely reinforced the arguments against the Maguires by repeating without critically examining the questionable evidence introduced against them at their trial.

November 17

A Greek terrorist group known as November 17 waged a campaign against both the Greek government and the U.S./European imperialist targets for nearly 30 years. The origins for November 17 go back to opposition groups to the military junta in power in Greece from 1967 through 1974. This terrorist group took its name from a violent and tragic 1973 student uprising that helped eventually fell the junta. It was and is the perception of those in the November 17 that the junta only stayed in power for as long as it did because of the backing of the U.S. government. Consequently, even as the junta fell from power, November 17 turned its attentions to American targets, as well as others allied with the United States, especially those within NATO (the North Atlantic Treaty Organization). In that period of time, this group was responsible for numerous bombings and shootings, including 23 assassinations in Athens, starting in 1975 with the then CIA Station Chief Richard Welch. Of note for our purposes in the symbolism of implements and tools of terror is the fact that most of these assassinations were carried out with one of two .45 caliber handguns—a Browning or a Smith and Wesson—both of which could be identified (such that they became the group's calling cards) and both of which were made in America. This last point was most especially significant, as the members of this group wanted American targets to understand that they would be attacked with American weapons.[16] The handguns became symbols of violence by America being directed back at Americans.

Terror From Above: The USSR and Afghanistan

In the period of time that the former Soviet Union suffered through its own kind of Vietnam experience, special forces troops in the employ of the Soviet state practiced a form of terrorism on Afghanis suspected of having ties to the warring Mujahideen fighters. The Soviet Army, allegedly in Afghanistan at "the request" of the Afghani government (which itself had come to power after a coup in April 1978 with the full backing of the USSR), found itself in a rapidly worsening military conflict that would keep them there from December 1979 through February 1989—a decade!—at a cost of 15,000 Soviet soldiers (and those are only the ones in the official government accounting) and approximately 1 million Afghanis. Soviet troops employed a wide variety of conventional military weapons in Afghanistan, such as rocket launchers with Russian names such as GRAD (translates to "hail") and URAGAN (translates to "hurricane"), large-caliber machine guns called DShKs, automatic rifles such as the AK47 and the AK74, MIG and SU fighter jets, and the enormous MI-18 and MI-24 helicopters, which could be used as flying gunships. As the United States had attempted in Vietnam, the Russian forces also attempted a form of psychological warfare in Afghanistan, designed to undermine popular support for the Mujahideen.

One example of this Soviet-style warfare, which would otherwise be called by its rightful name as state-sponsored *terror from above,* was the practice of concealing low-grade explosives in children's toys.[17] These toys were then dropped from the air (making this a literal terror from above) or left in villages suspected of sympathizing with the Mujahideen. The purpose was for children to find and attempt to play with them before being killed or maimed by the explosive devices inside. The assumption was that the child might take the explosive-charged toy back to the area where the Mujahideen were hiding and, when triggering the explosive, kill all within a certain blast radius. More often than not, however, children were the victims, and these toys became symbols of ruthless violence without conscience. The toys, like those children who were maimed but not killed, became symbols of lost innocence and senseless brutality. In either capacity, the goal had been to intimidate villagers and discourage them from assisting the Mujahideen; however, the opposite effect was achieved. The Mujahideen, consistently outnumbered and underestimated by the Soviet military, became emboldened, even with heavy losses. The Soviet exodus from Afghanistan in 1989 could scarcely be called a triumph for the USSR.[18] Sadly, it is now alleged that the Russian Army has used this same tactic of explosives hidden within toys in its military conflict with Chechnya.[19]

Suicide Bombers in Israel and Palestine

Similarly, in modern Israel and Palestine, the most recent violence in the West Bank confrontations between Israeli settlers, Israeli military, and Palestinians living in areas ceded to the Palestinian Authority has created a trend toward a different kind of weapon—the so-called suicide bomber. Ironically, in this example, children, instead of becoming the target of toys that contain hidden bombs, become bombs themselves. Many young Palestinians, including in one instance boys as young as 14 years old,[20] now feel compelled to become "human bombs," sacrificing themselves in the same terrorist act that also kills Israeli targets, both military and civilian. In this tragic and enduring conflict, which sometimes appears beyond political solution, the weapon of terror is combined with a human body, transforming the rhetorical symbolism in both. For some Israelis, the suicide bomber represents viciousness and inhumanity, but for many more, the suicide bomber is a symbol of the hopelessness and vulnerability of their situation—all in spite of vast military superiority and the backing of the United States. Regardless of all the security that comes with such advantages, Israelis are still forced to ask, How do you defend against this kind of terror without removing every possible suspect from the Israeli border? For many Palestinians, the suicide bomber becomes a symbol of heroism and martyrdom. They do not see this as an act of terror or murder as much as a kind of military response to Israeli occupation and denial of political freedom. And even for Palestinians who reject the concept of using this weapon against Israeli occupation, the symbolic power of the bomber as a martyr makes it very difficult to openly criticize the act or the individual martyr. Worse for both sides, with the ongoing symbolic value of these bombers— admittedly different for both communities—there is little to suggest that the bombing will stop. If Israel makes concessions in the face of this terrorism, it will be perceived as legitimizing the efficacy of the terror, suggesting that it might be an effective weapon after all. There is no current political will to take any such stance in Israel today. Likewise for Palestinians, this kind of terror becomes a response to occupation that guarantees carnage and headlines. It forces world attention—but may not always garner American sympathy—on their plight and condition. It may even become the instrument that, if impossible to respond to, results in diminished public confidence for those in power in the Israeli government, maybe someday forcing a change in leadership.

The Ku Klux Klan in America

The example of the Ku Klux Klan (KKK) shows that the implements and tools of terrorism may also extend to the clothing of terrorists, as well as other artifacts in their possession. In the United States, the Klan has operated in various incarnations since 1867. I say *various incarnations* because it is often assumed that the KKK today is the same Klan that existed 135 years ago. In fact, organizationally, the Klan has had three different existences.

The Klan was initially conceived in the mid-1860s as a private club of six men in Tennessee, most of whom were college educated and had been officers in the Confederacy. As far as is known, their original purpose was not clearly defined beyond enjoying dressing in costumes and riding between towns at night. The name they selected for themselves came from the ancient Greek word *kuklos,* which means "circle." They dressed as they imagined knights might have looked, and they remained a relatively secret club. They were more officially organized in 1867 under the leadership of Nathan Bedford Forrest. Forrest had been a respected and admired general of the defeated Confederate Army. According to some historical accounts, the original Klan was supposed to be composed of men like Forrest—ex-officers, wealthy and respected gentlemen who stood in opposition to suffrage for black Americans.[21] Forrest's tenure with the initial version of the Klan, however, lasted only a year or so, and he later resigned from its leadership and tried to disband the organization. By that point, however, membership in the Klan was filled with men who believed in violence of any kind, including assassination by shooting, stabbing, beating, or lynching, not to mention tarring, feathering, and whipping, to punish blacks and to drive the so-called Northern carpetbaggers from the South during the Reconstruction period immediately following the Civil War. During the next few years, the Klan was active in nine states, from Tennessee and the Carolinas to Mississippi, Texas, and Arkansas. Politically, the Klan was used as an organization in this period to control the black (at the time referred to as Negro) population, particularly with reference to suffrage.

In a fight between the federal Congress and the various state legislatures of many southern states, Democrats had been removed from power and replaced with so-called radical governments, usually made up of southerners who had been opposed to secession from the Union and who now embraced a form of suffrage for blacks. The real role of the Klan in this time was to undermine these new governments by attacking blacks and thinning the number of voters who might support the new regimes. By 1877, however, President Rutherford B. Hayes had withdrawn the last of his federal army from the South (originally there to enforce the terms of Reconstruction), and the pressure to oppose impositions from the North seemed to subside. There was still a considerable residue of hatred for the North and plenty of vitriol for blacks still living in the South, but by this time, the perceived necessity for a Klan such as what has been described earlier was lessening.

A second incarnation of the Klan occurred in the 1920s, although the seeds for this new Klan had been sown some 15 years earlier. In 1905, Thomas Dixon published a best-selling book titled *The Clansman*, which romanticized the earlier Klan that had fought against Reconstruction and presented its members as a kind of noble class striving to defend the civilized South in a post–Civil War period. In 1914, the rights for this book were sold to filmmaker D. W. Griffith, who then made a movie from the story (Griffith's version was, of course, the well-known *Birth of a Nation*), which "completed the process of rationalizing and romanticizing the Klan."[22] The positive reaction to the film helped create an environment within which the Klan could rise again, this time to be led by a 35-year-old veteran with a drinking problem and a checkered past in the Methodist Church: William Joseph Simmons. It was Simmons who actually created a new Klan and with it a new organization. The newer incarnation of the Klan was almost like a fraternal organization such as the Masons, which, not coincidentally, had been in Simmons's background as well.

A new organization with the appearance of a fraternal organization perhaps, but when it came to terrorism, the new Klan was the same old Klan, with the same kind of unchecked vigilantism that had featured in the Reconstruction period earlier. A slight difference in this second incarnation, however, was an expanded list of targets for the Klan, including Jews, Catholics, and immigrants of nonwhite European descent. Terrorism against these groups, especially the last of them, went largely unnoticed in this period because of public support for America's involvement in World War I. In fact, under Simmons, the new Klan even allied itself with the volunteer citizen-spying-on-citizen group called the Citizen's Bureau of Investigation.

Simmons later decided to improve the public image of the Klan by engaging the services of a public relations/advertising agency. As we shall discuss in greater detail in Chapter 6, this move helped construct the public face of the Klan and shaped public discourse about the Klan activities of the time. By 1921, tens of thousands of eager recruits were signing up to join the Klan,[23] and by 1923, its membership was reported to be somewhere between 3 and 6 *million* people, with Klan chapters now in the northern and western United States as well as still in the South.[24] So pervasive was the Klan's influence in this period that it became politically acceptable to associate with the group, even for an American president. According to Wyn Craig Wade, even President Warren G. Harding entered the ranks of the Klan in a ceremony held in the White House.[25] By the end of the 1920s, however, and on the cusp of the Great Depression, the influence of the second Klan had again begun to wane. Public tolerance for the group's violence and extremism had again subsided. By the end of the decade, Klan membership had again dropped, this time to barely 100,000. Through the next decade, Klan targets for their terrorism included the usual victims but also now communists (or socialists—Klan members seldom made the distinction) and unionists.

The third incarnation of the Klan really began with the U.S. Supreme Court decision of *Brown v. Board of Education*,[26] which declared segregation in public schools unconstitutional. Klan membership activity again increased, this time combining targets from the past, with Jewish lawyers and allegedly communist judges who were seen as responsible for spurring the oncoming civil rights movement. In this last incarnation of the Klan, membership began to taper once more, and the Klan began making more alliances with white supremacy groups, some of which have lasted to this day.

Although each of these incarnations of the KKK has to some extent been shaped by its historical period, the eccentricities of its leadership, and the general tolerance (or lack thereof) of the public, there have been some consistencies throughout each period, most notably those that relate to symbolism and Klan artifacts.

From the time of the first Klan, members wore the distinctive white robes and hoods, initially claiming that these resembled the clothing of the much romanticized knights of an earlier period in European (and, really, British) history. What these original members of the Klan quickly discovered, however, was that the white uniforms had the effect, especially when worn at nighttime, of terrifying those who were the Klan's victims.[27]

At night, the robe and hood took on the appearance of ghostly apparitions, seemingly floating just above the ground or on horseback. And like the souls of legend that haunted the earth in the afterlife, these uniforms were symbols of death, serious injury, and destruction. Seeing them in the context of lynching, flogging, castration, shooting, stabbing, beating, and burning only reinforced this symbolism.

Photo 4.5   The Klan makes use of the symbolism of a burning cross.

The same was true of a different Klan symbol: the burning cross. Members of the Klan (and even its own archivists) have long defended the use of the cross on religious grounds, asserting that the only symbolic value in this is the traditional one associated with Christianity. The records of Klan initiation and ritual tell a similar but mixed story. For example, in a document known as the *Kloran*,[28] also known as "The Book" (like a Bible) of the Invisible Empire, the ritual of the burning cross is explained in the following way. At a meeting (also called the *Kloncave)* of the Klan, the leader—the *Exalted Cyclops* (or EC, translated to mean a county commissioner)—will directly ask for a sacred altar to be prepared, with a Bible opened to Romans 12 and the altar flag of the Klan, along with a sword and a cross. Chapter 12, verse 21 of Romans reads, "Do not be conquered by evil, but conquer evil with good." The entire chapter actually addresses "the duties of a Christian," with focus on sacrifice of the body and mind,[29] many parts but one body,[30] and mutual love.[31] All this may seem somewhat misplaced in reference to the violent tendencies of the Klan, but it is intended to symbolize the relationship between a Klan member's responsibilities to the Klan and his society and the responsibilities of a Christian in addressing evil.

> The cross is then ignited by a Klan officer called a *Klokard*, who addresses the EC and says, "Your excellency, the sacred altar of the Klan is prepared, the fiery cross illuminates the *Klavern*."
>
> The EC is then to respond with these words: "Faithful Klokard, why the fiery cross?"
>
> The Klokard replies: "Sir, it [the fiery cross] is the emblem of that sincere, unselfish devotion of all Klansmen, the sacred purpose and principles we have espoused."
>
> The EC then says: "My Unit Leaders and Klansmen, what means the fiery cross?"
>
> All assembled then reply in unison: "We serve and sacrifice for the right."[32]

Accordingly, the burning cross is intended to symbolize a connection between Christianity and the Klan, between Christian duties and Klan responsibilities, and between service and sacrifice.

What does the burning cross symbolize for those victims of the Klan's terrorism through the past 130-plus years? I have regularly put this question to my students in a law class dealing with the Constitution. For many African American students with familial roots in the South, which go back at least one generation, the answer to my question will almost always be the same. In a word— *lynching*. The context of the symbol of terror provides one explanation for this.

The symbol of the burning cross means something quite different when placed in the context of the aforementioned violence and destruction. It was not uncommon for the burning cross to appear at a Klan gathering in the old South prior to a lynching.

Beyond context, one may also wish to reconsider the cross itself as a symbol. For Christians, it is a symbol of the resurrection, reinforcing the belief that Christ died and rose again in sacrifice for all who follow him. The cross itself, however, was in truth an instrument of torture and death. Crucifixion was intended as a means of capital punishment, with long and slow suffering before death, in a public display for all to see. Taken in the absence, for a moment, of the connection to the death and resurrection of Christ, the cross becomes a symbol of public execution. Adding the element of fire for a nighttime visit from the local Klan would only illuminate the symbol of the cross, again as a precursor to death.

The Dirty Bomb

Sometimes referred to as a "poor man's nuke,"[33] this weapon becomes more powerful because of its symbolic properties. A dirty bomb is actually a radiological dispersal device (or RDD), consisting of little more than any common explosive such as dynamite or semtex (a trade name for a type of plastic explosive manufactured in the Czech Republic), combined with any form of radioactive material. A dirty bomb is deadliest when combined with elements such as weapons-grade plutonium or spent nuclear reactor fuel, but these can be difficult (although not impossible) to obtain.[34] The greater likelihood is for a bomber to make use of other low-level radioactive materials, such as cobalt-60, cesium-137, strontium-90, or iridium-192, many of which can be found in workplaces such as hospitals (a byproduct of machines that offer diagnosis and treatment), research facilities (a byproduct of research work), or industrial and construction sites (e.g., sterilizing equipment and check-of-welding equipment).[35] In theory, these lower-level radioactive elements are attractive to a bomb maker because they can be had in either granulated or pellet form; if attached to sufficient explosive material, they can be dispersed in the immediate environment. In this sense, they are akin to a pipe bomb packed with nails, also a favored weapon of terrorists or guerrillas who must make use of common materials to fashion a weapon. A pipe is packed with explosive and nails and sealed at both ends; when it detonates, the nails are dispersed in different directions—each nail individually becoming an additional and potentially lethal weapon beyond the blast. For dirty bombs, in theory, a powerful enough blast would disperse radioactive material that was already in powdered or pelleted form to be absorbed into the atmosphere and become potentially poisonous to anyone in contact.[36] If there was enough radioactive material and a very large amount of explosive (such as a truck packed with dynamite), it might be possible to contaminate a city block or two, killing anyone in the immediate vicinity and forcing an immediate evacuation and closing of the area for a significant period of time.

At least, that is the theory. In practice, however, the record with dirty bombs is spotty. They are potentially attractive to terror groups for the reasons enunciated above, but their practical application as a weapon capable of killing a large number of people is in fact suspect. To begin with, in most situations, the dispersal of radioactive elements such as those listed above will quickly create absorption into the atmosphere, spreading the radiation over a larger area but weakening its lethal potential. Can exposure to material such as cesium-137 make you sick or even die? Yes, potentially, if your exposure is to a highly concentrated amount at close distance; but take a smaller amount (such as what would be extracted from hospital diagnostic equipment) and spread it over a larger area (even a square mile), and each individual amount of radiation becomes less threatening. Additionally, the ability of a bomber to spread the radiation over a larger area turns on both a large enough explosive and some help from prevailing winds to carry the radioactive dust farther away from the blast source. The combination of these realities, along with the fact that terrorists are only likely to obtain small amounts of this material, means that dirty bombs would likely fail to kill many people (if any) from radiation poisoning or exposure-induced risk for cancer.[37] That is to say, the more likely way a dirty bomb would be a lethal weapon is in the risk it poses to any victim unfortunate enough to be near the bomb blast.

In that sense, a dirty bomb is really a lethal weapon in the same way a conventional bomb is deadly: the blast kills or injures anyone in its radius.

So why all the anxiety over dirty bombs?

The answer, as suggested in the introduction to this section, owes less to its physical potential and more to the symbolic properties of such a weapon.

Photos 4.6 and 4.7   A dirty bomb disperses radioactive elements with an explosion, while an atomic weapon like the bomb (also known as "fat boy") dropped on Hiroshima works on nuclear fission to generate its enormous blast.
Source: U.S. National Archives.

As should be obvious by now, a dirty bomb is *not* an atomic bomb. It isn't even close. A dirty bomb or RDD operates on the rather simple principle of dispersing radiation with an explosion; an atomic bomb, in contrast, works by creating *nuclear fission* to generate enormous blasts such as those engendered by the first-generation nuclear weapons the

United States used on Hiroshima and Nagasaki. The latter of these weapons (used against Japan) also created the iconic symbol that haunted generations of people in the decades following Japan's surrender: the mushroom cloud.

It is the mushroom cloud we associate with an atomic bomb, a weapon that not only kills all those in its blast radius but also many hundreds of thousands more by the effects of radiation poisoning. The United States is the only country to have ever made use of these kinds of weapons in a wartime situation. To get a sense of their scale, consider that when the first bomb was dropped on Hiroshima on August 6, 1945, the temperature at the center of the blast area reached 5,400 degrees Fahrenheit, eviscerating anyone and anything in the immediate vicinity while also burning others to literal cinders farther away. From a greater distance, those who looked in the direction of the bright light created by the bomb blast had their eye grounds burned away.[38] Hair was also burned off and skin blackened. Hospitals filled with individuals whose extremities (e.g., ears, nose, and eyes) had burned away. Death was slow and painful,[39] and radiation sickness was to follow for those who survived the blast. Their short-lived future would include nausea, vomiting, convulsions, delirium, bleeding in the urine, from the eyes, the rectum, and the respiratory passages. Before death, there would be decay and failure of internal organs.[40] By the end of 1945, the Hiroshima bomb known as "fat boy" had been responsible for 140,000 deaths; by 1950, that total would grow to 200,000 people, most of whom were civilians. The Nagasaki bomb, dropped one week after the bombing of Hiroshima, would eventually claim 140,000 lives after 5 years as well.

In a way that is truly terrifying, the technology we would eventually develop for later generations of nuclear weapons would produce bombs capable of much greater damage and loss of life.

A dirty bomb is not one of these weapons; yet when dirty bombs are mentioned, the public worries because they hear the word "radiation" associated with these bombs, instantly connecting them to the mushroom cloud. This kind of association in the end is what gives a dirty bomb—or more surely, *the threat* of using a dirty bomb—its real force and power.

To date, no terrorist group has actually employed a dirty bomb, although there have been a few circumstances in which their use has been threatened. For example, in 1995, Shamil Basayev, at the time a leader of the Chechen rebels labeled "terrorists" by the Russian government, phoned a Moscow television station to alert them about where a container of cesium-137 was buried in Ismailovsky Park, a public park in Moscow.[41] The container was dug out and recovered without having been blown up. Basayev's call to the station was not intended as a last minute act of conscience; quite the opposite, it was intended to communicate a threat with a symbolic weapon. The goal was to create public anxiety, which it surely accomplished. He was also astute enough to recognize that notifying the Russian authorities directly might only have resulted in the device being recovered—but the story of its existence, buried. By calling television media, he guaranteed its wider distribution to a public audience, including those who made the connection to atomic weapons noted above.

Similarly, in 2002, the then Attorney General John Ashcroft created a media frenzy when he announced that one Jose Padilla, also known as Abdullah al-Mujahir, had been arrested for attempting to build a dirty bomb. Padilla had served time previously in Florida and later converted to Islam while still in prison. After his release from prison, the government alleged that he traveled to the Middle East where he met representatives of al Qaeda who recruited him to scout locations for an attack in the United States. Padilla was arrested when his plane landed in Chicago at O'Hare airport, and he was later charged (among other things) with attempting to build a dirty bomb. By 2007, in the midst of Padilla's trial in federal court, government prosecutors dropped the charges that related to a dirty bomb because of a lack of solid evidence.[42]

A final point is worth making here as well: The threatened use of dirty bombs can indeed create terror, anxiety, and panic (undoubtedly a goal for terrorists) and create a potential for disruption of daily life and business, but the mere name *dirty bomb*, or its accompanying moniker *poor man's nuke*, again contributes to the perception as described in Chapters 1 and 3 of this book that terrorism itself is mostly only bottom-up and rarely top-down. This kind of a weapon—the kind a *poor man* would use—is indeed *dirty* because it lacks the sophistication, polish, and disciplined/restrained use of a real nuclear weapon, wielded by the disciplined army of a nation-state. In such ways subtle and reinforcing, the public is again reminded that terrorism is the province of individuals and radical dissenters outside the mainstream. How ironic that the only use of real nuclear weapons, against largely civilian populations accounting for some 340,000 deaths, came at the behest of a nation-state.

❖ SUMMARY

Thus far, we have considered how terrorism may be considered as symbolic violence. At the intersection of a terrorist/rhetor's intent, the context of the terrorist incident, and the relative ability of the target audiences' ability to recognize the symbolism in the violence, we find different possibilities to again see terrorism as rhetoric. In this particular chapter, we focused on how that symbolism may be seen in the act of violence and destruction itself, as well as the means and implements of terrorism—whether from the top down or the bottom up. In the next chapter, we will extend this considering how symbolism can also be found in the targets of terrorism—and how they too may be rhetorical.

❖ NOTES

1. See *United States v. O'Brien*, 391 U.S. 367 (1968), wherein the Court acknowledged as much but was loath to extend the First Amendment protection to every kind of nonverbal action. See also *Spence v. Washington*, 418 U.S. 495 (1974), in which the Court fashioned a legal test to determine when nonverbal conduct might be considered expressive within the meaning of free speech under the First Amendment. The Court's model here, called the "expressive conduct test," is still in use today.

2. Philip Emmert and Victoria J. Lukasko, *Interpersonal Communication* (New York: William Brown, 1984) at p. 47.

3. See, for example, Steven W. Littlejohn, *Theories of Human Communication* (Belmont, CA: Wadsworth, 1983) at pp. 5–7; see also Douglas M. Fraleigh and Joseph S. Tuman, *Freedom of Speech in the Marketplace of Ideas* (New York: St. Martin's Press, 1997) at pp. 281–282.

4. James Gilligan, *Violence: Our Deadly Epidemic and Its Causes* (New York: Putnam Books, 1996) at p. 61.

5. For more about the Japanese Red Army, see William R. Farrell, *Blood and Rage: The Story of the Japanese Red Army* (Lexington, MA: Lexington Books, 1990).

6. Initially, this group, run by a disillusioned law student named Raul Sendic, aimed at social revolution, government reform, and the creation of economic opportunities. In 1963, the group's official name was the National Liberation Movement (MLN), but over time, the group embraced violence as a means for social change and felt the need to have a name with a more popular appeal, as well as one that would connect their violent means to a historic context. They settled on the name Tupamaros, after the heroic Inca chieftain Tupac Amuru. Amuru had been killed in a revolt against Spanish conquerors 200 years earlier.

7. John B. Wolf, *Fear of Fear* (New York: Plenum Press, 1981) at p. 82.

8. Arturo C. Porzecanski, *Uruguay's Tupamaros* (New York: Praeger, 1973).

9. Eric Arnesen, *Encyclopedia of U.S. Labor and Working-Class History* (Boca Raton, FL: CRC Press, 2006) at pp. 918–919.

10. Kevin Kenny, *Making Sense of the Molly Maguires* (New York: Oxford University Press, 1998) at pp. 20–22.

11. Michael Woodiwiss, *Organized Crime and American Power* (Toronto, Ontario, Canada: University of Toronto Press, 2001) at p. 118.

12. See Thomas Dublin and Walter Licht, *The Face of Decline: The Pennsylvania Anthracite Region in the Twentieth Century* (Ithaca, NY: Cornell University Press, 2005) at p. 30.

13. Arnesen, *Encyclopedia of U.S. Labor and Working-Class History, op. cit.,* at p. 219.

14. See Susan Campbell Bartoletti, *Growing Up in Coal Country* (Boston: Houghton Mifflin Harcourt, 1999) at p. 108.

15. This originally appeared as part of the official appendix for Franklin B. Gowen's *Argument Before the Joint Committee of the Legislature of Pennsylvania,* 1875. You can also find it reprinted along with other examples of coffin notices in Kenny's *Making Sense of the Molly Maguires* (1998) in Appendix 4.

16. Significant success in breaking up this group have only recently been achieved, as of summer 2002, with the assistance of the Greek government and law enforcement. Some have speculated, however, that this cooperation from Greek officials came about only because of the prospect of the Athens Olympics in 2004 and a desire to alleviate pressure from influential participant nations such as the United States. For more, see Anthee Carassava, "Greeks Claim a Victory Against a Small Band of Political Assassins," *New York Times,* July 19, 2002, p. A3.

17. For more, see Michael Elliot, "Down and Dirty," *Time,* October 14, 2002. Retrieved May 27, 2009, from www.TIME.com.

18. For more on the USSR military campaign in Afghanistan, see Vladimir Tamarov, *Afghanistan: A Russian Soldier's Story* (Berkeley, CA: Ten Speed Press, 2001).

19. See staff article for "Powerless to Act? Not So: The West Cannot Ignore Its Duty to Chechnya," *Guardian,* November 6, 1999. Retrieved May 27, 2009, from www.cdi.org/russia/johnson/3609.HTML.

20. David Rohde, "Passions Inflamed, Gaza Teenagers Die in Suicidal Attacks," *New York Times,* June 25, 2001, pp. A1–A15.

21. Thomas Gossett, *Race: The History of an Idea in America* (New York: Oxford University Press, 1997) at pp. 258–261.

22. Shawn Lay, "Introduction: The Second Invisible Empire," in *The Invisible Empire in the West: Toward a Historical Reappraisal of the Ku Klux Klan of the 1920s,* ed. Shawn Lay (Urbana: University of Illinois Press, 1992) at p. 4.

23. Ibid., p. 7.

24. Gossett, *Race: The History of an Idea in America, op. cit.,* at p. 371.

25. Wyn Craig Wade, *Fiery Cross: The Ku Klux Klan in America* (New York: Simon & Schuster, 1987) at p. 165.

26. 347 U.S. 483, 74 S.Ct. 686, 98 L.Ed. 873 (1954).

27. John Hope Franklin, *From Slavery to Freedom* (New York: Knopf, 2000); see also Gossett, *Race: The History of an Idea in America, op. cit.,* at p. 260.

28. It is not clear if this pun was intentional or the result of putting the "Kl" in front of as many words as Klan members are accustomed to do (e.g., they meet at a *Klonklave,* and the meeting is called to order by a *Klaliff*), but here the word *Kloran* is similar in appearance to another recognizable holy book— the *Koran.*

29. Romans 12:1–2.

30. Romans 12:3–8.

31. Romans 12:9–21.

32. For a complete text of the Kloran, see W. H. Weller, *Under the Hood: Unmasking the Modern Ku Klux Klan* (North Manchester, IN: DeWitt Books, 1998) at pp. 127–148.

33. David J. Whitaker, *Terrorists and Terrorism in the Contemporary World* (New York: Routledge, 2004) at p. 122.

34. Graham T. Allison, *Nuclear Terrorism: The Ultimate Preventable Catastrophe* (New York: Macmillan, 2005) at p. 230.

35. Gopal B. Saha, *Physics and Radiobiology of Nuclear Medicine* (Berlin, Germany: Springer-Verlag, 2006) at p. 261.

36. James F. Broder, *Risk Analysis and the Security Survey* (Oxford, UK: Butterworth-Heinemann, 2006).

37. Richard A. Muller, *Physics for Future Presidents* (New York: W. W. Norton, 2008) at p. 40.

38. Michihiko Hachiya, *Hiroshima Diary,* trans. and ed. Warner Wells (Chapel Hill: University of North Carolina, 1955 at p. 131.

39. Ibid., at p. 117.

40. The Committee for the Compilation of Materials on Damage Caused by the Atomic Bombs in Hiroshima and Nagasaki, *Hiroshima and Nagasaki: The Physical, Medical, and Social Effects of the Atomic Bombings,* trans. Eisei Ishikawa and David L. Swain (New York: Basic Books, 1981) at p. 115.

41. Paul J. Murphy, *The Wolves of Islam: Russia and the Faces of Chechen Terror* (Dulles, VA: Brassey's, 2004) at p. 25.

42. Gary Ackerman and Jeremy Tansett, *Jihadists and Weapons of Mass Destruction: A Growing Threat* (Boca Raton, FL: CRC Press, 2009) at p. 186.

5

Symbolism in the Targets of Terrorism

❖   ❖   ❖

The symbol in an act of terrorism may also be communicated through the specific target of the terror act. Whether by the terrorist's intent or because of the meanings that a target audience consciously or subconsciously attaches to the target, the symbolic value may still be present and discoverable. To see how this works in practice, let us begin by examining how targets can be situated within certain contexts to imbue them with specific meaning; first , we will examine temporal contexts for targets of terrorism. Next, we will return to two specific examples of terror targets and use some of the aforementioned methods of criticism to discover how and why they are rhetorical.

❖   TEMPORAL TARGETS FOR TERRORISM

On occasion, a target for terrorism may be defined by its chronological or temporal dimensions; a specific location and/or group of individuals take on new significance depending on where one finds them on the calendar. By way of example, in recent times we have sadly, all too often, observed an increase in terrorist attacks coinciding with religious holidays—especially involving two of the world's older religions: Judaism and Islam. Extremist interpretations of both religions have exacerbated tensions between Israelis and Palestinians for many years—and sometimes combined with the symbolic meaning of religious holidays to manifest in violent terrorism and death. Consider the following examples, one from 1994 and the other from 2008, as illustrations of this point.

In 1994, Dr. Baruch Goldstein (MD), an American-born Israeli and settler living in Kiryat Arba, a West Bank settlement near Hebron, committed an act of terrorism by randomly firing his military rifle into a crowd of Palestinian Muslim worshippers, who had gathered for prayer at the mosque in the Cave of the Patriarchs. In addition to being a doctor, Goldstein was an Israeli Defense Force (IDF) reservist and a member of the extremist Kach movement. Earlier in his life, Goldstein had been a friend and follower of the controversial extremist Rabbi Meir Kahane.

The Cave of the Patriarchs—known in Hebrew as *Me'arat HaMachpela* (meaning Cave of the Double Tombs)—is believed to house the remains of Abraham, Sarah, Isaac, and other early significant individuals whose importance is felt by three of the world's larger religions: Judaism, Christianity, and Islam. The large structure atop these caves was at different points in the past 3,000 years a shrine built by the ancient Israelites, converted to a church by the crusaders, and also a mosque by the Muslims, who took control of Hebron in the 7th century. For Muslims, this location is known as the Mosque of Abraham (*Ibrahimi Mosque* in Arabic).

Adding to the symbolic texture of the context for the terrorism that was to occur on that fateful day was the fact that in 1994 it so happened that the Jewish holiday of *Purim* coincided with the beginning of the monthlong religious observance in Islam known as *Ramadan*; here, the former overlapped with the beginning of the latter.

For Jews, Purim is easily the most festive and joyous celebration of the year; indeed, sometimes American Jews have playfully referred to it as the "Jewish Mardi Gras." Purim recounts the story of how Jews living in Persia were saved from death and extermination through the efforts of Esther and her cousin Mordecai. As told in the Book of Esther, the story recounts how (with Mordecai's persuasive encouragement) Esther agrees to speak to King Ahasuerus[1] of Persia (into whose harem she had been placed), in the process foiling a plot by the king's evil advisor Haman to kill all Jews in Persia. The story concludes with Haman's plot being reversed against him and the advisor being killed on the very gallows he had intended for Mordecai.

Jews celebrate this is as a story of deliverance and revenge against the evil Haman—who is believed to have descended from Agag, the King of the Amalekites. The Amalekites, in turn, are also mentioned in the Book of Exodus[2] and in Deuteronomy[3] and are seen as the traditional enemies of the Jewish people.

Ramadan, in contrast, occurs during the nineth month of the Muslim calendar and is seen as a time for a cleansing of the soul for devout Muslims. Marking the time when Allah first revealed the verses of the Quran to the Prophet Muhammad, during Ramadan Muslims are directed to fast during the day and to be introspective about their beliefs and actions, as well their commitment to Allah. In addition to fasting, they are encouraged to mend damaged relationships, to give charity, and to grant and seek the forgiveness of others.

On February 25, 1994, more than 700 Muslim Palestinians (adults and children) had gathered in the mosque at the Cave of the Patriarchs for morning prayers, starting the observance of Ramadan. At that same time, Dr. Goldstein arrived at the site dressed in his IDF uniform and carrying a Galil assault rifle (the Israeli version of an AK-47), along with numerous clips of ammunition, with 30 rounds in each. The mosque was reportedly packed to capacity, with the Muslim worshippers kneeling on plastic mats, their backs to him. According to reports after the crime, he aimed at people's heads and began firing.[4] Pandemonium ensued as people struggled in vain to avoid the barrage of 5.56 mm rounds. Goldstein sprayed the room and repeatedly changed clips. In 10 minutes, he had fired 110 shots. While he was trying to reload again, some of the worshippers subdued him, and one bludgeoned him to death using a fire extinguisher. Before he was killed, he had managed to murder 29 Palestinians and wound 150 more.

Although Goldstein did not say anything during his attack to explain his actions, it is known that the night before his assault he had attended a service at the Jewish side of the Cave of the Patriarchs, where after listening to the traditional reading from the Scroll of Esther, he told others there that they should all behave like Esther.[5] The timing of his attack the next day at the same site hardly seems the product of happenstance or coincidence. It was the day of Purim. Moreover, although his actions seemed to be the product of a mind that had snapped or become depraved, there did not seem to be any sign that he was suffering from a mental disorder.[6] His actions were deliberate and intentional. Goldstein was troubled by the ongoing peace negotiations between Israel and the Palestinians in Oslo and openly concerned that a Palestinian state was about to be created. His attack on Muslim worshippers at the same site, while Purim coincided with Ramadan, was an attempt to cast himself symbolically in the story as Mordecai.[7] Indeed, that was exactly the way his actions were interpreted by other settlers at Kiryat Arba,[8] and in the years to come after 1994, there would be numerous instances in which the settlers would celebrate Purim by also invoking Goldstein's memory and image in a provocative manner.[9] His act of terror had ripple effects throughout Israel and the Palestinian community. The Oslo Peace accords were badly damaged by his actions, and militant groups such as Hamas used the incident as an opportunity to both recruit new fighters and step up the violence against Israelis. In the days after the tragedy, Palestinians in Hebron, Gaza, Ramallah, and Jerusalem rioted against Israeli occupation, and the ensuing violence actually killed more Palestinians (33) than had been murdered at the Cave of the Patriarchs. The Israeli government, embarrassed and horrified that an Israeli citizen had committed an act of terror against Palestinian civilians at a time of worship, was quick to condemn Goldstein and the massacre and eventually outlawed his right-wing group (Kach). One additional legacy of this violence was the role it would play in increasing the stature of Hamas as a foil to Yasser Arafat and, of course, to Israel itself.

Fourteen years later in 2008, the religious school known as *Mercaz Harav Yeshiva* in Jerusalem was the site of a similar, shocking and equally repellant act of terrorism. This yeshiva is generally regarded as one of the leading institutions for religious study in Israel and is often linked with conservative right-wing groups—including many of the settlers in the occupied territories. As to this last point, many of the students at Mercaz Harav belonged to the settlement movement.[10] On March 6, 2008, some 80 students had gathered in the school library for prayers before intending to celebrate the holiday of Purim with a party. At the same time this was happening, a young Palestinian named Alaa Abu Dheim made his way through the yeshiva gates, dressed in a long coat beneath which he concealed a military assault rifle, at least one pistol and several clips with ammunition.

In the days following the incident at Mercaz Harav, it would be noted that Abu Dheim was an otherwise happy and ordinary 25-year-old man. As a resident of Jerusalem with an Israeli identification card, he was able to work as a driver, and had plans for marriage. His family would later allege that he had been disturbed by reports of violence in Gaza between Israelis and Palestinians. He came from a middle-class family that lived in Jabal Mukabar, the Arab quarter of Jerusalem. Abu Dheim was not known to be affiliated with any group such as Hamas or Hezbollah, but like many Palestinians living inside Israel, he took an interest in what was happening in places such as Gaza.[11] According to the accounts of survivors, the gunman found his way to the library, where he encountered the students and began firing. Students immediately began diving for cover; some leapt from the windows. By all reports, Abu Dheim aimed to shoot his victims in the head in order to make certain they were dead.[12] Abu Dheim was eventually shot by one of the students (who had also been armed) and then killed by an Israeli soldier. At that point, he had already murdered eight students and wounded nine more; seven of the dead were between the ages of 15 and 19.

While the attack at the yeshiva generated intense public outrage and sadness inside Israel, much of the public discourse focused on the fact that Abu Dheim had been a Palestinian resident of Jerusalem, and it raised questions about what this might mean for future threats from Palestinians or Arabs living within Israel. In the months to come, there would also be much discussion about whether the police response had been timely or adequate. Surprisingly, there was very little connection made in public discourse about the attack to link it to the Purim holiday or observation of its striking similarities to Baruch Goldstein's attacks at the Cave of the Patriarchs. In retrospect, the symbolic connections were everywhere.

Abu Dheim chose to strike students at the yeshiva—a prominent seminary with very strong links to the settlers' movement; Baruch Goldstein was a settler who took the law into his hands in murdering 29 Palestinians. Abu Dheim's primary weapon was a Kalashnikov (also known as an AK-47); Goldstein's weapon was the Israeli Galil—modeled after the AK-47. Both men aimed for the heads of their victims to be certain they were dead. Perhaps most significantly, both men used the occasion of Purim to attack their target victims at a physical location with special religious significance, given the holiday. Abu Dheim attacked the students on their campus shortly before they celebrated Purim, while Goldstein attacked Muslim worshippers at the beginning of Ramadan, at the Muslim side of the Cave of the Patriarchs—also on the day of Purim. Goldstein's terror was a symbolic realization of the story of Purim, while Abu Dheim's actions were a deconstruction and rejection of the same.

❖ SYMBOLISM AND THE CHECHEN TERRORIST ATTACK ON A MOSCOW THEATER

Allegedly, the Dubrovka Theater was not really the first choice for the Chechen rebel leader Mosvar Barayev; he wanted to take the

Kurchatov Institute, one of Russia's most important nuclear design centers, to make his point for Chechen independence. The Kurchatov Institute had 26 working nuclear reactors and enough highly enriched uranium to create hundreds or even thousands of nuclear weapons,[13] but attacking a nuclear design center was too difficult. For the goals the Chechen terrorists had in mind, a more central, accessible, and public forum would be a better choice, and for these reasons, the decision was made to target the Dubrovka Theater in Moscow.[14] Preparation for the terror event at the theater was meticulous and thorough: two to three months of advance planning included the necessary time for recruitment of experienced fighters to build a team of more than 50, as well as time to travel to the theater area and take up jobs as construction workers in the Central Station nightclub located in the theater complex. Weapons and explosives were smuggled into the theater and hidden, and a thorough reconnaissance of the three-story building was undertaken.[15] Some members of the terrorist team also attended performances of the musical *Nord-Ost* at the theater, studying the audience placement and the entrance/exit points.

On the night of October 23, 2002, the Chechen terrorists—who called themselves the Riyadus-Salikhin Suicide Battalion (or RAS)—staged their raid on the Dubrovka Theater, in southeast Moscow, only three blocks from the Kremlin. The theater was still showing a performance of *Nord-Ost*, a popular musical chronicling the lives of two Russian explorers in a travel adventure set during the era of Stalin. Some 700 people were in the audience, most of them Russian. An additional 75 were foreign nationals from 14 other countries, including Australia, Germany, the Netherlands, Ukraine, the United Kingdom, and the United States.

Nineteen members of the RAS terror group were women, ranging in age from 16 to 43 years; many of them claimed to be Chechen widows of men who had been killed in the Russian/Chechen conflict. They formed a striking and rhetorically potent group of suicide bombers, nicknamed the *Black Widows* in the media accounts of the assault, and their responsibilities would include guarding the hostages (cast, crew, and audience) in the theater and being willing to detonate their explosives if given the go-ahead by the leaders of the operation. They held nearly 800 hostages. Immediately, a standoff with Russian security forces ensued, as the RAS made its demand that Russian military forces cease operations, immediately and permanently withdraw from Chechnya, while also granting Chechen independence. Failure to comply would result in the deaths of the hostages in an explosion that would destroy the theater.

Aware of the media spectacle that was unfolding in Moscow—the capital of Russia—the government initially chose to try and negotiate with the RAS, hoping to avoid losing any of the hostages. On the third day of the crisis, however, Russian special forces pumped a chemical narcotic gas through the theater's ventilation system; anyone exposed to the gas for a prolonged period would be rendered unconscious. Elite special force commandos, known as *Spetsnaz*, then stormed the theater from multiple directions. All the male members of the RAS moved to the foyer and balcony areas to engage the Russian forces, only to be outnumbered and overwhelmed.

Inside the theater auditorium, the *Black Widows* had been left to guard and theoretically kill the hostages, if necessary, by detonating their explosives. But as *Spetsnaz* forces charged into the auditorium, they found all the *Black Widows* unconscious and executed them on the spot.[16] The Russians would later claim that they executed the unconscious terrorists to prevent them from awakening and detonating their explosives. The firefight in the foyer and balcony also left most of the male members of the RAS dead.

Tragically, the gas also rendered many of the hostages unconscious, and by the time the *Spetsnaz* forces had secured the theater, many of the hostages began experiencing difficulty breathing; over a short period of time, 126 hostages would die from a series of complications brought on by the gas, which turned out to be a highly potent opioid called fentanyl, often used for anesthesia in hospitals. An antidote for this is nalaxone, and if it had been provided, many of the exposed hostages could have been saved. Their deaths were an embarrassment to the government, and when it was later disclosed that the explosive detonation devices in the theater auditorium were in fact nonoperational (and apparently never had been), more questions were raised about whether the Russian assault had been necessary to resolve the crisis.

As we contemplate this incident in hindsight, a different set of questions can be asked: Why did Chechen terrorists target this theater and this audience to make their point? What, if any, symbolism could be found in targeting this theater? What was the rhetorical significance of the symbolism?

For this analysis, let's return to one of the methods of rhetorical criticism suggested in Chapter 2—*dramatism*—and make use of the method known as the *Pentad*, suggested by the rhetorician Kenneth Burke.[17] Dramatism is the name given by Burke to describe his theories about how human motivation can be rhetorically analyzed by applying the key elements of drama.

According to Burke, dramatism operates on two assumptions: first, that the use of language or symbols constitutes action and not simply motion (action in this way corresponds with the intentional, neurological ability of a human to acquire language and symbol systems) and, second, that humans craft and present messages in ways that are parallel to the manner in which a play is presented and performed. According to Burke, humans use rhetoric to create an argument or constitute a perspective in the same way a play presents a perspective or describes a situation and setting. In this way, an individual's rhetoric can be seen as employing five basic elements of drama: *act, agent, agency, scene,* and *purpose.* The combination of these five elements gives rise to Burke's *pentad* and can be used to describe completely any symbolic action.

In order, *act* refers to what took place, in thought or deed; *agent* refers to the person(s) who performed the act; *agency* refers to the means or instruments used to perform the act by the agent; *scene* refers to the place and context in which the act occurs; and *purpose* obviously enough refers to the intentions and reasons behind the act. In common parlance, these are also seen as the who (agent), what (act), how (agency), why (purpose), and where (scene) behind human motivation for symbolic action and behavior.

Applying this method of criticism to the Chechen takeover of the Dubrovka Theater yields the following:

Act: The assault on the Dubrovka Theater, yielding some 800 hostages

Agent(s): RAS Chechen terrorists, including the Black Widows

Agency: By force, including the use of explosives, suicide bombers, and guns; also making an example by executing and/or wounding (by shooting) three hostages

Scene: The Dubrovka Theater, in southeast Moscow

Purpose(s): At least three in this act: (1) force the Russian government to cease military operations in, withdraw from, and grant independence to Chechnya; (2) force the Russian government to kill Russian hostages by ending the Theater crisis; and (3) make martyrs of the Chechen RAS terrorists

Pentadic analysis also requires some perspective on which element or elements of the pentad were dominant; understanding this will usually give way to an explanation of how the symbolism in the act was rhetorical. If we follow this method here, we can see that *purpose* was primarily dominant for several reasons.

To begin with, in this instance, the purposes of this act inform and influence every other element of the pentad. In order, the triple *purposes* of wanting to force a change in Russian military and foreign policy toward Chechnya, forcing the Russian government to kill Russians, and making martyrs of the members of the Chechen RAS could all be served by the *act* of creating an assault in a public and accessible place such as the Dubrovka Theater and taking some 800 hostages. Realizing these purposes could only be attained if the *agents* involved were willing to commit an act of terror; willing to take and kill hostages; and, most important, willing to die themselves. These purposes required the *agency* of the use of force, both by example (the terrorists did execute one hostage and shoot two others as a means of making an example) and by threat (their explicit message to the government was that all hostages would be killed if their demands were not met), and required the tools of guns and explosives in a public demonstration. Finally, and perhaps most significant, these triple purposes also dictated the *scene* or location and context within which the act occurred—at the Dubrovka Theater, during a production of the musical *Nord-Ost*. Not to be missed here is the fact that the location of this act was itself a theater; in many respects, the triple purposes in this explain the rhetorical, symbolic significance of this scene as well.

By selecting the theater, the RAS Chechens were not only picking a building that housed hostages; they were also making use of a structure that gave them a stage and created an act of theater for a domestic Russian (and ultimately global) audience. Indeed, when the RAS forces first appeared in the theater auditorium, they initially walked onto the stage in the midst of the performance. Actors on stage seemed initially confused by the presence of new individuals—who quickly waved them off stage with the point of their guns. Several people in the live audience thought at this moment that the Chechens were actually a part of the show.[18] Cast and crew members were then herded into the seats with the regular audience, merging into a form of a literally captive audience, while the real drama was to be played for those outside the theater.

In a more subtle way, the fact that they did this during the production of *Nord-Ost* also added a dimension of rhetorical symbolism. As indicated before, this play tells the story of two Russian explorers, set in a time period during the era of Stalin. As a musical and as a love story, it perhaps romanticizes some of that era in the pursuit of telling its story. For Chechens, this same time period (the Stalin era) features heavily in the context of their grievance with Russia.

It is true that the modern and contemporary struggle for Chechen independence points to the breakup of the old Soviet Union and the two wars between the Chechens and the Russians, since that time, over the subject of Chechnya's desire to be free of Russian domination; but in many ways, the real source of their mutual animus traces back to World War II. In that period, Chechens were accused by Josef Stalin of collaborating with the Nazis—an act of political and moral treason that demanded (according to Stalin) the most extreme of reactions: the forced relocation and in some cases mass murder of an entire population of Chechens (and the neighboring Ingush). Sadly, this treatment of both the Chechens and the Ingush (as well as some others) was more the rule than the exception during Stalin's era.[19] The truth is that a small number of Chechens watched as German soldiers entered their territory and debated about which monster/master would be worse to serve: Hitler or Stalin? Some elected to assist the former (Hitler), but they were small in number and most assuredly did not speak for the majority of the Chechens.[20]

Measuring this by numbers, the opposite was true; the Russian army had a disproportionately high number of Chechens and Ingush serving as regular troops, all of whom saw extensive combat against the Germans.[21] There was no disloyalty there.

Stalin, however, made no such distinctions, and he used the allegations of collaboration to justify (with the assistance of his NKVD [People's Commissariat for Internal Affairs], Chief Lavrenti Beria) a policy of forced deportation, dispossession of property, forced labor, and mass murder on the Chechen population. Literally overnight, trucks and trains carried Chechens out of their cities and country, whisking them away to outer provinces and further east; many of those forced into the train container cars eventually died from exposure, starvation, and typhoid. Those who survived were forced to work in labor camps. During this period of time, it is estimated that from a population of some 300,000 who were deported, the combined loss of life and lost population growth amounted to a total demographic loss of some 200,000 Chechens.[22]

In the meantime, their country and cities and villages were filled with Russian emigrants. Road signs were changed to Russian; schools were taught only in the Russian language. Deliberately and systematically, all evidence of Chechen existence was being erased and wiped away. It remained that way until Stalin died, and Nikita Khrushchev came to power with the intent of de-Stalinizing the Soviet Union. One of his acts was to slowly allow the Chechen people—those who had survived—to try and return home. And so they came, but when they arrived, they found other people living in their country. Resettlement was slow and painful, and the stigma of their forced exodus lingered in their collective psyche.[23] Even with repatriation in the 1950s, the memory of their ordeal fueled a hatred for Soviets and, later, Russians.

It was this hatred that made the RAS terrorists demand that Russian military forces withdraw from Chechnya, just like it was this hatred that made the terrorists create a situation in which the Russian security services would likely be forced to kill the Russian hostages in an effort to end the ordeal.

With the benefit of hindsight, it is also dubious to believe today that any of the RAS terrorists for a moment believed that their grand act of theater would produce a shift in Russian foreign policy; Vladimir Putin had never given in before—why would this event prove different for a man who had vowed to crush the Chechen "rebels?" The greater likelihood is that this purpose was a surface argument made to shelter the real purposes behind this assault—which was to produce Russian casualties at the hands of Russian forces, as well as limited public sympathy for (and fear of) the Chechens, who were willing to die and be martyred for their cause. Although they didn't anticipate the use of gas pumped into the ventilation system as the means to their end, the RAS terrorists still achieved these purposes to some extent when so many of the hostages died from complications caused by the gas—and so many terrorists were killed in the *Spetsnaz* assault.

❖ SYMBOLISM, THE WORLD TRADE CENTER, AND THE PENTAGON

In the time, immediately following the attacks of September 11, much of the media and public attention focused on the damage done to the World Trade Center (WTC) and specifically to the Twin Towers, which were the most significant components of the WTC complex. Of course, the WTC was only one of the targets struck on that fateful day. The Pentagon in Washington, D.C., was also a target, and it is believed that the White House or the Capitol Building was intended to be an additional target. In spite of this, most of our attention was drawn to New York. Why? The answer may have to do with the symbolism of the specific target in New York.

If we were to consider the WTC as a symbolic target, we might want to evaluate the intent of those who allegedly planned the attack. Why was the WTC targeted on September 11? Perhaps for no more complicated a reason than that it had been targeted in a bomb attack before.[24] Maybe there was a sense of needing to complete an incomplete act, given that the prior bombing had caused loss of life and significant damage but nothing on a large scale. Or perhaps the WTC was targeted because the Twin Towers were two of the most recognizable buildings in the profile of New York—the sort of profile typically featured in photographs of the city. New York City is often regarded as a gateway to the United States from the East, and its diversity is often representative of all that is American. Damaging that profile and damaging the city was striking a blow against America perhaps.

Or maybe the WTC was targeted because the towers were two of the largest buildings in the city and an attack there would be likely to cause more damage, loss of life, and injury than attacks on other targeted buildings. At the very least, with their incomparable height, the towers may have been targets because tall buildings are easier to hit with a plane.

The WTC had been the dream of the Rockefellers—David, the then chairman of Chase Manhattan Bank, and Nelson, the then governor of New York—who had wanted to name the two towers after themselves. New York City Mayor John Lindsay had insisted that the name of the entire complex be the World Trade Center. The buildings were designed by the Japanese architect Minoura Yamasaki, who in the Twin Towers created what many felt was an overly orthodox, plain, and visually dull set of monolithic structures (for which many in the city initially criticized him). In addition to the towers, the WTC complex had five other smaller office buildings. When completed, each tower had 110 stories, and the South Tower, 1,362 feet high, and the North Tower, 1,368 feet high, were the tallest buildings in the world at the time. The construction of Chicago's Sears Tower and Malaysia's Petronas Towers would eventually change that.

The WTC became home to many in the Western and global business community, not to mention specific American companies. Of all the businesses in the WTC, six banks, five investment firms, and three insurance companies had their headquarters there. The Bank of America had a significant presence there, and American Express occupied three floors. Both the Secret Service and the FBI had office space in the towers, as did 29 nations with trade missions and (ironically) virtually every major U.S. airline. In all, more than 50,000 people worked in the towers, and more than 200,000 tourists moved through all the buildings every day.

The WTC thus was always busy, filled with activity and people. Would these factors explain the terrorists' fascination—perhaps preoccupation—with the WTC? In truth, this level of inquiry assumed that we would be able to discover the symbolic value of the targeting on September 11 by examining the terrorists' intent. But even after our war in Afghanistan and even after all the incarceration, "debriefing," and questioning of former Taliban and al Qaeda personnel, we have little hard evidence of the actual reasons for choosing these specific targets—and especially the WTC.

Forgetting the terrorists' motives at this point, would the above factors in the background of the WTC explain our own fixation with the target site after September 11? Not necessarily. The Pentagon is also a significant and well-known structure, and on that date, it too was struck and significantly damaged, also with loss of life. Possibly more horrible was the fate of those passengers on United Flight 93, which crashed in Shanksville, Pennsylvania, only after courageous passengers, made aware of their impending doom, charged the cockpit in an attempt to take control of the plane. We assume today that the crashed jet was targeting Washington, D.C., either the White House or the Capitol Building. As we wrestle in our own minds with the fears and anxiety of being attacked anywhere and anytime, can any of us imagine the horror of learning that our plane has been hijacked and later learning that it will be used as a weapon to destroy a large building and kill many people besides those in the plane? In short, there were many horrors on that date, and though New York's tragedy may certainly have been on a larger scale, with greater loss of life and damage, the loss was relative. The Pentagon was an equally significant target, and the suffering of the WTC victims was surely no greater or more horrific than that of the passengers on the flight that crashed in Pennsylvania. So what is it about New York and the Twin Towers that was and is different?

Perhaps the answer to this question—and an answer to why the WTC was targeted in the first place—can be found in the rhetorical significance of the structures. Many have proclaimed architecture as rhetoric before[25]—whether comparing buildings and structures,[26] amusement and theme parks,[27] or even memorial structures and their meaning.[28] Nowhere is this rhetorical dimension of architecture more pronounced than in the division of modernist architecture and postmodern architecture. Modernist architecture—which can be seen in structures such as public housing projects or tall business buildings, for example, skyscrapers—symbolizes both the rejection of classical and historical thought and the celebration of "twentieth century's achievements and dominance of technological innovation, rationality and corporate power."[29] Modernist architecture has focused less on form or aesthetic style and more on function, efficiency, and order—not unlike that philosophy around which corporate business was organized and developed in the past century.[30] Thus, modernist architecture is often simple, with relatively clean lines for design and much forethought devoted to that which is functional and rational—even if boring and dull.

Postmodern architecture, in contrast, is often seen as a reaction to modernist architecture. With design styles that defy a definable or universal standard or genre, the postmodern architectural style is more easily identified by its rejection of modernity; implicitly, therefore, it is a rejection of rationality, technology, and corporatism. Design styles in postmodern architecture do not celebrate simplicity, symmetry, efficiency, or function as ends unto themselves or goals toward which our society should aim. Postmodern architecture—which can be seen in examples such as the Vietnam Veterans' Memorial in Washington, D.C., or San Francisco's relatively new Museum of Modern Art—suggests that architecture must be considered in relation to other structures as well as the general environment and that a building or structure must be evaluated as "part of a cultural and physical context."[31] The postmodern architecture must interact with others in that context. In these ways, postmodern architecture must be viewed as inherently political.[32]

Seen in this light, the WTC generally and the Twin Towers specifically may be considered as clear examples of modernist architecture. The towers were, as previously referenced, relatively simple and dull monolithic structures. They were, as the name of the complex (World *Trade* Center) ultimately suggested and as the list of building occupants clearly demonstrated, celebrations of corporatism on both an American and a global scale.

Am I suggesting here that the towers were targeted because they were symbolic examples of modernity? Not entirely. Or am I suggesting that our fascination and concern with them as a target of terrorism represents a public concern with terrorism targeting modernity? Again, the answer is no. Words such as *modernism* and *postmodernism* are mostly used by academics (and not even then do all of the users understand the terms entirely!). What I would claim, however, is that the symbolic value of the Twin Towers changed on the day of September 11 and that the towers moved from being examples of the modern in structure to examples of the postmodern in the moment of their destruction—and that in that way, the terrorist attack on these symbols was inherently rhetorical. The *destruction* of these buildings was a *deconstruction* of their symbolic meaning and a subsequent rearrangement of a new symbol that had serious political meaning for the United States.

To understand this, let us refine our explanation of the Twin Towers as examples of modernist architecture and also consider them as symbols of something else. In simple, visual form, the Twin Towers stood out because they were big and tall—but most important, because they were towers (plural) and not a tower in the singular sense. There were two of them, and although the North Tower was a few feet taller than the South, they were for the most part identical from the outside. In that way, they resembled not so much identical towers as they did posts to a fence, or perhaps a gate.

If we were for the moment to consider the other targets of terrorism on that day, we might discover that they too formed symbolic components of a fence or wall, metaphorically speaking, surrounding and (falsely perhaps) insulating the United States from the rest of the world. The Pentagon, for example, could be considered symbolic of the military might behind the United States, without which we might not be the one remaining and undisputed global superpower in the world.

Likewise, the White House and the Capitol Building are symbolic of our political strength at the national level, without which, again, we would not be considered a global superpower. Indeed, reconsidered in this way, the towers themselves were symbols of corporatism, and in that way, they were part of the third leg of the real American triad— economic strength. Without economic strength, the United States would be no better than Russia (still armed to the teeth but with only a developing economy and still emerging political control).

The symbolism of each target on that day makes more sense when you consider each target in relation to one other. In context, all were symbols of the strength (or veneer of strength) behind American superiority. By attacking these symbols, terrorists on that day undermined the value of this strength, causing us all to reconsider our role in the world, not to mention our individual security.

Conceptualizing the towers as the gateposts to this wall (military, economic, political), securing our country makes more sense if we also consider that a gatepost controls both the entrance and the exit to a place. Our economy is likewise the most accessible point of origin for our society. The concept of "the American Dream" rests on the idea that people from anywhere can come to the United States and, within a generation, improve their standard of living. For those who come to this country, the gate of economic opportunity—a central strength of our country—allows access.

Like the gateposts of mythology involving castles—or the city-states enclosed by walls—the Twin Towers were symbolic not only of our economic strength but also of our insulation and protection. Though our economy was and is accessible, it is still protected by laws and customs favoring American business and culture, reinforcing our dominant economic position in the world. In the gatepost towers of any castle or city-state, the towers themselves had to represent the tallest and most structurally sound portion of the wall barrier to guarantee the integrity of the gate.

In Homer's mythological description of the fall of Troy, it was not until Greek soldiers led by Odysseus and hidden within the fabled Trojan Horse were brought into the city-state and revealed themselves in a surprise attack on the city that the gate was opened for the larger Greek invasion and destruction of the same.[33] When our towers collapsed following the attack on September 11, it was as if the gate had been crushed and forced open and the soundness of our impregnable position exposed. In that way, the meaning of the symbol changed, from one celebrating modernity and the triumph of corporatism in our economic strength to something else entirely. In that pile of rubble and debris, later known as *Ground Zero* (yet another rhetorical labeling), was a new symbol of our vulnerability.

❖ SUMMARY

As suggested in the last chapter, terrorism as an act of violence and destruction can also be understood by the symbolic value attached to the terror act. When we describe something as a symbol, or declare that it possesses symbolic value, we are suggesting that this thing—whether an object, a word, a sound, or conduct—may be interpreted to mean something more than itself. All nonverbal acts are to some degree expressive and thus inherently symbolic. By employing communication tools looking for the intent of the actor, the context of the situation, and the relativity of the message, we may discover what that symbolic meaning is.

In terrorism, we have seen that symbolism and rhetorical meaning may be found in the specific targets of the terror act—whether situated in the context of time or location—both of which significantly contribute to the manner in which we construct what terrorism means for us. In the next chapter, we consider how our public discourse about this meaning is further affected and (if we aren't careful) manipulated by the official rhetoric that can be found in speeches by political leaders.

❖ NOTES

1. Today most scholars refer to this king as Xerxes I.
2. See Exodus 17:8–16, wherein God vows to have war with Amalek "from generation to generation."

3. See Deuteronomy 25:17–19, in which those assembled are commanded to "blot out the remembrance of Amalek from under heaven."

4. Isaac Cronin, *Confronting Fear: A History of Terrorism* (New York: Thunder's Mouth Press, 2002) at p. 306.

5. Roger Friedland and Richard Hecht, *To Rule Jerusalem* (Berkeley: University of California Press, 2000) at p. 493.

6. Robert S. Robins and Jerrold M. Post, *Political Paranoia: The Psychopolitics of Hatred* (New Haven, CT: Yale University Press, 1997) at p. 164.

7. Mathew Levitt, *Negotiating Under Fire: Preserving Peace Talks in the Face of Terror Attacks* (Lanham, MD: Rowman & Littlefield, 2008) at p. 29.

8. See Anton La Guardia, *War Without End: Israelis, Palestinians and the Struggle for a Promised Land* (New York: St. Martin's Press, 2003) at p. 293: "For many of Hebron's Jews, the massacre was a reenactment of the Purim story contained in the Scroll of Esther. . . . To the settlers, the Arabs are the embodiment of the evil vizier Haman, who schemed to wipe out the Jews of Persia. Goldstein took on the role of Mordecai, the Purim hero who destroyed the Jew-killers."

9. For more on this, see Ehud Sprinzak, *Brother Against Brother* (New York: Simon & Schuster, 1999) pp. 257–259.

10. See *USA Today* reprint of Associated Press wire story of the shooting "Israel on Alert after Seminary Shooting," March 7, 2008; this story can be accessed online at http://www.usatoday.com/news/world/2008-03-07-israel-attack_N.htm.

11. Joel Greenberg, "'Optimistic' gunman didn't fit profile of typical jihadist," *The Chicago Tribune*, March 8, 2008. Retrieved May 27, 2009, from www2.canada.com/ottawacitizen/news/story.html?id=a45d8bf7-a403–439b-a0ed-da28f4e6f848.

12. Mathew Wagner, "Mercaz Harav Rabbis Call to Settle the 'Land,' Change the government; Tamir verbally assaulted as 'murderer and traitor'; Yeshiva rejects visit request by PM," *Jerusalem Post*, March 10, 2008, at p. 1.

13. Graham Allison, *Nuclear Terrorism* (New York: Times Books) at p. 32.

14. Adam Dolnik, Keith Fitzgerald, and Gary Noesner, *Negotiating Hostage Crises With the New Terrorists* (Santa Barbara, CA: Greenwood Publishing Group, 2007) at p. 75.

15. Ibid., at p. 73.

16. Michael Wines, "Hostage Drama in Moscow: The Aftermath; Hostage Toll in Russia over 100; Nearly All Deaths Linked to Gas," *New York Times*, October 28, 2002, p. A1.

17. For more on Burke and dramatism, see Kenneth Burke, *Language as Symbolic Action: Essays on Life, Literature, and Method* (Berkeley: University of California Press, 1966); Kenneth Burke, *The Philosophy of Literary Form: Studies in Symbolic Action* (1941; reprinted, Berkeley: University of California Press, 1973); Kenneth Burke, *A Grammar of Motives* (1945; reprinted, Berkeley: 1969); and Kenneth Burke, "The Five Master Terms: Their Place in a 'Dramatistic' Grammar of Motives," *View*, 2, June 1943: 50–52.

18. In an interview for a BBC documentary on the incident, one of the hostages said later "I thought great acting; just look at the fear on their faces. It

wasn't until they sat down in front of us that I realized it wasn't a game." For the link to the original documentary, go to www.truveo.com/DUBROVKA-THEATRE-TERROR/id/3977332058 (accessed May 26, 2009).

19. Indeed, although history records Adolph Hitler as the most powerful and far-reaching promoter of genocide and state terrorism—a case could certainly be made for Josef Stalin, whose atrocities rival and perhaps surpass Hitler with the deaths of more than 20 million of his own countrymen, during the time of his rule. See Simon Sebag Montefiore, *Stalin: The Court of the Red Tsar* (Essex, UK: Vintage Books, 2005) at p. 649.

20. John B. Dunlop, *Russia Confronts Chechnya: Roots of a Separatist Conflict*, 2nd ed. (Cambridge, UK: Cambridge University Press, 1998) at pp. 56–84.

21. Ibid., at p. 60.

22. Tozun Bahcheli, Barry Bartmann, and Henry Felix Drebrnik, *Defacto States: The Quest for Sovereignty* (New York: Routledge, 2004) at p. 120.

23. Sebastian Smith, *Allah's Mountains: Politics and War in the Russian Caucasus*, 2nd ed., (London: Tauris Parke Paperbacks, 2005) at p. 60: "The scar is deep, not only on the generation which survived the train journey and the generation born in exile, but on their descendants. Because this was punishment based on race, the deportations have become part of the national identity of Chechens, Ingush, Karachai, and Balkars. Like Jewish Holocaust survivors, it is an event which quietly dominates both individuals' lives and the nation as a whole. Everyone without exception is a victim."

24. The original bombing occurred in 1993. Using some 1,300 pounds of explosives placed in the garage, terrorists killed 6 people and injured approximately a 1,000 more.

25. See, for example, Umberto Eco, "Function and Sign: The Semiotics of Architecture," in *Signs, Symbols and Architecture*, pp. 11–69, ed. Geoffrey Broadbent, Richard Bunt, and Charles Jencks (New York: John Wiley, 1980).

26. See, for example, Darryl Hattenhauer, "The Rhetoric of Architecture: A Semiotic Approach," *Communication Quarterly*, 32, 1984: 71–77.

27. See, for example, Elizabeth Walker Mechling and Jay Mechling, "The Sale of Two Cities: A Semiotic Comparison of Disneyland With Marriot's Great America," *Journal of Popular Culture*, 37, 1973: 253–263.

28. See, for example, Carole Blair, Marsha S. Jeppeson, and Enrico Pucci, Jr., "Public Memorializing in Post-Modernity: The Vietnam Veterans Memorial as Prototype," *Quarterly Journal of Speech*, 77, 1991: 289–308.

29. Ibid., p. 291.

30. Steven Connor, *Postmodern Culture: An Introduction to Theories of the Contemporary* (Oxford, UK: Basil Blackwell Press, 1989) at p. 76.

31. Robert Stern, "The Doubles of Post-Modern," *Harvard Architectural Review*, 1, 1980: 75–87.

32. Blair et al., "Public Memorializing," *Quarterly Journal of Speech*, 77(3), 1991: 263–288.

33. Homer, *The Odyssey of Homer*, trans. Richmond Lattimore (New York: Harper Perennial, 1991), at pp. 4.271–289, 8.499–520, and 9.523–537.

6

Methods for Studying Public Oratory About Terrorism

❖　❖　❖

In Chapter 3, we briefly reviewed the development of rhetoric, some of which centered on the contribution of the ancient Greeks and the schism between the Sophists and, later, Plato and Aristotle, the latter of whom felt that public speaking and rhetoric were less ends unto themselves and more the sine qua non of good citizenship. In developing a modern theory of rhetoric, we also referenced neoclassical theory, the contemporary application of Aristotle's ideas about oratory and persuasion. In this chapter, we will examine the relationship between public oratory and the general discourse we have concerning terrorism and how we construct its meaning—or how that meaning is constructed for us. By *public oratory,* I am referring not just to any speeches made on the subject of terrorism but to those speeches for a public audience made by our leaders or those of other countries, decision makers, and individuals in authority (including, by extension, the leaders of those groups we designate as terrorist). Any of these individuals are likely to shape public opinion. Naturally, I could be referring to any senior member of government (e.g., in this country, a president or a secretary of state); a former authority figure (e.g., a former leader like President Clinton); an expert recognized by the public (e.g., a well-known academic whose advice is relied on by people in government); the leader of a state that practices terror (e.g., the leader of a country that employs terrorism against its own populace); the leader of a dissent terror group (e.g., the leader of al Qaeda); and so on. In the interest of space and economy, however, I will here focus on only two speakers for this analysis: a former president, whose speeches on terrorism should be well-known to the reader at this time, and the most famous (or infamous) leader of a terror group.

In the next chapter, we will look at two speeches given by President George W. Bush in response to terrorism and the events of September 11. As leaders and authority figures, presidents occupy unique positions in American and global politics. A sitting president is the leader of our country but, by the rules of our Constitution, must share political power with the legislative branch of government (the Congress), and both the president and the Congress must have that power checked by the judicial branch of government (hence the old concept of *checks and balances*). Nevertheless, the president enters the game of shared power with considerable resources at his (and someday her) disposal—one of which concerns foreign affairs. It has been our custom throughout the history of our country to allow the president to speak with a single voice for all of us in matters of foreign affairs. It is true that Congress, controlling appropriations (i.e., the money to pay for things), still has influence in foreign matters and that the federal judiciary (and most especially the Supreme Court) will ensure that nothing a president does even in the foreign arena blatantly violates our Constitution; but these facts notwithstanding, foreign affairs are still the president's domain. This authority is bolstered by the fact that the Department of State is folded under the executive branch of government, as well as the fact that the president has the title of commander-in-chief of all the armed forces. In times of foreign conflict—especially involving war or the threat of war—the president's authority is unmatched. Even though our Congress passed a law called the War Powers Act[1] after our conflict in Vietnam, requiring more of a role for the Senate in the making of war, the act was filled with loopholes and is today a post facto measure, for the Senate does not get involved until after the fact and only if the president formally declares war or has committed American troops for combat beyond a certain statutory period.[2] Smart presidents since that time have been loath to declare war (although in some crises their rhetoric comes awfully close to *sounding* like a declaration of war) and have also been careful about time periods for deployment of troops or what language they would use in describing the reasons for sending troops in the first place. The result has been that the president acts and speaks for us in a relatively unchecked, single-minded manner. For all these reasons, presidents make ideal subjects for studying the effects of public oratory on matters of public concern—especially a topic such as terrorism, which, when committed on American soil, has the feel of war declared on America. Although in this book I will focus our examination on two of the more rhetorically significant addresses given by President George W. Bush in the aftermath of the terrorist attacks on September 11, let me stress that there are many acts of terror against this country and others (both *terror from above* and *terror from below*) that could be evaluated in the context of the public oratory they incite and how it shapes discourse. I have elected to use only these two examples because of time and space constraints. For the sake of understanding how these kinds of oratory engage the discursive process eliciting other kinds of rhetoric, including more oratory, in the next chapter I have also included a speech by Osama bin Laden—given three years after Bush's second speech in this chapter. Bin Laden's speech is clearly a response to Bush and, as we shall see, is an attempt to influence the 2004 presidential election.

Before I discuss the three speeches, however, I think it is important to first return to the subject of rhetoric—our rhetorical strand for this aspect of terrorism as a communication process—and address how we evaluate public oratory to discover its rhetorical function.

❖ A METHOD OF RHETORIC FOR PUBLIC ORATORY

Using the notion of neoclassical theory as a springboard, I will suggest the following methodology in this section, first by examining the notion of rhetoric, public speaking, and persuasion as being *audience centered;* then by examining the development of specific *rhetorical appeals* to affect that persuasion; and finally by considering how these appeals translate into actual persuasive messages with the assistance of *rhetorical figures* of speech and with the occasional use of *rhetorical fallacies*. Let's consider each of these in turn.

Public Speaking and Persuasion as Audience-Centered Rhetoric

Although it would seem that any discussion of this subject (especially one employing a modern application of Aristotle's ideas) should begin with an examination of appeals in the speech message proper, I feel that this puts the cart before the horse. In truth, effective public speaking and persuasion recognizes that its rhetoric must be created for and targeted to a specific audience (or audiences). Before we can talk about the persuasive message itself, therefore, we have to begin our discussion by understanding what and who the audience is, because considerations of audience drive the creation of effective persuasive messages in the first place. Out of necessity, we must begin our discussion of methodology with a comment about the significance of audience and how it is analyzed by the speaker/rhetor before the creation of the message. By understanding how and why speechwriters and speakers (not always the same person) make assumptions about audience, we can begin the process of deconstructing a public speech to understand how it works its influence on the intended audience. How does the creator of the speech message make assumptions about his or her audience?

The first question that must be asked is *"Who is the specific audience for this speech?"*[3] On occasion, there will be only one audience, but in truth, for most public speeches such as the kind given by a president, there will be multiple audiences. These may include (but are not limited to) members of the president's own party or those of the opposition party; they may include all the members of the armed forces—the Army, Navy, Air Force, Marines, Coast Guard, and so on, members of the White House and the executive branch, or members of the Congress; they may include foreign governments of countries who are our allies, those who are neutral to the interests of the United States, or even our supposed enemies; and they may also include any and/or all the residents of those countries on whose support the leadership of their governments depends. Audiences may include important captains of industry in our business sectors or important bankers and investment officials who need to be comforted or reassured by the president's words. They may include the leaders of state governments or state and local law enforcement personnel, whose cooperation the president may require for an initiative. Audiences may also include lobbyists and the leaders of special-interest groups who regularly contribute money and resources to campaigns for politicians who support their positions while campaigning vigorously against those who oppose them. Most fundamentally, audiences may obviously include the American people—regardless of party affiliation—whose interests the president is supposed to represent and serve and on whose good graces a reelection bid may hang.

Understanding more about who the audience is can be facilitated by asking questions about *audience demographics*[4] (e.g., age, race, ethnicity, cultural background, religion, education, and political orientation);

size of the audience[5] (how many people will be in the audience); *when the speech will be seen by the audience*[6] (both for those in attendance and for those who may be watching on television, listening on radio, or doing either on the Internet); *how much time will be allotted for the speech*[7] (i.e., for how long one can speak to the audience); and *where the speech will take place*[8] (i.e., questions about forum, which are most relevant for a live audience but can also play a role when the event is witnessed on television and the location creates a sense of background scenery/context for the speech).

Next, the creator of the speech may inquire, "*Is there any possibility for common ground between the speaker/rhetor and the audience?*"[9] In practice, this means considering whether there is anything in the background or situation of the audience that may also be found in the background or situation of the speaker. For example, if the president was addressing a group of concerned parents about the problems of teenage drinking, he might make a reference to the challenges he has faced as a parent concerned with alcohol use by his own teenage daughters. Doing so suggests that a common ground or bond exists between the speaker and the audience; he understands their concerns or situation because these are his concerns or his situation too.

Another audience-centered question the creator of the speech may ask is "*Has the audience heard the speech message before?*"[10] This is also known as "prior exposure to the message," and it deals with whether the audience has already been exposed to the speech message and has formed some kind of opinion or position in response. Has the audience heard this before? If so, what was the reaction? Was it what the speaker wanted? If it was a negative reaction, why did this happen? Surprisingly, some speakers are foolish about repeating speech messages that have proven unpopular or ineffective with audience members in the past. Sometimes, speakers do this because they are dogmatic and stubborn about their own positions; other times, they do this because they failed to consider the audience and prior exposure. In either event, it is a general rule of crafting speeches for specific audiences that what has worked in the past rhetorically will work again in the future, assuming that conditions and circumstances for the audience have not changed. For example, the senior George Bush, former president of the United States, decided to emphasize a traditional message in his speeches for election in the campaign of 1988. These included references to themes that his predecessor, President Reagan, had evoked in the previous campaigns of 1980 and 1984, such as the need for a strong defense, decreasing the tax burden, diminishing the role of the federal government in the private life of a citizen (or a business!), and return of greater political power to states and localities. It made sense for Bush, a former vice president under a popular president (Reagan), to repeat these same ideas in his speech messages in 1988. Of course, by 1992, conditions and circumstances had changed. How? The Soviet Union had broken up, and the Berlin Wall had crumbled. The concept of a political enemy in the Soviet communists was a strong rationale in much of the rhetoric used to advocate a stronger defense and more military spending. But, by 1992, that rationale wasn't effective for most voters because the old enemy no longer existed. In its place were new defense concerns, but President Bush's rhetoric never really effectively defined these in a way that resonated with voters. At the same time, he was accused—even by members of his own party—of going back on a pledge to never raise taxes. And of course, in that election year, the economy was still in recession, and many people felt vulnerable, while others suffered hardship from the downturn of events. Taken with that set of changed conditions and circumstances for the targeted audience of his reelection speeches in 1992, it is not hard to understand why Bush failed to connect with voters. Though it is true that messages that are effective can be repeated, it is also true that those messages should not be repeated if conditions and circumstances have changed the audience's disposition about the message. What worked for the senior Bush in 1988 was exactly what proved to be his undoing in 1992.

A final audience-centered question the creator of the speech message may wish to consider is *"What is the disposition of the audience to the speech message or to the speaker on a personal level?"*[11] Here, we would look to see if there was any evidence of audience disposition to be discovered from the other aspects of audience analysis we have discussed so far. How will the audience feel about the message the speaker is presenting? What is its disposition toward the speaker on a personal basis? In contemporary practice, we think of broad classifications to describe audience orientation to the message or speaker. These include classifying all or part of an audience as *hostile* to the message or speaker (meaning that audience members cannot be persuaded because they are so opposed to what is being said or to the speaker personally); *sympathetic* (meaning that they are, in effect, already persuaded because of their support, love, adoration, etc., for the message or speaker from previous experience); or *neutral* (meaning that no firm disposition exists toward speaker or message—the audience is yet to be persuaded). Though it is possible in theory for an entire audience to be classified as one or the other of these, more commonly—especially for public speeches delivered by presidents—elements of all three classifications may be found in the audience. Or to put this in a different way, it is more likely that for most presidential addresses, there will be multiple audiences, which are divided along the lines of hostility, sympathy, or neutrality. Knowing this ahead of time helps the creator of the message know what message is intended for what audience; likewise, it helps us understand, when we deconstruct a speech, why certain message choices were made.

Public Speaking, Oratory, and Rhetorical Appeals

Now that we have considered the audience, the next part of our methodology for public oratory is to consider the message itself. Here, we may reach back to Chapter 2 and our discussion of Aristotle and entertain three concepts he introduced in developing a theory of rhetoric. These concepts are still in use today by neoclassical theorists. They are the concepts of a persuasive speech message, classified as ethos, pathos, and logos. Of course, their effectiveness will depend on the audience; we are not all affected by ethos, pathos, and logos in the same ways.

In contemporary application, *ethos* refers to credibility—and specifically to the credibility of the speaker or rhetor, the messenger. When we say that a speech message is imbued with a strong sense of ethos, we are suggesting that the speaker, himself or herself, has a strong sense of credibility with the given audience. Of course, credibility can take many forms. For example, an individual may be credible because he or she is an *authority figure* (a person of power and responsibility), like a political leader or the leader of an organization or movement. Or a person may be credible because he or she is an *expert* on the subject addressed, like a scientist or a researcher. Or an individual may be deemed credible because he or she has *experience* with the subject being discussed—like Christopher Reeve, who, though not a medical expert on the subject of broken spines and paralysis, could still speak effectively because of his own experience. Perhaps, an individual may be found credible because he or she is trustworthy and honest, such as someone in whom you really trust and believe. (Can you think of any people like this? How about a close friend or family member?) If an individual possesses some amount of ethos, we may say that he or she will be effective with the audience, not necessarily because the speech message content itself is effective and persuasive but more because the speaker as an individual is credible. A powerful leader like the president will often have the ethos of credibility that comes from authority, but since the Watergate era, that has not always guaranteed that audiences would automatically believe anything a president had to say. Different presidents since that time have affected different forms of rhetorical ethos. For example, President Carter, though not perceived as an effective leader by the end of his administration, was nevertheless perceived to be an intelligent man and a very honest one, a perception confirmed in 2002, when he was awarded the Nobel Peace Prize. In contrast, President Reagan, Carter's successor, was a highly popular and likable leader, with an ethos that touched even his political opponents. Though many Democrats may have opposed Reagan's policies, most would still admit that they liked him on a personal level. The American people were no different; though many disagreed with Reagan's position on issues such as abortion or separation of church and state, they still liked him on a personal level and could be persuaded to vote for him. President Clinton, like President Reagan, was also an immensely popular leader—even to the point where his public support remained unflinchingly solid in the face of impeachment over whether he had perjured himself in an investigation over an alleged affair with Monica Lewinsky. Clinton's ethos, however, was different from Reagan's. How would we describe this ethos? Although both men shared enormous charisma, Clinton was often perceived as credible for his intelligence and command of detail, while Reagan—the so-called Teflon president—was more like a general or corporate CEO. Acting above the level of detail for which Clinton was known, President Reagan was seen as an authority figure who could see the big picture and make the larger decision.

A second form of rhetorical appeal identified for us by Aristotle is what he called *pathos* or the appeal of emotion. Here, we are describing speech rhetoric that persuades and affects an audience because it appeals to them on an emotional level. Not surprisingly, much of the rhetoric used by presidents in their speeches to different audiences employs pathos-centered appeals. For example, President Clinton, speaking in the aftermath of the violent tragedy at Columbine High School, made reference to the deaths of so many young people to make a larger point about the need for gun control. Though the President's point may have been logically connected to the gun control argument, the first way it hit many in the nation was emotionally because the memory of so many young victims was present in our consciousness.

Likewise, when the senior President Bush chose to make flag burning a political issue for the campaign in 1988, he employed rhetoric suggesting that support for the physical symbol of the flag was in some way a litmus test for an individual's patriotism to this country. Anyone who dared to support flag burning was unpatriotic and un-American. Ironically, a year later, the U.S. Supreme Court declared that burning the flag was symbolic, political expression protected by the First

Amendment.[12] It would not have been difficult for the senior Bush to have explained his argument in logical terms,[13] but he instead made this a mostly emotional argument, involving the aforementioned patriotism.

A third form of rhetorical appeal identified for us by Aristotle is *logos*—the appeal of logic or reasoning. In contemporary terms, we are describing rhetoric that succeeds with an audience because the message is rational and logical. There are many different ways to use logos appeals, but the kind with which you may be most familiar involves the use of *deductive reasoning*. This form of reasoning operates from the assumption that if certain statements—called argumentative premises— are true, then a certain conclusion must follow. If you have already enjoyed a class in critical thinking, you will undoubtedly have been exposed to this kind of argument before—usually in the form of what is called a *syllogism*. With a syllogism, there are two premises, the major premise and the minor premise, that must be true if a certain argumentative conclusion is to follow. For example, you may recall this syllogism from a class in critical thinking:

Major premise: All men are mortal.

Minor premise: Socrates is a man.

Conclusion: Socrates is mortal.

Note that when this kind of appeal is used in oratory, the speaker seldom (if ever) uses language to suggest that something is a "major premise" or a "minor premise." More often, we find these premises embedded in the text of the speaker's arguments as we deconstruct them.

Presidents, when trying to make a case to a certain audience, will sometimes use logos-based appeals with deductive reasoning in their speeches. More often, however, the use of these appeals must be kept relatively simple because the audience(s) for the president will be diverse and not always capable of understanding a complex argument in the same way. In such situations (which are common for speakers/ rhetors addressing large audiences), simple is better!

For example, it was, ironically, former President Richard Nixon— someone who had the ethos of a fighter and a staunch anticommunist— who later argued that negotiation with Communist China would not be possible without first improving relations with that country. His symbolic visit to China (the first by an American president since the communist revolution there) was the culmination of an argument he had already made to the Congress and to the country. The premises for this were relatively simple. Peaceful coexistence (and containment) of China required negotiation between our countries. Negotiation between the two countries, in turn, required normal relations. Therefore, it followed that peaceful coexistence with China would flow from normalizing relations. The more complex realities of using our improved relations with China to help drive a dividing wedge in the damaged relationship between China and the Soviet Union made for more complexity than Nixon wanted to convey.

If a president is to be effective, his or her decision to employ one or more of these appeals is ultimately driven by the assumptions made regarding the audiences to be addressed. As indicated before, not every appeal works with every audience member in the same way—if at all. Accordingly, it is rarely the case that a president's rhetoric reflects only *one* of these kinds of appeals. More commonly, there will be a blend of two or, perhaps, all three of the appeals, depending on the audience analysis that has already been conducted. Later in this chapter, I will discuss how these appeals are used in rhetoric about terrorism; for the moment, what would you assume would be the most common form of appeal to employ when discussing terrorism before an American audience?

Public Speaking, Oratory, and Rhetorical Figures

Understanding whether the speech message is ethos, pathos, or logos oriented for the specific audience(s) is an important step in deconstructing the public oratory of individuals like our political leaders—especially on topics such as terrorism. The next step is to examine how these messages are actually worded to create the desired rhetorical effect. To appreciate this, we will here consider how *rhetorical figures of speech and argument* are used. Rhetorical figures are the actual techniques for wording specific kinds of claims and arguments, and although there are literally hundreds of these, I will (for the sake of space considerations) focus on those that are most relevant to our discussion about terrorism. These include accumulation, anaphora, antithesis, catalog, personification, and prolepsis.

The first of these, *accumulation,* refers to a situation in which two or more clauses are used in succession within a speech, saying essentially the same thing. This is often done for emphasis and/or clarity. For example, during the 1960 presidential election, questions were raised about the fact that the presidential candidate John F. Kennedy was a Catholic, with some charging that his election would be dangerous for the United States because his first allegiance on different issues might be to whatever the Vatican's positions were. Answering this charge with an eloquent speech,[14] Kennedy used accumulation when he said,

> I am wholly opposed to the state being used by any religious group, Catholic or Protestant, to compel, prohibit, or persecute the free exercise of any other religion. And that goes for any persecution at any time, by anyone, in any country.[15]

Here, the words *religious groups* and *Catholics and Protestants* are saying essentially the same thing. The same is true for *compel, prohibit, or persecute*, and *at any time, by anyone*, or *in any country*.

An additional example from an ally of the United States can be seen in this passage from former British Prime Minister Margaret Thatcher's speech, only a month after her political party's (The Conservatives) conference had been bombed at the Grand Hotel in Brighton by the IRA. Thatcher said, "The terrorist is obsessed with power, but knows he cannot get it by democratic means. Reasoned debate means nothing to him. He despises it. He scorns the arts of persuasion. Democratic institutions he holds in contempt."[16] Each successive statement here echoes and reiterates Thatcher's claim that IRA terrorists reject democracy and reasoned discourse.

In contrast, another figure called *anaphora* deals with the repetition of a word or phrase at the beginning of successive phrases, clauses, or lines. Like accumulation, this is often done for emphasis and clarity— as well as for a sense of rhetorical style. For example, Lyndon Baines Johnson, who was sworn into office as president with the assassination of President Kennedy, addressed a joint session of Congress shortly thereafter,[17] in which he said,

> All I have I would have given gladly not to be standing here today. The greatest leader of our time has been struck down by the foulest deed of our time. Today, John Fitzgerald Kennedy lives on in the immortal words and works that he left behind. *He lives on* in the minds and memories of mankind. *He lives on* in the hearts of his countrymen [italics added to show anaphora].

The repetition of the words *he lives on* allows Johnson to emphasize Kennedy's memory and creates a sense of style for the pathos-oriented speech to multiple audiences.

A third rhetorical figure, called *antithesis*, deals with clauses in a speech set in opposition to one another, usually to distinguish between choices, concepts, and ideas. For example, in his first inaugural address,[18] President Richard Nixon closed his speech with antithesis, encouraging his audience to remember that "our destiny offers *not the cup of despair, but the chalice of opportunity*" [italics added to show antithesis]. Here, Nixon sets the *cup of despair* in opposition to the *chalice of opportunity*, leaving his large audience with a clear choice (after all, who would opt for despair over opportunity?) in this speech mixed with pathos and logos, along with the ethos of the presidency as an authority source.

In a similar way, consider the example of the Palestinian Liberation Organization (PLO) leader Yasser Arafat, who spoke to the United Nations General Assembly in 1974, declaring, "Today I have come bearing an olive branch and a freedom fighter's gun. Do not let the olive branch fall from my hand. I repeat: do not let the olive branch fall from my hand."[19] Here the olive branch was set in opposition to a gun, and the choice Arafat wants his audience to make is not even implied— it is directed with the last words.

A fourth example of a figure for our review is *catalog*, in which a speaker/rhetor offers a list of things, ideas, or arguments. Often, this is done in conjunction with a logos appeal to suggest evidence or support for a claim the speaker is making. Beyond making the message appear logical, this figure may also strengthen a speaker's/rhetor's ethos as an expert and a trustworthy source, by making the speaker appear as if he or she has considered all the possibilities. Political leaders often make use of this device. For example, former President Gerald Ford, in a speech[20] to a joint session of Congress, explained his vision for a new energy policy to cure the nation's energy problems.

> America's future depends heavily on oil, gas, coal, electricity, and other resources called energy. Make no mistake, we have an energy problem. The primary solution has to be at home . . . I have ordered today the *reorganization of our national energy effort* and the *creation of a national energy board*. It will be charged with developing a *single national energy program*. . . . *New legislation* will be sought after your recess to require use of *cleaner coal processes* and *nuclear fuel in new electric plants*, and the *quick conversion of existing oil plants*. . . . I will use the *Defense Production Act to allocate scarce materials for energy development*. . . . I will *meet with top management of the automobile industry* to assure. . . . a firm *program* aimed at *achieving a forty percent increase in gas mileage* within a 4-year deadline [italics added to illustrate catalog].[21]

Here, Ford lists aspects of his energy effort and program. The sum total of this list of initiatives is designed to rhetorically suggest that

Ford is actively trying to lead by comprehensively dealing with a complicated problem.

Another commonly used rhetorical figure is known as *personification*, the assigning of human characteristics to impersonal, nonhuman things. This is often used to create a positive or negative association with something by imbuing it with characteristics the audience may more easily understand. Regular product advertising and marketing campaigns often resort to this. For example, an ad at a service station selling gasoline with additives supposedly able to clean engine parts proclaimed, "Your car's parts are *happier* when they're *cleaner*" [italics added to show personification]. Of course, engine parts do not feel emotions any more than they have awareness of being dirty or clean, but wording it this way suggests that car parts have feelings like people, rhetorically suggesting that as consumers we should respect their wishes and spring for the more expensive gasoline! Likewise, politicians often employ personification in their speech making. For example, former President Jimmy Carter, while addressing the nation in his 1980 State of the Union speech, employed personification as he described the conflict with the hostage situation in Iran: "In response to the abhorrent situation in Iran, our nation has never been so *aroused* and unified greatly in peacetime. Our position is clear. The United States will not *yield* to blackmail" [italics again added to illustrate personification].[22] Can a "nation" be "aroused"? Can it "yield"? Or are these things that people do? How might it have changed Carter's speech if he substituted the word *people* for *nation*?

A final rhetorical figure we might consider is called *prolepsis*, which refers to anticipatory refutation. In this situation, the speaker/rhetor anticipates a criticism or counterargument to the one he or she presents and actually voices the response to it before the opposition can respond. If you have ever watched a student debate in a classroom or perhaps a debate between politicians in an election, you will have observed this in practice as one debater argues something to the effect of "In his next speech, my opponent will likely suggest this is not true. But let me tell you why he will be wrong." In this case, the entire reference is prolepsis because the debater anticipates the criticism and immediately counters it. This is often done to get the response out ahead of the counterargument and perhaps to discourage the opposition from even suggesting it.

Politicians will often use this in their speech making as well. For example, former President Reagan, two years into his first administration,[23] once explained his budgeting priorities and answered criticism (before it was made in response to his speech!) that he was unwilling to help the poor and less fortunate in American society. An exasperated Reagan observed,

> In the discussion of Federal spending, the time has come to put the sob-sister attempts to portray our desire to get government spending under control as a hard hearted attack on the people of America. In the first place, even with the economies that we've proposed, spending for entitlements—benefits paid directly to individuals—will actually increase by one third over the next five years. . . . Only here in this city of Oz would a budget this big and generous be characterized as a miserly attack on the poor. *Now where do some of these attacks originate? They're coming from the very people whose past policies, all done in the name of compassion, brought us the current recession* [italics added to show prolepsis].

Reagan was perfectly aware that his discussion of government spending would be criticized by Democrats in the Congress, and, anticipating their arguments, he addressed them directly, voicing the criticism and then supplying the response. Using prolepsis will not completely eliminate the opposition or criticism a speaker/rhetor faces, but it can be a very effective way of dulling the impact of such arguments in advance of their use.

Public Speaking, Oratory, and Rhetorical Fallacies

On occasion, speakers/rhetors may want to create the appearance of being rational and reasonable in their rhetoric but will employ tactics that are really anything but logical. When this occurs, rhetorical fallacies are in play. How do they work?

Fallacies are argumentative tactics that operate outside the presence of logic or reasoning. Sometimes explained as logical inconsistencies, these tactics will often be undetectable unless the audience member knows what to look for and demands more logic from the rhetoric. Again, if you have had a class in critical thinking, you will have been exposed to this before. You may be aware that there are literally hundreds of different types of fallacies used by speakers. It is not my intention to restate them all here. Rather, I will address a small list of the more common ones in use by political leaders, like the president, so that we may add them to our grouping of tools for deconstructing public oratory about terrorism. These fallacies are example reasoning, scare tactics, *post hoc ergo propter hoc* arguments, *reductio ad absurdum* claims, and *ad hominem* attacks.

The fallacy of *example reasoning* is the absence of deductive reasoning. Here, a speaker/rhetor purports to be logical in evidencing his or her conclusion by using evidence from some form of example. This becomes fallacious (and thus illogical), however, if it is clear that a single example or a limited set of examples has been used, rendering the approach inductive. For example, if the president says that the evidence for a new solution to resolve homelessness can be found in the example of an approach taken by a single city in America but it turns out that this city has a unique population, not typical of the rest of the country, and the approach has been in operation for only a month, we might say that this argument was a fallacy because of example reasoning. Quite simply, the example would not support the conclusion the president advocated.

Another kind of fallacy commonly used by our leaders is the *scare tactic*. Here, the speaker/rhetor typically overstates or exaggerates a claim for the purpose of trying to scare the audience into submission to his or her message. When your parents swore that they personally knew of someone who had lost an arm that had been waved out of a car window in traffic, they were using this kind of fallacy. It is highly unlikely that they knew of any such individual; their purpose was to scare you into believing that you should keep your hands in the car when they were driving! A president will often resort to the scare tactic fallacy when trying to urgently make a case for something (such as congressional support and funding for a financial bailout to investment companies in 2008) by suggesting dire consequences if he or she does not get what he or she wants. This is commonly detected when the language and word choice used by the president suggest exaggeration, with the effect of scaring the audience. President Clinton, who made a habit of having his way with the Republican-controlled Congress, often employed this fallacy in successive State of the Union addresses, as well as in Rose Garden press conferences, when arguing against Republican plans to cut his initiatives to "invest in the American future" by paying down the deficit. Clinton would often paint a future doomsday scenario in which generations of Americans would suffer horribly.

The fallacy of *post hoc ergo propter hoc,* although a mouthful to say out loud, is not as complicated as the name implies. Translated, it means, "after the fact, therefore because of the fact." This is a fallacy dealing with the appearance of logical causation. Here, the speaker/rhetor argues that because one result occurred in time *after* the presence of another factor, the factor must have caused the result. For example, you may recall that in any television murder mystery—such as *Matlock*—an innocent man (soon to be Matlock's client) would often be the "last person to have seen the deceased alive." As such, it was often assumed (fallaciously, of course) that because the murder occurred after the defendant had seen the victim, the defendant must have committed the murder! Programs such as this revolved around being able to show that this kind of causal argument would not stand up to reason.

Presidents sometimes use post hoc reasoning in their rhetoric, especially when in the midst of trying to assign blame for something. For example, President Reagan, in his first inaugural address, argued that the economic harm facing the nation as he took office (which included rampant inflation and high unemployment) was the direct result of too much reliance on the government for solutions. In Reagan's words "In the present crisis, government is not the solution to our problem; government is the problem." The President's argument, a centerpiece of his populist conservatism in the election, was that the failing economy he inherited in 1980 came about after Jimmy Carter's expanded role for the federal government from 1976 (especially with respect to taxation and regulation of energy importation and consumption) and that because the problems came after the federal buildup, they must have been caused by the buildup. The President's argument, however, presented a classic post hoc fallacy. The economic problems facing the country in 1980 were the result of myriad problems; some of them may have been traced to inadequate government policies, but they also included normal cycles of contraction in the economy; decades of poor—or nonexistent—planning at the federal, state, and local level for conservation; no investment in alternate energy forms; and a flailing foreign relations agenda that stretched back through numerous administrations.

The fallacy of *reductio ad absurdum* can be seen in arguments in which a claim is extended through to an extreme position, quite literally *reduced to the absurd*. These kinds of claims are common—especially in marketing and advertising rhetoric. How often are we told, for example, that failure to use certain products may lead to dire and/or embarrassing consequences? One television spot for a product to control the effects of diarrhea argues for its effectiveness but then suggests that failure to use it may subject an individual suffering from diarrhea to the worst of consequences. In the advertising spot, a father who failed to use this particular product is being buried in the sand during a day at the beach when he becomes afflicted. At the last instant, in a moment that is funny but patently absurd, he is suddenly struck with the diarrhea but unable to move because he is buried up to his neck!

Presidents and other political leaders will, on occasion, rely on this kind of fallacy in their rhetoric as well. In a famous address critical of television news media, former Vice President Spiro Agnew once complained that there was too much liberal bias in television news (not always true, even when Agnew was in office); that television news exerted too much influence (somewhat accurate—television news was and is extremely influential, as we shall explore in Chapters 8 and 9); and that decisions about what to show in the news were always based on telling a story that showcased "controversy" (again, a fair claim for television news, even today). But he then further opined that the only reason there were so many demonstrations in the streets in protest against the country's involvement in Vietnam was because television news cameras were present. Agnew asked, "How many marches and demonstrations would we have if the marchers did not know that the ever faithful TV cameras would be there to record their antics for the next news show?" Agnew's conclusion presented a typical reductio fallacy. He began by making reasonable claims (at least in part) but gradually spun the argument until it reached a more absurd conclusion— that the only reason for people to demonstrate en masse against the war in Vietnam was that they thought they might get on television. His claim, of course, ignored the possibility that the large public demonstrations against the war were due to a sizable number of Americans having serious doubts about what the United States was doing or accomplishing in Southeast Asia.

The fallacy of *ad hominem* attacks occurs when a speaker/rhetor resorts to name-calling to advance a claim. We call this approach fallacious because the speaker is suggesting that a course of action be followed or avoided, not for any rational reason but simply because an individual or institution associated with the message is a "nasty you-know-what." In many ways, this is more common in the heat of campaigns, when the mudslinging between political camps has increased and the number of days left before the election is limited. The temptation to engage in this fallacy is overwhelming.

Even though it is more typically found in campaigns, this fallacy is often also employed by presidents during their administrations. For example, President Reagan, in a speech now famously remembered for increasing the stakes in the Cold War, once referred to the Soviet Union as the "evil empire." In a similar fashion, President Bush Sr. once referred to the government in Iraq as "Nazi." Both claims were fallacious arguments, designed to create public support for U.S. foreign policy against the U.S.S.R. and Iraq. Reagan's argument was fallacious because calling a country an "evil empire," without explaining what constituted evil, amounted to simplistic name-calling. Likewise, Saddam Hussein's regime may have been repressive and was most assuredly a dangerous dictatorship, but to claim that it was the same as a fascist regime promoting racial purity and world domination was a real stretch. Bush chose the word because Nazism was and is unpopular, and he wanted to make that association in the minds of Americans to ensure public support for the Gulf War.

❖ SUMMARY

Public oratory about terrorism is one of the additional rhetorical strands that envelop the discursive process as we negotiate the meaning of terrorism or a terrorist act. This can include both the public oratory for large audiences by a political leader (like a president or a prime minister) and that from the leader of a group or country we have labeled as terrorist (such as a dictator or the leader of a dissent group). In this chapter, we have examined some methods for using a neoclassical approach to deconstructing the meaning of this oratory, including those for audience analysis, rhetorical appeals, rhetorical figures, and fallacies. In the next chapter, we will apply these methods to two speeches on terrorism by former President George W. Bush, as well as one by Osama bin Laden.

❖ NOTES

1. War Powers Act of 1973, Public Law 93-1-48.

2. Section 5(b) of the War Powers Act requires that the president report on military activities to the Congress and adds, "Within sixty calendar days after a report is submitted or required to be submitted . . . the President shall terminate use of U.S. Armed Forces unless the Congress (1) has declared war or has enacted specific authorization for such use of U.S. Armed Forces, (2) has extended by law such sixty day period, (3) is physically unable to meet as a result of an armed attack on the United States."

3. For a complete and thorough description of the audience analysis in public speaking and persuasion, see Joseph S. Tuman and Douglas M. Fraleigh, *The St. Martin's Guide to Public Speaking* (New York: St. Martin's Press, 2002) at pp. 89–115.

4. Ibid., pp. 97–102.

5. Ibid., pp. 92–93.

6. Ibid., pp. 93–94.

7. Ibid., pp. 93–94.

8. Ibid., pp. 95–96.

9. Ibid., pp. 102–103.

10. Ibid., pp. 104–105.

11. Ibid., pp. 105–107.

12. See *Texas v. Johnson*, 109 S. Ct. 2533 (1989).

13. For example, in ibid., Chief Justice William Rehnquist, writing a dissenting opinion, offered a historical perspective on the use and meaning of the flag to defend the legality of laws preventing its destruction by burning.

14. This speech was made at a campaign appearance before the Greater Houston Ministerial Association in September 1960. The address, titled "Religion in Government," gave Kennedy a chance to put the issue of his religious faith behind him for good. For a text of this speech, see Joseph S. Tuman, *Political Communication in American Campaigns* (Thousand Oaks, CA: Sage, 2008) at pp. 257–260.

15. Ibid., p. 259.

16. This is from a speech by Margaret Thatcher at the Lord Mayor's Banquet, November 12, 1984. The text of this speech can be found at www.margaretthatcher.org/speeches/displaydocument.asp?docid=105786 (accessed May 25, 2009).

17. The speech, titled "Let Us Continue," was delivered on November 27, 1963, only five days after Kennedy's death. It was as much a speech to the nation and the world as it was an address to the Congress, and it provided everyone a real glimpse of Johnson in an entirely new role and in a new light in a time of genuine crisis. For a text of this speech, see Theodore Windt, *Presidential Rhetoric*, 5th ed. (Dubuque, IA: Kendall Hunt, 1994) at pp. 53–55.

18. This speech was delivered January 20, 1969. For text, see ibid., pp. 123–127.

19. From Yasser Arafat's speech to the United Nations, November 13, 1974. For a full text of the speech, see *Journal of Palestine Studies*, Beirut, vol. IV, no. 2, Winter 1975, pp. 181–192.

20. This speech, titled "Win!", was delivered to a special joint session of the Congress on October 8, 1974, as inflation rates climbed out of control and as many, with serious doubts about the pardoning of Richard Nixon, began to question Ford's ability to lead the nation. For text, see Windt, *Presidential Rhetoric, op. cit.*, pp. 242–249.

21. Ibid., p. 244.

22. This 1980 State of the Union address by President Carter is often recalled as the speech that announced the "Carter Doctrine" for American foreign policy. Ibid., p. 297; the full text of the speech is on pp. 296–302.

23. This address, titled "The Conservative Cause," was made to the Conservative Political Action Committee (an obviously sympathetic audience for Reagan) on February 26, 1982. Ibid., p. 339; the full text of the speech is on pp. 335–342.

7

Case Studies for Public
Oratory About Terrorism

❖ ❖ ❖

N ow that we have considered different tools for rhetorically deconstructing a public address or oratory, we can apply these same tools to public speeches by a government official and a terrorist, both of whom speak on the same subject: terrorism. In this chapter, I will use two speeches by President George W. Bush, both made in the aftermath of the attacks on September 11, 2001. Next, I'll make use of a speech delivered by Osama bin Laden, some three years after Bush's speeches; bin Laden's speech is made on the eve of the 2004 presidential election. For all three speeches, the paragraphs are numbered, with the number boldfaced and in parentheses at the beginning of each paragraph; this is done so that when I reference the passage in the analysis following each speech, I can identify it for you by the paragraph number. After each speech, I provide a full commentary, including audience analysis, description of rhetorical appeals, use of rhetorical figures, and identification of any fallacies. Let's consider each of these in turn.

❖ PRESIDENT BUSH'S SPEECH TO THE NATION
   IMMEDIATELY AFTER THE ATTACKS OF 9/11

In this first speech, President Bush addresses the nation on the evening
of 9/11:

(1) Good evening. Today, our fellow citizens, our way of life, our very
freedom came under attack in a series of deliberate and deadly
terrorist acts. The victims were in airplanes, or in their offices;
secretaries, businessmen and women, military and federal
workers; moms and dads, friends and neighbors. Thousands of
lives were suddenly ended by evil, despicable acts of terror.

(2) The pictures of airplanes flying into buildings, fires burning, huge
structures collapsing, have filled us with disbelief, terrible
sadness, and a quiet, unyielding anger. These acts of mass murder
were intended to frighten our nation into chaos and retreat. But
they have failed; our country is strong.

(3) A great people has been moved to defend a great nation. Terrorist
attacks can shake the foundations of our biggest buildings, but
they cannot touch the foundation of America. These acts shattered
steel, but they cannot dent the steel of American resolve.

(4) America was targeted for attack because we're the brightest
beacon for freedom and opportunity in the world. And no one
will keep that light from shining.

(5) Today, our nation saw evil, the very worst of human nature. And
we responded with the best of America—with the daring of our
rescue workers, with the caring for strangers and neighbors who
came to give blood and help in any way they could.

(6) Immediately following the first attack, I implemented our
government's emergency response plans. Our military is powerful,
and it's prepared. Our emergency teams are working in New York
City and Washington, D.C. to help with local rescue efforts.

(7) Our first priority is to get help to those who have been injured,
and to take every precaution to protect our citizens at home and
around the world from further attacks.

(8) The functions of our government continue without interruption.
Federal agencies in Washington which had to be evacuated today
are reopening for essential personnel tonight, and will be open for
business tomorrow. Our financial institutions remain strong, and
the American economy will be open for business, as well.

(9) The search is underway for those who are behind these evil acts.
I've directed the full resources of our intelligence and law

enforcement communities to find those responsible and to bring them to justice. We will make no distinction between the terrorists who committed these acts and those who harbor them.

(10) I appreciate so very much the members of Congress who have joined me in strongly condemning these attacks. And on behalf of the American people, I thank the many world leaders who have called to offer their condolences and assistance.

(11) America and our friends and allies join with all those who want peace and security in the world, and we stand together to win the war against terrorism. Tonight, I ask for your prayers for all those who grieve, for the children whose worlds have been shattered, for all whose sense of safety and security has been threatened. And I pray they will be comforted by a power greater than any of us, spoken through the ages in Psalm 23: "Even though I walk through the valley of the shadow of death, I fear no evil, for You are with me."

(12) This is a day when all Americans from every walk of life unite in our resolve for justice and peace. America has stood down enemies before, and we will do so this time. None of us will ever forget this day. Yet, we go forward to defend freedom and all that is good and just in our world.

(13) Thank you. Good night, and God bless America.

Audience Analysis of President Bush's September 11 Speech

Here, President Bush spoke several hours after the attacks on New York and Washington, D.C., and the crash in Pennsylvania. He was aware that he had not been seen or heard from for much of the time immediately following the attacks and that speculation about his whereabouts (and those of Vice President Dick Cheney) had caused additional anxiety about what was happening.

What can be said about the audience or audiences for his speech? First, we know that even though the speech was broadcast in the evening, the President and his speechwriters could absolutely assume that they had the attention of almost anyone within sight of a television set or computer monitor or within earshot of a radio. Unlike most presidential addresses (even popular ones such as a State of the Union or the Inaugural Address), this was a relatively short speech that would command widespread attention. The President speaks to multiple audiences in this address.

First and foremost, he addresses all Americans, including both political allies and opponents. After a day's worth of extensive media coverage of the attacks (and most especially, the video footage of the jets flying into the World Trade Center [WTC]), he could be sure that everyone in the domestic audience had already seen the attacks, or knew of them, and would be concerned. As mentioned in the previous chapter, in times of political crisis with international repercussions, the President generally speaks with a single voice for the country at large. On this night, he could also safely assume that no one, including his opponents in the Democratic party who might still have been questioning his legitimacy after the Florida election results, would challenge his leadership or what he had to say about the attacks on our country. Though he acknowledges members of the Congress in Paragraph **10**, he does not address political insiders as allies or opponents in this speech. Instead, he simply assumes that they are all part of the larger domestic audience of Americans, as shaken and concerned as anyone else. Within that context, his message (as we shall see when we assess his use of appeals) could be general for all Americans. Using the terminology addressed before, we could categorize this initial audience as sympathetic—even if it contained traditional opponents.

A second audience for this speech includes the larger international community of nations, although here Bush is more careful to divide his comments between America's friends and opponents. Friends and allies of America are defined in this speech in Paragraph **11** as those who want peace and security in the world. Although Bush does not identify any allied nations by name, he assumes that most people in the audience will already have been exposed to news reports of international condemnation for the attacks by other countries across the globe. Like the domestic audience, we might consider this audience to be sympathetic to the speech message.

In contrast, in Paragraph **9**, he labels our opponents as either those who have directly participated in this terrorism or those countries who, by giving sanctuary to terrorists, have allowed the attacks to occur. Again, here he does not name names because at this point in the day, there is still no hard and clear evidence about exactly who is responsible for what (at least, if there is such evidence, Bush isn't sharing it in this speech). Nevertheless, the President addresses this audience of opponents who might have given sanctuary or support to terrorists, emphasizing the beginnings of a new policy for the United States: that in hunting down those responsible for the attacks, the United States will not distinguish between sponsors, nation-hosts, sanctuary givers, and the actual terrorists themselves.

Finally, the President's speech also addresses those directly responsible for the terror of that day. Although he does not (and perhaps cannot at this point) identify them specifically, he simply refers to them and their actions as "evil" in Paragraphs **1** and **9**.

Selection of Rhetorical Appeals

Given that the first and, perhaps, most important audience Bush addresses is the American public, he quickly fashions a message that addresses their (our) immediate concerns of the day. In Paragraphs 1 to 4, Bush acknowledges the prior exposure via mass media of this audience to the attacks of the day, but he quickly argues that although the country has been shaken by the terror, it has not been fundamentally diminished or weakened. Bush's description of the attacks is vivid and graphic—though no different from what people have already been exposed to on television. These specific references are largely pathos oriented, designed to remind the country of the mood it is feeling, which, in the words of the President in Paragraph 2, hovers between "disbelief, terrible sadness, and a quiet, unyielding anger."

In Paragraph 4, the President feigns an attempt at a logos-centered claim when he attempts an explanation for why the United States was attacked. Here, he suggests that we were targeted because "we're the brightest beacon for freedom and opportunity in the world." If this were reconstituted as a syllogism with premises and a conclusion, it would look like the following:

Major premise: Terrorists target and attack those who promote freedom and opportunity.

Minor premise: America is the brightest beacon for freedom and opportunity.

Conclusion: Terrorists targeted America because we (America) are the brightest beacon for freedom and opportunity.

Does this use of logos make sense to you? Both premises must be accurate and defensible for the conclusion to follow and the syllogism to be effective. Are both premises defensible here? Taking them in reverse order for the moment, the second premise (the minor premise) may be defensible, depending on how one defines "freedom and opportunity." Ours is a relatively free society and generally open and accessible to all who make it here legally.

What about the major premise? Is it true that terrorists attack those who promote freedom and opportunity? Here, the logic is less compelling. Bush never explains why terrorists would oppose either freedom or opportunity. He never gives other examples or offers any evidence for this claim—and as such, it comes off sounding flat. But that may not really matter for the initial audience of Americans. The President's use of pathos in the first few paragraphs has identified for us how we are feeling; intellectualizing the reasons for a terror attack can come later.

Bush's other primary appeal to this initial audience involves a greater blend of ethos. Remember that many were wondering who was in charge immediately after the attacks. Of course, today we know that the Secret Service was merely following protocol in sequestering the President in the face of the attack and making sure he was kept separate from the Vice President (so that both would not be targeted for assassination at the same time, creating a void at the top of the executive branch). But on that night, the President needed to reassure people that he was in charge and in control of the situation. In a sense, he needed to use language to communicate his ethos as leader and authority figure. He does this in Paragraphs 6 to 9 as he describes the initiatives he has set into motion in responding to the crisis.

To America's allies, who look to the United States as the dominant superpower in the world, Bush offers thanks for their condolences and assistance in Paragraphs 11 to 12, and he tries to reassure them that this country has not been permanently damaged economically in Paragraph 9, suggesting that the economy remains strong and "will be open for business." These are mostly ethos appeals, as Bush tries to impute the personal strength he suggests for himself to the country as a whole.

For America's enemies, the President's use of the foregoing is intended to suggest that the attacks have not achieved their objectives (shutting us down, paralyzing us), and in Paragraph 9, the President offers a blend of ethos (speaking as the commander-in-chief) and pathos when he suggests that those responsible will be brought to justice and punished.

Figures and Fallacies in the September 11 Speech

This speech is short and fairly to the point. The single attempt at logos is, as indicated before, at worst weak and at best underevidenced or explained. In that way, Bush's use of logic is to some degree fallacious, but we must remember that in this speech, the audience analysis was not necessarily dictating a lengthy, logical message. Americans needed to be reassured that they had a strong leader who empathized with their suffering and anger. Our allies needed to know that we appreciated their concern and that we were still the same superpower they had depended on 24 hours earlier. Our enemies needed to know that the United States would not let this attack go unpunished. In that rhetorical situation, logic and reasoning were beside the point.

The President does, however, make use of some figures to get his message across to the multiple audiences. In Paragraphs 6 to 9, he uses catalog to list all the actions he has taken to respond to the attacks as a way of communicating his ethos as a leader.

In Paragraph **5**, he employs antithesis when he sets clauses in opposition to each other. Here, he casts "evil" and "the very worst of human nature" in opposition to the "best of America" to illustrate the moral correctness of our position as victims of terror and again to communicate to the terrorists that ultimately they have failed in their attempts.

In Paragraph **12**, President Bush also employs personification, assigning human, personal characteristics to a nonhuman, nonpersonal thing, when he suggests that "America has *stood down* enemies before." Used in this way, America is compared with a single, strong individual, unafraid to stand up to bullies and villains. This is meant to boost confidence in the American audience, while again suggesting to the terrorists what fate awaits them in the future.

❖ BUSH'S SPEECH TO THE CONGRESS, THE NATION, AND
THE WORLD, SEPTEMBER 20, 2001

The second speech we will examine from President Bush is an address dated September 20, 2001:

(1) Mr. Speaker, Mr. President Pro Tempore, members of Congress, and fellow Americans:

(2) In the normal course of events, Presidents come to this chamber to report on the State of the Union. Tonight, no such report is needed. It has already been delivered by the American people.

(3) We have seen it in the courage of passengers, who rushed terrorists to save others on the ground—passengers like an exceptional man named Todd Beamer. And would you please help me to welcome his wife, Lisa Beamer, here tonight. (Applause.)

(4) We have seen the state of our Union in the endurance of rescuers, working past exhaustion. We have seen the unfurling of flags, the lighting of candles, the giving of blood, the saying of prayers—in English, Hebrew, and Arabic. We have seen the decency of a loving and giving people who have made the grief of strangers their own.

(5) My fellow citizens, for the last nine days, the entire world has seen for itself the state of our Union—and it is strong. (Applause.)

(6) Tonight we are a country awakened to danger and called to defend freedom. Our grief has turned to anger, and anger to resolution. Whether we bring our enemies to justice, or bring justice to our enemies, justice will be done. (Applause.)

(7) I thank the Congress for its leadership at such an important time. All of America was touched on the evening of the tragedy to see

Republicans and Democrats joined together on the steps of this Capitol, singing "God Bless America." And you did more than sing; you acted, by delivering $40 billion to rebuild our communities and meet the needs of our military.

(8) Speaker Hastert, Minority Leader Gephardt, Majority Leader Daschle and Senator Lott, I thank you for your friendship, for your leadership and for your service to our country. (Applause.)

(9) And on behalf of the American people, I thank the world for its outpouring of support. America will never forget the sounds of our National Anthem playing at Buckingham Palace, on the streets of Paris, and at Berlin's Brandenburg Gate.

(10) We will not forget South Korean children gathering to pray outside our embassy in Seoul, or the prayers of sympathy offered at a mosque in Cairo. We will not forget moments of silence and days of mourning in Australia and Africa and Latin America.

(11) Nor will we forget the citizens of 80 other nations who died with our own: dozens of Pakistanis; more than 130 Israelis; more than 250 citizens of India; men and women from El Salvador, Iran, Mexico and Japan; and hundreds of British citizens. America has no truer friend than Great Britain. (Applause.) Once again, we are joined together in a great cause—so honored the British Prime Minister has crossed an ocean to show his unity of purpose with America. Thank you for coming, friend. (Applause.)

(12) On September the 11th, enemies of freedom committed an act of war against our country. Americans have known wars—but for the past 136 years, they have been wars on foreign soil, except for one Sunday in 1941. Americans have known the casualties of war—but not at the center of a great city on a peaceful morning. Americans have known surprise attacks—but never before on thousands of civilians. All of this was brought upon us in a single day—and night fell on a different world, a world where freedom itself is under attack. Americans have many questions tonight. Americans are asking: Who attacked our country? The evidence we have gathered all points to a collection of loosely affiliated terrorist organizations known as al Qaeda. They are the same murderers indicted for bombing American embassies in Tanzania and Kenya, and responsible for bombing the USS Cole.

(13) al Qaeda is to terror what the Mafia is to crime. But its goal is not making money; its goal is remaking the world—and imposing its radical beliefs on people everywhere.

(14) The terrorists practice a fringe form of Islamic extremism that has been rejected by Muslim scholars and the vast majority of Muslim clerics—a fringe movement that perverts the peaceful teachings of Islam. The terrorists' directive commands them to kill Christians and Jews, to kill all Americans, and make no distinction among military and civilians, including women and children.

(15) This group and its leader—a person named Osama bin Laden—are linked to many other organizations in different countries, including the Egyptian Islamic Jihad and the Islamic Movement of Uzbekistan. There are thousands of these terrorists in more than 60 countries. They are recruited from their own nations and neighborhoods and brought to camps in places like Afghanistan, where they are trained in the tactics of terror. They are sent back to their homes or sent to hide in countries around the world to plot evil and destruction.

(16) The leadership of al Qaeda has great influence in Afghanistan and supports the Taliban regime in controlling most of that country. In Afghanistan, we see al Qaeda's vision for the world.

(17) Afghanistan's people have been brutalized—many are starving and many have fled. Women are not allowed to attend school. You can be jailed for owning a television. Religion can be practiced only as their leaders dictate. A man can be jailed in Afghanistan if his beard is not long enough.

(18) The United States respects the people of Afghanistan—after all, we are currently its largest source of humanitarian aid—but we condemn the Taliban regime. (Applause.) It is not only repressing its own people, it is threatening people everywhere by sponsoring and sheltering and supplying terrorists. By aiding and abetting murder, the Taliban regime is committing murder.

(19) And tonight, the United States of America makes the following demands on the Taliban: Deliver to United States authorities all the leaders of al Qaeda who hide in your land. (Applause.) Release all foreign nationals, including American citizens, you have unjustly imprisoned. Protect foreign journalists, diplomats and aid workers in your country. Close immediately and permanently every terrorist training camp in Afghanistan, and hand over every terrorist, and every person in their support structure, to appropriate authorities. (Applause.) Give the United States full access to terrorist training camps, so we can make sure they are no longer operating.

(20) These demands are not open to negotiation or discussion. (Applause.) The Taliban must act, and act immediately. They will hand over the terrorists, or they will share in their fate.

(21) I also want to speak tonight directly to Muslims throughout the world. We respect your faith. It's practiced freely by many millions of Americans, and by millions more in countries that

America counts as friends. Its teachings are good and peaceful, and those who commit evil in the name of Allah blaspheme the name of Allah. (Applause.) The terrorists are traitors to their own faith, trying, in effect, to hijack Islam itself. The enemy of America is not our many Muslim friends; it is not our many Arab friends. Our enemy is a radical network of terrorists, and every government that supports them. (Applause.)

(22) Our war on terror begins with al Qaeda, but it does not end there. It will not end until every terrorist group of global reach has been found, stopped and defeated. (Applause.)

(23) Americans are asking, why do they hate us? They hate what we see right here in this chamber—a democratically elected government. Their leaders are self-appointed. They hate our freedoms—our freedom of religion, our freedom of speech, our freedom to vote and assemble and disagree with each other.

(24) They want to overthrow existing governments in many Muslim countries, such as Egypt, Saudi Arabia, and Jordan. They want to drive Israel out of the Middle East. They want to drive Christians and Jews out of vast regions of Asia and Africa.

(25) These terrorists kill not merely to end lives, but to disrupt and end a way of life. With every atrocity, they hope that America grows fearful, retreating from the world and forsaking our friends. They stand against us, because we stand in their way.

(26) We are not deceived by their pretenses to piety. We have seen their kind before. They are the heirs of all the murderous ideologies of the 20th century. By sacrificing human life to serve their radical visions—by abandoning every value except the will to power— they follow in the path of fascism, and Nazism, and totalitarianism. And they will follow that path all the way, to where it ends: in history's unmarked grave of discarded lies. (Applause.)

(27) Americans are asking: How will we fight and win this war? We will direct every resource at our command—every means of diplomacy, every tool of intelligence, every instrument of law enforcement, every financial influence, and every necessary weapon of war—to the disruption and to the defeat of the global terror network.

(28) This war will not be like the war against Iraq a decade ago, with a decisive liberation of territory and a swift conclusion. It will not look like the air war above Kosovo two years ago, where no ground troops were used and not a single American was lost in combat.

(29) Our response involves far more than instant retaliation and isolated strikes. Americans should not expect one battle, but a

lengthy campaign, unlike any other we have ever seen. It may include dramatic strikes, visible on TV, and covert operations, secret even in success. We will starve terrorists of funding, turn them one against another, drive them from place to place, until there is no refuge or no rest. And we will pursue nations that provide aid or safe haven to terrorism. Every nation, in every region, now has a decision to make. Either you are with us, or you are with the terrorists. (Applause.) From this day forward, any nation that continues to harbor or support terrorism will be regarded by the United States as a hostile regime.

(30) Our nation has been put on notice: We are not immune from attack. We will take defensive measures against terrorism to protect Americans. Today, dozens of federal departments and agencies, as well as state and local governments, have responsibilities affecting homeland security. These efforts must be coordinated at the highest level. So tonight I announce the creation of a Cabinet-level position reporting directly to me—the Office of Homeland Security.

(31) And tonight I also announce a distinguished American to lead this effort, to strengthen American security: a military veteran, an effective governor, a true patriot, a trusted friend—Pennsylvania's Tom Ridge. (Applause.) He will lead, oversee and coordinate a comprehensive national strategy to safeguard our country against terrorism, and respond to any attacks that may come.

(32) These measures are essential. But the only way to defeat terrorism as a threat to our way of life is to stop it, eliminate it, and destroy it where it grows. (Applause.)

(33) Many will be involved in this effort, from FBI agents to intelligence operatives to the reservists we have called to active duty. All deserve our thanks, and all have our prayers. And tonight, a few miles from the damaged Pentagon, I have a message for our military: Be ready. I've called the Armed Forces to alert, and there is a reason. The hour is coming when America will act, and you will make us proud. (Applause.)

(34) This is not, however, just America's fight. And what is at stake is not just America's freedom. This is the world's fight. This is civilization's fight. This is the fight of all who believe in progress and pluralism, tolerance and freedom.

(35) We ask every nation to join us. We will ask, and we will need, the help of police forces, intelligence services, and banking systems around the world. The United States is grateful that many nations and many international organizations have already responded—with sympathy and with support. Nations from

Latin America, to Asia, to Africa, to Europe, to the Islamic world. Perhaps the NATO Charter reflects best the attitude of the world: An attack on one is an attack on all.

(36) The civilized world is rallying to America's side. They understand that if this terror goes unpunished, their own cities, their own citizens may be next. Terror, unanswered, cannot only bring down buildings; it can threaten the stability of legitimate governments. And you know what—we're not going to allow it. (Applause.)

(37) Americans are asking: What is expected of us? I ask you to live your lives, and hug your children. I know many citizens have fears tonight, and I ask you to be calm and resolute, even in the face of a continuing threat.

(38) I ask you to uphold the values of America, and remember why so many have come here. We are in a fight for our principles, and our first responsibility is to live by them. No one should be singled out for unfair treatment or unkind words because of their ethnic background or religious faith. (Applause.)

(39) I ask you to continue to support the victims of this tragedy with your contributions. Those who want to give can go to a central source of information, libertyunites.org, to find the names of groups providing direct help in New York, Pennsylvania, and Virginia.

(40) The thousands of FBI agents who are now at work in this investigation may need your cooperation, and I ask you to give it.

(41) I ask for your patience, with the delays and inconveniences that may accompany tighter security; and for your patience in what will be a long struggle.

(42) I ask your continued participation and confidence in the American economy. Terrorists attacked a symbol of American prosperity. They did not touch its source. America is successful because of the hard work, and creativity, and enterprise of our people. These were the true strengths of our economy before September 11th, and they are our strengths today. (Applause.)

(43) And, finally, please continue praying for the victims of terror and their families, for those in uniform, and for our great country. Prayer has comforted us in sorrow, and will help strengthen us for the journey ahead.

(44) Tonight I thank my fellow Americans for what you have already done and for what you will do. And ladies and gentlemen of the Congress, I thank you, their representatives, for what you have already done and for what we will do together.

(45) Tonight, we face new and sudden national challenges. We will come together to improve air safety, to dramatically expand the number of air marshals on domestic flights, and take new measures to prevent hijacking. We will come together to promote stability and keep our airlines flying, with direct assistance during this emergency. (Applause.)

(46) We will come together to give law enforcement the additional tools it needs to track down terror here at home. (Applause.) We will come together to strengthen our intelligence capabilities to know the plans of terrorists before they act, and find them before they strike. (Applause.)

(47) We will come together to take active steps that strengthen America's economy, and put our people back to work.

(48) Tonight we welcome two leaders who embody the extraordinary spirit of all New Yorkers: Governor George Pataki, and Mayor Rudolph Giuliani. (Applause.) As a symbol of America's resolve, my administration will work with Congress, and these two leaders, to show the world that we will rebuild New York City. (Applause.)

(49) After all that has just passed—all the lives taken, and all the possibilities and hopes that died with them—it is natural to wonder if America's future is one of fear. Some speak of an age of terror. I know there are struggles ahead, and dangers to face. But this country will define our times, not be defined by them. As long as the United States of America is determined and strong, this will not be an age of terror; this will be an age of liberty, here and across the world. (Applause.)

(50) Great harm has been done to us. We have suffered great loss. And in our grief and anger we have found our mission and our moment. Freedom and fear are at war. The advance of human freedom—the great achievement of our time, and the great hope of every time—now depends on us. Our nation—this generation—will lift a dark threat of violence from our people and our future. We will rally the world to this cause by our efforts, by our courage. We will not tire, we will not falter, and we will not fail. (Applause.)

(51) It is my hope that in the months and years ahead, life will return almost to normal. We'll go back to our lives and routines, and that is good. Even grief recedes with time and grace. But our resolve must not pass. Each of us will remember what happened that day, and to whom it happened. We'll remember the moment the news came—where we were and what we were doing. Some will remember an image of a fire, or a story of rescue. Some will carry memories of a face and a voice gone forever.

(52) And I will carry this: It is the police shield of a man named George Howard, who died at the World Trade Center trying to save others. It was given to me by his mom, Arlene, as a proud memorial to her son. This is my reminder of lives that ended, and a task that does not end. (Applause.)

(53) I will not forget this wound to our country or those who inflicted it. I will not yield; I will not rest; I will not relent in waging this struggle for freedom and security for the American people.

(54) The course of this conflict is not known, yet its outcome is certain. Freedom and fear, justice and cruelty, have always been at war, and we know that God is not neutral between them. (Applause.)

(55) Fellow citizens, we'll meet violence with patient justice—assured of the rightness of our cause, and confident of the victories to come. In all that lies before us, may God grant us wisdom, and may He watch over the United States of America.

(56) Thank you. (Applause.)

Audience Analysis of the September 20, 2001, Speech

Here, President Bush is addressing many of the same audiences he did in the speech on September 11. Again, there is the appeal to Americans and to our allies, as well as a more pointed message to the nations sponsoring or hosting terrorists and, of course, the terrorists themselves. These are sympathetic audiences (Americans and allied countries of the United States) and hostile audiences (terrorists and nations that sponsor or give refuge to terror), respectively. But in this speech, one finds that the President has decided to broaden the range of audiences.

First, in Paragraphs **21** to **26**, Bush turns to an audience segment that may cut across sympathetic, neutral, and hostile audience groups, depending on where these audience members reside, as he addresses Muslims both in the United States and abroad. Mindful that within days after 9/11, some American citizens of Muslim faith were harassed because of false assumptions about their faith and an assumed connection to the attacks, as well as rampant media speculation about which other nations might have been connected to the attacks (most of the speculation centering on nations with large Muslim populations), the President is careful to distinguish the perpetrators of the attacks from Muslims generally. When he says, "The enemy of America is not our many Muslim friends; it is not our many Arab friends. Our enemy is a radical network of terrorists, and every government that supports them," he is attempting to narrow the list of those responsible, making it possible for people to fill the ranks of the neutral or sympathetic audience for his message.

At the same time, there were, by inference, neutral audience members to this speech as well—most likely in those nations that might feel sympathy for victims of the terrorist attacks but that might not otherwise feel inclined toward U.S. foreign policy in the Middle East politically or be much inclined to sign on to a military campaign generally. When Bush states in Paragraph **29** that "either you are with us, or you are with the terrorists," he is putting these audience members on notice that they can no longer be neutral in this affair; they will have to pick sides, and the consequences for picking the wrong side will be severe.

Notice that while this speech follows Bush's previous address by only nine days, the amount of detail and the extent to which he is forthcoming are much greater in this second speech. Now, many of the answers he was unwilling or unable to provide in the immediate aftermath of the attacks are made clearer. The motivations for this can be found again in the audiences Bush addresses. Bush is aware that much media attention and general public discourse has been devoted to speculation about who was responsible and why they attacked. In this speech, he does his best to answer those questions for the more general American audience, while also using the answers he gives as a beginning justification for the argument he will make to other nations, allies and enemies, about picking sides. Bush is also much more direct about who he believes our allies and our enemies to be. Unlike the address of 9/11, this speech identifies countries, terrorist groups, and specific individuals.

Selection of Rhetorical Appeals

As before, it is critical that the American audience perceive Bush the messenger as a strong, authoritative leader. Understandably, 9/11 was perhaps too soon after the attack for him to be anything but general in his remarks about the attacks. Although he had announced some initiatives as of 9/11, here he is far more specific about what he wants to do in response to the threat from terrorism. In Paragraphs **30** and **31**, he announces the creation of a new cabinet-level position, called the Office of Homeland Security, to be headed by Tom Ridge and charged with the coordination of federal, state, and local efforts involving homeland security.

In Paragraphs **19** to **20, 22,** and **27** to **29,** he makes the case for demanding immediate concessions from Afghanistan and threatening (or really, promising) war on al Qaeda. Both the creation of the new cabinet position and the promise of war are targeted to showcase Bush's ethos with the audience and to reinforce his authority as our leader.

Additionally, and in contrast to his address of 9/11, Bush here resorts to a familiar rhetorical approach to ethos, typical of traditional presidential addresses such as a State of the Union speech. Notice in Paragraph **3** how Bush makes reference to the sacrifice of Todd Beamer, one of the individuals killed in the plane crash in Pennsylvania as passengers sought to retake the plane, and later, in Paragraph **52,** how he makes reference to Officer George Howard, one of the rescuers killed in the attack on the WTC. He references these two men by name and then indicates Beamer's widow and Howard's mother, who are present at the speech. Bush derives ethos from both men and their respective families. They were heroes and martyrs, and Bush derives strength from their examples. Notice also that he opens his speech this way and closes it in the same way—both of which indicate the degree to which he perceives this kind of derived ethos is significant to the American audience.

Like the address of 9/11, this speech is filled with pathos-oriented rhetoric, targeted not only to the American audience but also to the different countries in the international community. Both the aforementioned examples of Beamer and Howard also serve as pathos in this speech, for they are sad, emotional examples of sacrifice and courage. Additionally, in Paragraph **4,** Bush references the symbolic responses of people in America (unfurling flags, lighting candles, giving blood, and praying), and later, in Paragraphs **9** to **11,** he describes the international response of support from Europe, parts of Asia, Africa, Australia, and Latin America. Each international episode he cites (prayers of sympathy offered at a mosque in Cairo, the U.S. national anthem being played at the Brandenburg Gate in Berlin, even the presence of British prime minister Tony Blair in the audience for Bush's speech) are designed to be emotional and showcase support for the position he will advance in his war against terrorism.

Of necessity, Bush does go back to a logos message in this speech as well when he attempts to explain who was responsible for the attacks. In Paragraphs **12** to **16,** he identifies al Qaeda as the terrorist organization responsible for the attacks, Osama bin Laden as the leader of al Qaeda, and Afghanistan as the country responsible for hosting al Qaeda. He creates the appearance of logos in these passages by suggesting that "evidence we have gathered points to a collection of loosely affiliated terrorist organizations known as al Qaeda." In Paragraph **18**, he focuses on Afghanistan, which will be the initial theater for military operations in the "war on terror," and constructs what appears to be another attempt at deductive logic when he explains that those who aid and abet murder are themselves guilty of murder. This time, his implied syllogism appears to be more defensible. It looks like this:

Major premise: All those who aid and abet murder are guilty of committing murder.

Minor premise: The Taliban (the authority in Afghanistan at the time) aids and abets murder by giving sanctuary to al Qaeda.

Conclusion: By aiding and abetting murder, the Taliban is guilty of committing murder.

As a matter of criminal law and public understanding in this country, the major premise is not a controversial statement. Federal and state criminal laws[1] recognize such a distinction and routinely prosecute those who aid and abet murder. Likewise, the minor premise—suggesting that the Taliban aids and abets al Qaeda by giving it sanctuary—is openly recognized. If these premises are accurate, the conclusion regarding the Taliban and committing murder must follow. At least, that is the way it appears at first blush.

This use of logos is necessary not only for the American audience, whose backing Bush will need in the coming war in Afghanistan, but also for the international community of allies, whose logistical, political, and/or military support he may require in the military campaign that is all but preordained in this speech. Americans have to be satisfied that there is a reason (beyond revenge) to go into a war that may, in the President's words, become a "lengthy campaign" (Paragraph **29**), within which America may well suffer real casualties. Likewise, our international allies need to be assured that there is a semblance of reason and fact (beyond the impulse for a pound of flesh) for a military campaign, lest they be accused of backing America in an imperialist campaign against a smaller, poorer nation. Especially important here are those allies in Arab countries such as Egypt, whose support the United States has in this affair but whose people may share a different perspective, fearing American retaliation against Afghanistan as a plot against Islam, another perceived effort at imperialism, or yet another case of what they see as an American foreign policy that favors Israel over other Middle Eastern countries. For leaders in countries such as Egypt to be able to sell their support of the U.S. position, logos informed by facts and evidence may be a better tool than ethos or pathos.

Rhetorical Figures and Fallacies

Stylistically, the President employs a series of rhetorical questions throughout the speech to advance the general structure of his address. At Paragraphs **12**, **23**, **27**, and **37**, he voices questions that he assumes his American audience would like to ask. In a way, this approach is a form of prolepsis in that here he anticipates the questions (which have already been voiced as criticisms from Americans who do not understand why the attacks occurred or what the administration is planning to do about them). Bush voices the questions and then supplies the answers in a way that not only speaks to the American audience but creates a framework for the messages to the other audiences as well. For example, when in Paragraph **12** he says, "Americans are asking: Who attacked our country?" he then supplies the answer, identifying al Qaeda, as a means to suggest for the larger audience what he will do to terrorists and what he may do to Afghanistan. It is there that Bush reminds all other nations that they must pick sides in this fight.

Bush makes use of many other figures in this speech as well. First among these is the use of anaphora in Paragraphs **3** and **4**, where he suggests, "We have seen it," and in Paragraph **50**, where he notes that "*we will* rally the world to this cause by our efforts, by our courage. *We will* not tire, *we will* not falter, and *we will* not fail." By continually beginning each portion with "we will," he makes our response a collective response, for both the United States and the international community.

Another figure featuring prominently in this speech is antithesis, which Bush uses in Paragraphs **6** ("Whether we *bring our enemies to justice, or bring justice to our enemies*"), **49** ("But our *country will define our times, not be defined by them*"), and **50** ("*Freedom* and *fear* are at war"), each time to show sharp contrast between the United States's options for dealing with terrorism. When he describes the first of these in Paragraph **6**, the contrast is meant to indicate that we may go through traditional legal channels to arrest and prosecute those responsible or that we may use our military superiority to attack and eliminate the threat in a way that (as the euphemism suggests) "brings justice." Likewise, when he suggests in Paragraph **49** that our country will define our times rather than be defined by them, he is really arguing that our government will not be passive and reactive but rather active and assumptive in dealing with terror. The final use of antithesis, in

Paragraph **50**, is meant to reduce and simplify our conflict with terror to a simple choice between "freedom" (for the United States and her allies) and "fear" (practiced and spread by terrorists as a means of achieving their goals). The antithesis here is perhaps overly simplistic, but Bush intends to inspire his sympathetic American and allied-country audiences and to warn those neutral audience members that their choice is not just between the United States and terrorists but implicitly between freedom and fear.

The President employs accumulation in Paragraph **27** when he uses several examples, all of which are basically diplomatic and military tools at the disposal of the United States, that he asserts will disrupt and defeat global terror.

Catalog is employed by Bush in Paragraphs **2** to **4** to list all the ways Americans have demonstrated courage, sacrifice, and patriotism, and later in Paragraphs **9** to **11** as he lists the examples of support from the international community. Here, the emphasis is on volume, trying to give depth to the emotional appeal of the individual examples he cites.

Bush also uses personification in this address: In Paragraph **6**, he suggests that the country is "awakened to danger," treating our country as an individual and imbuing it with individual characteristics, such as awakening or coming to a new sense of awareness. The impact of this is to suggest that we are a collective whole, all thinking the same way on this issue. He makes use of personification again in the closing words to the speech when he reminds us that he will not forget the "wound to our country" (Paragraph **53**).

The President also makes extensive use of fallacies in this speech, including ad hominem attacks, example reasoning, post hoc ergo propter hoc, reductio ad absurdum, and scare tactics.

In Paragraph **13**, the President compares al Qaeda with the Mafia, a well-known criminal network. The effect is to give the American audience a way to understand "who attacked our country" by instantly labeling the terrorists with a comparison to something they already know and fear. Some may argue the comparison is not fallacious because both terrorists and Mafiosi are prone to violence, but the parallels are not so strong. The Mafia engages in criminal enterprise, including the use of violence, for profit; terrorists, in contrast, have widely different motivations for their use or threats of violence. Comparing the terrorists of al Qaeda with the Mafia, however, allows us to draw on representations of gangsters and organized criminals in popular culture and to see terrorists in the same light.

In Paragraph **35**, Bush employs the fallacy of example reasoning when he cites the NATO Charter to demonstrate why all nations have a stake in battling terrorism and says, "An attack on one is an attack on all." This kind of evidence for his claim of international support perhaps makes the most sense for our allies in western Europe who are currently members of NATO, but he references other continents (e.g., Asia and Africa, as well as the Islamic world—by which, one presumes, he means the Middle East), that are not and will never be members of NATO, as regions whose nations might also believe this. In point of fact, many of these other countries, though perhaps feeling sympathy for the United States in the 9/11 attacks, have their own problems at home with terrorism and seldom act in unified ways to respond to them. Equally important, not even NATO members always agree about responding collectively when the interests of NATO member nations are challenged.[2]

A post hoc fallacy can be seen in the President's attempt at logic as he builds the argument that those who aid and abet murder are actually murderers themselves. In Paragraphs **17** to **19**, he begins by suggesting that the Taliban was responsible for giving shelter to al Qaeda and therefore for helping cause the violence this terrorist group practiced. Because the attacks of 9/11 came *after* the Taliban's willingness to host this group, Bush argues that the Taliban must have helped cause the attack (after the fact, therefore because of the fact). Of course, there is no proof offered at this point in the speech (or any speech he had given to that date) that the Taliban actively approved of and sponsored the attacks of 9/11. And Bush seems to be aware he will be accused of fallacious argumentation if he persists in this, for it is at this point that he shifts his argument to the syllogism articulated earlier. Whether or not the Taliban actually participated in the sponsoring of the attack, Bush says, giving any aid to those who commit murder makes the individual who gives the aid equally responsible for the murder.

Finally, the President also employs an example of reductio ad absurdum fallacy in Paragraph **26** when he suggests that terrorists are like those who used ideology to rationalize murder earlier in the past century and then calls these groups by name—fascists, Nazis, totalitarians—and adds that, like them, terrorists will find their ideologies in the graveyard of "discarded lies." At this point, however, the President has provided no evidence or explanation of the motives for these attacks, other than claiming that these terrorists hate freedom and countries (such as the United States) that promote freedom. He has also already added that they cannot claim Islam as the religious, ideological basis for their motivation, so what is the ideology they practice? Why is it like fascism, or Nazism? The further Bush goes with this point, the less it makes sense, although one must admit that it sounds and reads well.

Despite a critical review of the rhetorical approach used by the President, this speech was still very effective in reaching its different audiences—most especially the primary sympathetic audience in America and her allies, as well as the possibly neutral audience of some countries in the international community who were noncommittal about a military incursion into Afghanistan. Although Bush is actually quite lean on specific details and the evidence he claims to have, he does name names and identify nation-sponsors and a terror organization in this speech. The details give those in the sympathetic audience enough to frame the outline of our discourse about 9/11, correcting and smoothing out the rough speculation we may have learned from endless priming in news and popular media. By the conclusion of this speech, the sympathetic audience has the President's official version of the facts: Osama bin Laden and his organization (al Qaeda) were responsible for the attacks, and Afghanistan is the country that played host to them and therefore the country that must now give them up or face the wrath of the United States and her allies. Of course, this suggests that a physical response from the United States will be forthcoming, and although the President can speak for the nation in foreign affairs, it is evident that he wants their (our) blessings before proceeding. To that end, he is careful to still cast the attack *and our response* in moral terms, reducing this to a simple fight between good and evil. In the President's rhetoric, all terrorism and terrorists are evil, whereas the United States (now the victim) represents what is good and decent. Domestically, at least, the President's reduction of terrorism and 9/11 to a fight between good and evil again helps to shape public discourse by implying that the choice for understanding terrorism and what must be done in response is relatively simple. Some may point out that this only reflects the President's style, which is to speak in plain language, but the reduction of this complex problem to something so simple also helps mute criticism of the administration or its response. When the President says this is about good and evil—and he speaks for us—then we talk about 9/11 in the same way, perhaps with the same simplicity. What critical questions do we ask when the discourse is at this level? Are there questions about prior American foreign policy and the Taliban? Or are there questions about the involvement of our own CIA with the Mujahideen in their fight against the old Soviet Union? Is there discussion about our foreign policy in the Middle East toward wealthy oil-producing nations such as Saudi Arabia, or toward Israel?

It is in this last point that the President begins to find some disagreement in the international community; some countries (including some in Europe) do not feel the problem of terrorism is anywhere near as simplistic as he represents. Many feel that the problem he has identified is genuine and acknowledge the right and responsibility of the United States to respond with force but also suggest that the problem is complicated and may require a more nuanced, sophisticated analysis. By framing the argument about terrorism as the President has done, the complexity in the issue is left to the larger international audience, and, given the media coverage of the issue, not always in a manner that allows for diverse points of view.

For our discourse at home, reducing this equation to a choice between simplistic extremes was also reinforced by making support for the President's position a measure of one's patriotism. Indeed, one strong effect of both terror violence and destruction on 9/11, *as well as* the President's statements about the same, has been to encourage many in the American audience to reconsider what patriotism and love of this country mean. Part of the American public discourse about the terrorism of 9/11 was to rediscover a sense of patriotism, often expressed in the symbol of the American flag. In the weeks and months following the attacks of 9/11 and the President's own rhetoric about the subject, large national chain stores such as Wal-Mart began reporting that all their supplies of American flags, usually reserved for holidays such as the Fourth of July, were selling out.[3] Millions of Americans began displaying flags—on houses, in yards, on automobiles, and even pinned to lapels or as prints on shirts, shorts, hats, and bathing suits—to express themselves as patriots. The American flag, long an honored symbol in this country, was rediscovered attached to another new symbol post-9/11 when it was attached to the sides of fire engines driving throughout different cities across the country. Even in places of critical introspection about the meaning of terms like *patriotism,* in cities such as Berkeley, California, people were engaging in discourse about terrorism by expressing themselves symbolically with the flag.[4]

❖ SPEECH BY OSAMA BIN LADEN, DATED 11/1/2004:
   JUST BEFORE THE 2004 GENERAL ELECTION
   IN THE UNITED STATES[5]

(1) Praise be to Allah who created the creation for his worship and commanded them to be just and permitted the wronged one to retaliate against the oppressor in kind. To proceed:

(2) Peace be upon he who follows the guidance: People of America this talk of mine is for you and concerns the ideal way to

prevent another Manhattan, and deals with the war and its causes and results. Before I begin, I say to you that security is an indispensable pillar of human life and that free men do not forfeit their security, contrary to Bush's claim that we hate freedom.

(3) If so, then let him explain to us why we don't strike for example—Sweden? And we know that freedom-haters don't possess defiant spirits like those of the 19—may Allah have mercy on them. No, we fight because we are free men who don't sleep under oppression. We want to restore freedom to our nation, just as you lay waste to our nation. So shall we lay waste to yours. No one except a dumb thief plays with the security of others and then makes himself believe he will be secure. Whereas thinking people, when disaster strikes, make it their priority to look for its causes, in order to prevent it happening again. But I am amazed at you. Even though we are in the fourth year after the events of September 11th, Bush is still engaged in distortion, deception and hiding from you the real causes. And thus, the reasons are still there for a repeat of what occurred. So I shall talk to you about the story behind those events and shall tell you truthfully about the moments in which the decision was taken, for you to consider.

(4) I say to you, Allah knows that it had never occurred to us to strike the towers. But after it became unbearable and we witnessed the oppression and tyranny of the American/Israeli coalition against our people in Palestine and Lebanon, it came to my mind.

(5) The events that affected my soul in a direct way started in 1982 when America permitted the Israelis to invade Lebanon and the American Sixth Fleet helped them in that. This bombardment began and many were killed and injured and others were terrorized and displaced.

(6) I couldn't forget those moving scenes, blood and severed limbs, women and children sprawled everywhere. Houses destroyed along with their occupants and high rises demolished over their residents, rockets raining down on our home without mercy.

(7) The situation was like a crocodile meeting a helpless child, powerless except for his screams. Does the crocodile understand a conversation that doesn't include a weapon? And the whole world saw and heard but it didn't respond.

(8) In those difficult moments many hard-to-describe ideas bubbled in my soul, but in the end they produced an intense feeling of rejection of tyranny, and gave birth to a strong resolve to punish the oppressors. And as I looked at those demolished towers in Lebanon, it entered my mind that we should punish the oppressor in kind and that we should destroy towers in America in order that they taste some of what we tasted and so that they be deterred from killing our women and children.

(9) And that day, it was confirmed to me that oppression and the intentional killing of innocent women and children is a deliberate American policy. Destruction is freedom and democracy, while resistance is terrorism and intolerance.

(10) This means the oppressing and embargoing to death of millions as Bush Sr. did in Iraq in the greatest mass slaughter of children mankind has ever known, and it means the throwing of millions of pounds of bombs and explosives at millions of children—also in Iraq—as Bush Jr. did, in order to remove an old agent and replace him with a new puppet to assist in the pilfering of Iraq's oil and other outrages.

(11) So with these images and their like as their background, the events of September 11th came as a reply to those great wrongs, should a man be blamed for defending his sanctuary? Is defending oneself and punishing the aggressor in kind, objectionable terrorism? If it is such, then it is unavoidable for us. This is the message which I sought to communicate to you in word and deed, repeatedly, for years before September 11th.

(12) And you can read this, if you wish, in my interview with Scott in *Time* Magazine in 1996, or with Peter Arnett on CNN in 1997, or my meeting with John Weiner in 1998. You can observe it practically, if you wish, in Kenya and Tanzania and in Aden. And you can read it in my interview with Abdul Bari Atwan, as well as my interviews with Robert Fisk. The latter is one of your compatriots and co-religionists and I consider him to be neutral. So are the pretenders of freedom at the White House and the channels controlled by them able to run an interview with him? So that he may relay to the American people what he has understood from us to be the reasons for our fight against you?

(13) If you were to avoid these reasons, you will have taken the correct path that will lead America to the security that it was in before September 11th. This concerned the causes of the war. As

for its results, they have been, by the grace of Allah, positive and enormous, and have, by all standards, exceeded all expectations. This is due to many factors, chief among them, that we have found it difficult to deal with the Bush administration in light of the resemblance it bears to the regimes in our countries, half of which are ruled by the military and the other half which are ruled by the sons of kings and presidents.

(14) Our experience with them is lengthy, and both types are replete with those who are characterized by pride, arrogance, greed and misappropriation of wealth. This resemblance began after the visits of Bush Sr. to the region. At a time when some of our compatriots were dazzled by America and hoping that these visits would have an effect on our countries, all of a sudden he was affected by those monarchies and military regimes, and became envious of their remaining decades in their positions, to embezzle the public wealth of the nation without supervision or accounting.

(15) So he took dictatorship and suppression of freedoms to his son and they named it the Patriot Act, under the pretence of fighting terrorism. In addition, Bush sanctioned the installing of sons as state governors, and didn't forget to import expertise in election fraud from the region's presidents to Florida to be made use of in moments of difficulty.

(16) All that we have mentioned has made it easy for us to provoke and bait this administration. All that we have to do is to send two Mujahidin to the furthest point east to raise a piece of cloth on which is written al Qaeda, in order to make the generals race there to cause America to suffer human, economic, and political losses without their achieving for it anything of note other than some benefits for their private companies.

(17) This is in addition to our having experience in using guerrilla warfare and the war of attrition to fight tyrannical superpowers, as we, alongside the Mujahidin, bled Russia for 10 years, until it went bankrupt and was forced to withdraw in defeat. All Praise is due to Allah. So we are continuing this policy in bleeding America to the point of bankruptcy. Allah willing, and nothing is too great for Allah.

(18) That being said, those who say that al Qaeda has won against the administration in the White House or that the administration has lost in this war have not been precise, because when

one scrutinizes the results, one cannot say that al-Qaeda is the sole factor in achieving those spectacular gains.

(19) Rather, the policy of the White House that demands the opening of war fronts to keep busy their various corporations—whether they be working in the field of arms or oil or reconstruction—has helped al Qaeda to achieve these enormous results. And so it has appeared to some analysts and diplomats that the White House and us are playing as one team towards the economic goals of the United States, even if the intentions differ.

(20) And it was to these sorts of notions and their like that the British diplomat and others were referring in their lectures at the Royal Institute of International Affairs. [When they pointed out that] for example, al Qaeda spent $500,000 on the event, while America, in the incident and its aftermath, lost—according to the lowest estimate—more than $500 billion. Meaning that every dollar of al-Qaida defeated a million dollars by the permission of Allah, besides the loss of a huge number of jobs. As for the size of the economic deficit, it has reached record astronomical numbers estimated to total more than a trillion dollars.

(21) And even more dangerous and bitter for America is that the Mujahidin recently forced Bush to resort to emergency funds to continue the fight in Afghanistan and Iraq, which is evidence of the success of the bleed-until-bankruptcy plan—with Allah's permission.

(22) It is true that this shows that al Qaeda has gained, but on the other hand, it shows that the Bush administration has also gained, something of which anyone who looks at the size of the contracts acquired by the shady Bush administration-linked mega-corporations, like Halliburton and its kind, will be convinced. And it all shows that the real loser is . . . you.

(23) It is the American people and their economy. And for the record, we had agreed with the Commander-General Muhammad Ataa, Allah have mercy on him, that all the operations should be carried out within 20 minutes, before Bush and his administration notice. It never occurred to us that the commander-in-chief of the American armed forces would abandon 50,000 of his citizens in the twin towers to face those great horrors alone, the time when they most needed him. But because it seemed to him that occupying himself by talking to the little girl about the goat and its butting was more important than occupying himself with the planes and their butting of the skyscrapers, we were given three times the period required to execute the operations—all praise is due to Allah.

(24) And it's no secret to you that the thinkers and perceptive ones from among the Americans warned Bush before the war and told him: "All that you want for securing America and removing the weapons of mass destruction—assuming they exist—is available to you, and the nations of the world are with you in the inspections, and it is in the interest of America that it not be thrust into an unjustified war with an unknown outcome."

(25) But the darkness of the black gold blurred his vision and insight, and he gave priority to private interests over the public interests of America. So the war went ahead, the death toll rose, the American economy bled, and Bush became embroiled in the swamps of Iraq that threaten his future. He fits the saying "like the naughty she-goat who used her hoof to dig up a knife from under the earth."

(26) So I say to you, over 15,000 of our people have been killed and tens of thousands injured, while more than a thousand of you have been killed and more than 10,000 injured. And Bush's hands are stained with the blood of all those killed from both sides, all for the sake of oil and keeping their private companies in business. Be aware that it is the nation who punishes the weak man when he causes the killing of one of its citizens for money, while letting the powerful one get off, when he causes the killing of more than 1,000 of its sons, also for money.

(27) And the same goes for your allies in Palestine. They terrorize the women and children, and kill and capture the men as they lie sleeping with their families on the mattresses, that you may recall that for every action, there is a reaction.

(28) Finally, it behoves you to reflect on the last wills and testaments of the thousands who left you on the 11th as they gestured in despair. They are important testaments, which should be studied and researched. Among the most important of what I read in them was some prose in their gestures before the collapse, where they say: "How mistaken we were to have allowed the White House to implement its aggressive foreign policies against the weak without supervision."

(29) It is as if they were telling you, the people of America "Hold to account those who have caused us to be killed, and happy is he who learns from others' mistakes."

(30) And among that which I read in their gestures is a verse of poetry. "Injustice chases its people, and how unhealthy the bed of tyranny." As has been said "An ounce of prevention is better than a pound of cure."

(31) And know that: "It is better to return to the truth than persist in error." And that the wise man doesn't squander his security, wealth and children for the sake of the liar in the White House.

(32) In conclusion, I tell you in truth, that your security is not in the hands of Kerry, nor Bush, nor al-Qaeda. No. Your security is in your own hands. And every state that doesn't play with our security has automatically guaranteed its own security.

(33) And Allah is our Guardian and Helper, while you have no Guardian or Helper. All peace be upon he who follows the Guidance.

Audience Analysis of bin Laden's Speech

This was not the first time bin Laden had released a videotaped speech post-9/11; there had been several.[6] In most of those other instances, however, there were arguably multiple audiences for his rhetoric, including people in the Arab/Muslim community within the Middle East, other members of worldwide Islam, those nations that had allied with the United States to battle al Qaeda, those that had been critical of the United States, and the United States itself. This speech is unique because it is directly targeted to an American audience. This much is obvious for two reasons. First, bin Laden very plainly says as much in Paragraph **2** when he declares, "People of America this talk of mine is for you." Additionally, the timing of this speech situates it within a specific context that has unique meaning and purpose for the United States: It came only a few days before Americans went to their polling places to cast ballots in the 2004 presidential election. Osama bin Laden intended to speak directly to American voters before they voted.

He surely understood that he would have little common ground with his viewers and listeners—and that he was facing a decidedly hostile audience.

Rhetorical Appeals in bin Laden's Speech

At various points it appears as if bin Laden is trying to use logos on his American audience, as a means of rationalizing the attacks of 9/11. He spends much time at the beginning of his speech explaining the cause behind 9/11, in the process implying that what we have called terrorism in the West was merely (from his perspective) an act of self-defense. Here, he challenges the existing characterization of 9/11 as an act of terrorism. He then spends the bulk of his speech critiquing President Bush's decision to take America into war with both Afghanistan and Iraq. Some of his points here echo arguments and criticism that were made of the Bush administration during the 2004 campaign season.[7] Additionally, in places, he does launch into what seemed to be a minor pathos appeal, when he reminds voters of the loss of life on 9/11 (in Paragraphs 2 and 23), the specter of American bankruptcy from spending on a failed war in Iraq (Paragraph 21), and the growing list of American casualties—mostly in Iraq (Paragraph 26). These are intended to frighten and upset the audience.

We would be missing the larger and more dominant form of appeal in this speech, however, if we assumed that bin Laden was trying to use logic to persuade Americans that they (we) deserved to be attacked on 9/11 or that any action in pursuit of al Qaeda was foolhardy and would only lead to financial ruin and more loss of life. In a way that may not appear obvious, the dominant rhetorical appeal in this speech is ethos. After several years of hiding and playing cat and mouse with American security forces, bin Laden is only too well aware of how he is perceived around the world, and most especially in the United States. At different points he has been labeled both as an evil genius and a fanatic, as well as someone who seeks to hijack his religion.[8] At other points he has been described as our "worst nightmare"[9]—and the "most wanted man" in the world.[10] His face and likeness have become the symbolic "other" referenced in Chapter 3 of this book.

With this as a rhetorical backdrop, he had no hope or expectation of rehabilitating his ethos or persuading Americans of the correctness of his position and actions. So what was his real motivation for this speech?

Rather clearly, the answer can be seen if we again consider the context for this address—*a few days before the 2004 election*. Osama bin Laden traded on his ethos in this speech to attack President Bush. The more he attacks and criticizes him, the more he makes President Bush appear sympathetic to an American audience. Osama bin Laden's ethos, laden with words such as *evil* and *fanatic*, as much guarantee a contrast with the President. If bin Laden is evil, Americans are reminded that the President must be the opposite (good); if he is a fanatic, President Bush must be seen as rational and measured.

These assumptions may seem somewhat heretical and perhaps counterintuitive; after all, why would President Bush's worst enemy want to make the President more sympathetic for voters?

Why indeed? The answer to that may become clear once we dispense with analysis of figures and fallacies.

Rhetorical Figures in bin Laden's Speech

It is important to note at the outset of this analysis that we are deconstructing a translation of bin Laden's words from Arabic into English, and thus, the rhetorical figures we may detect here are the product of choices made in the translation. Nevertheless, this was the text of his speech that was printed and broadcast here, shortly before the election; in that sense, it is still fair to analyze the translated words since these were the words that would have an impact on the same audience.

In this speech, we find a variety of figures that advance bin Laden's rhetorical appeals with his American audience. For example, in Paragraph 3 he makes use of antithesis when he contrasts al Qaeda's efforts to "restore freedom" with America's intention to "lay waste" to his nation (by which he means Islam and the Middle East); this is intended to lay a foundation for a form of logos, rationalizing the attack of 9/11. Similarly and quite significantly, he employs both a form of prolepsis (since he knows his argument will be critiqued by U.S. government officials after the speech is broadcast) and rebuttal to President Bush's previous speech in this chapter, when he challenges the assumption that he and al Qaeda fighters attacked America because they hate freedom. As he says in Paragraph 2, "free men do not forfeit their security, contrary to (President) Bush's claim that we hate freedom." Playing with labels such as "freedom" and "terrorism," he then observes with sarcasm that what America (which practices democracy and cherishes freedom) has done to his nation amounts to destruction, while those who defend his nation are accused of intolerance and terrorism. In his words at the end of Paragraph 9, "Destruction is freedom and democracy, while resistance is terrorism and intolerance."

Rhetorical Fallacies in bin Laden's Speech

There are individual instances of rhetorical fallacies in bin Laden's speech. Chief among these are post hoc ergo propter hoc/false cause fallacies, scare tactics, and ad hominem attacks. For example, while explaining his reasons for plotting the attacks of 9/11, bin Laden claims in Paragraphs **4** to **8** that the attacks against the WTC were revenge for the bombing by the U.S. Navy (in support of Israel) on different buildings in Lebanon in 1982. Later, he claims that the American-led embargo against Iraq was an additional yet different reason for the 9/11 attack. In effect, he is arguing that the 9/11 attack came after these acts by the United States, and therefore these acts were the cause of 9/11. His reasoning, however, is fallacious. The reference to burning buildings in Lebanon does not explain why he targeted specific buildings such as the WTC or the Pentagon or (presumably) the White House with those aircraft on 9/11. As indicated in Chapter 5, those were symbolic targets that had a very unique meaning. Equally so, his claim that the American-led embargo against Iraq presumes his sympathy for Iraq and Saddam Hussein, but there is no evidence today to suggest any affiliation, much less support and sympathy, from bin Laden or al Qaeda for Iraq or Hussein in this period. These weak claims are intended to rationalize his attacks, yet he knows that Americans will never be persuaded that they (we) deserved the tragedy of 9/11.

In a similar vein, bin Laden also employs scare tactics when he threatens the United States with financial ruin and bankruptcy over the war in Iraq. Here, the argument is fallacious because the intended purpose is to scare the audience into agreeing with his position, and while there is evidence that a great deal of money was (and is still being) spent in Iraq, suggesting bankruptcy here overclaims the final impact of this particular conflict. As the most recent recession has demonstrated, the American economy is complex and multifaceted, and ultimately one of the more resilient economies in the world.

These fallacies help with logos, but as suggested above, the dominant appeal in this speech is ethos. Bin Laden is unable to work around this—he is dealing with an intensely hostile audience—so instead, he chooses to work with his ethos. By employing ad hominem attack, he trades off his negative ethos with Americans as he attacks President Bush. Two examples in this speech are prominent. In one place, he compares Bush with a "naughty she-goat"—who is not only naughty, but also foolish (Paragraph **25**). Not coincidentally, this dovetails with his statement of ridicule that while the 9/11 attacks were happening and after he had been informed, the President was busy reading stories to Florida school children about a goat (Paragraph **23**). These attempts to demean President Bush by comparing him with an animal, much less a foolish animal (and not to be ignored within a sexist culture, *a female animal*) end up doing exactly the opposite—they make the

President appear sympathetic. Americans are unable to process these verbal insults without filtering them through their awareness of bin Laden's ethos as an evil enemy of the United States.

Real Intentions for bin Laden's Speech

If we conclude, then, that this speech was not about persuading Americans that the United States deserved what happened on 9/11, what was bin Laden's real intention here? The answer has to do with the proximity of this speech to the 2004 presidential election. Osama bin Laden mentions both President Bush and his Democratic challenger John Kerry in Paragraph **32**, but it is only Bush that he criticizes and insults throughout the speech. His goal was to make the President more appealing for voters—by tearing him down. As indicated above, this caused American voters who might have been undecided in the week before the campaign to reconsider Bush's candidacy with some sympathy engendered by their hostile reaction to bin Laden. For some, Bush was an unpopular president in 2004, but he was *our* unpopular president. When bin Laden attacked him, he was attacking us. Public reaction would be obvious; many voters would rally to support Bush.

Inside our government, intelligence analysts understood what I have suggested with rhetorical analysis above: bin Laden's strategic objective was to help (not hinder) President Bush's reelection. Deputy Director of the CIA John McLaughlin was reported to have said after analyzing bin Laden's speech, "bin Laden certainly did a nice favor today for the President."[11] Poll numbers taken just before the election told the story. In the week leading up to the election, President Bush led challenger John Kerry by the thinnest of margins; in the *Newsweek* poll of that week, Bush led Kerry by only 48% to 46%, with 6% still undecided. A 2% lead in a survey with ± error ratio of 3% means a statistical tie. For the same poll service, taken *after* bin Laden's speech, but *before* the final vote, Bush's numbers changed to 50% versus 44% for Kerry.[12] President Bush was reelected.

It might be overstating the impact of bin Laden's speech to claim that it alone spelled victory for Bush. Indeed, there is plenty to suggest that the President's campaign, coupled with the work of surrogate groups such as the *Swift Boat Veterans for Truth*, had been enormously effective in raising questions for voters about Senator Kerry's patriotism and ability to make decisions; but the fact remains, the race was close going into the last week of the campaign season. In a close election, little things can move undecided voters one way or another. Osama bin Laden's speech, so close to the final result, was indeed influential in the outcome.

And why did he do it? Only bin Laden knows for sure, but one point seems obvious enough. Osama bin Laden was President Bush's symbolic "other," as implied by the analysis in Chapter 3, but the opposite is true as well: President Bush was bin Laden's symbolic "other," too. Just as the President found his purpose with 9/11 and the war on terror and made a political issue and campaign cause of fighting terrorism and bin Laden, so bin Laden used President Bush to raise his stature among Arabs and Muslims and to find sympathy, volunteers, and support for al Qaeda. In a twisted way, each man needed and used the other, his "other."

❖ SUMMARY

In this chapter, we have reviewed how our own discourse about public issues such as terrorism is influenced and manipulated by public oratory from leaders of the state. To that end, we have explored how important an analysis of the rhetorical audience is for the creation of the oratorical message generally and for terrorism specifically, as well as the ways in which assumptions about the audience(s) influence the message choices the orator will make. We have examined some of the many possible uses of rhetorical figures used in oratory, how they can affect an audience, and how some of the more common intentional uses of rhetorical fallacies manipulate audiences exposed to oratorical addresses. All this was done to offer you some tools for critical evaluation of public speeches that describe terrorism in this country. Using two dominant public addresses from President Bush about the attacks of September 11, we then employed some of these tools to engage in critical analysis of how his speeches helped shape and, to some degree, limit our discourse about terrorism. Additionally, we considered an important speech by Osama bin Laden on the eve of the 2004 presidential election, in which he purported to rationalize 9/11 and challenge the defining of terrorism—while also helping President Bush's reelection efforts. To this point, I have provided all of the analysis for using these tools with the President's speeches on terrorism. I would encourage you to read more speeches from President Bush, President Obama, and other leaders addressing terrorism, or those leaders like bin Laden we have accused of terrorism, this time using the same rhetorical tools (audience analysis, selection of appeals, rhetorical figures, and rhetorical fallacies) to critically evaluate each speech and understand how it affected our discourse.

As you read these, consider the following questions. What assumptions would you make about the audience(s)? How are rhetorical appeals employed to target this (these) audience(s)? How many figures and fallacies do you find in the speech, and why do you think the speaker is using them? Finally, what impact does this speech have on our discourse about terrorism? Does it extend the effect of the previous speeches, or is there something different in play?

❖ NOTES

1. The concept of a felony-murder rule dates all the way back to English common law, and today, all states in the union have a version of this rule, as does the federal government (18 U.S.C. A7 §1111). The application of such a rule holds that anyone who is involved in the commission of a felony may be held responsible for any death that occurs as a result of the felony. For example, the driver of the getaway car (who himself or herself does not use a weapon or participate directly in an armed robbery) can still be found guilty of first-degree murder if anyone is killed in the commission of the crime. By operating the car, the driver facilitates and aids in the robbery and thus shares in its consequences.

2. For example, during the horrible violence in Bosnia, NATO members were not of one mind about how (or indeed if) to respond to the conflict.

3. See Will Evans, "Flag Merchants See Little Let-up Since September 11," *Sacramento Bee,* July 3, 2002, which noted that from September 11, 2001, to May 23, 2002, Wal-Mart had sold 4.96 million flags, up from 1.18 million the year before.

4. Merrill Collett, "Old Glory Beckons a Berkeley Peacenik," *Los Angeles Times,* September 24, 2001.

5. This is a translation of the version that appeared on Al Jazeera Television.

6. For more on this, see Chapter 9, dealing with bin Laden's use of new and free media.

7. For more on this, see Joseph S. Tuman, *Political Communication in American Campaigns* (Thousand Oaks, CA: Sage, 2008).

8. Look back to Paragraphs 13 to 16 of President Bush's second speech in this chapter.

9. The Editors of Salon.com, *Afterwords: Stories and Reports From 9/11 and Beyond* (New York: Books Pocket Books, Simon & Schuster, 2002) at p. 95.

10. Thomas R. Mockatis, *The "New" Terrorism: Myths and Reality* (Greenwood Publishing Group, 2007) at p. 52.

11. See Ron Suskind, *The One Percent Doctrine: Deep Inside America's Pursuit of Its Enemies since 9/11* (New York: Simon & Schuster, 2006) at p. 336.

12. For a complete review of these numbers, go online to www.telegraph.co.uk/news/worldnews/northamerica/usa/1475515/Bush-takes-a-six-point-lead-after-new-bin-Laden-tape.html.

8

Theories of Mass Media for Terrorism

❖ ❖ ❖

U p to this point, we have considered how terrorism can be rhetorical by examining the defining and labeling of terror as a rhetorical act; the symbolic messages in terror violence, means, and targets; and the public rhetorical discourse about terror. A final, equally significant factor to consider is the way this rhetoric is to some degree preconditioned in the minds of different audiences by images and representations in mass media. Without the assistance of media, terrorist rhetoric would influence only those in the immediate vicinity of terrorist violence and destruction. Conversely, with the assistance of media, terrorism reaches a much broader, sometimes global audience, and in an era in which most people (at least in the United States) get their political information from television, mass-mediated depictions of terrorism can have a profound effect on the way we think about and engage in discourse about terrorism. As the political science professor Abraham Miller once noted,

> Terrorism and the media are entwined in an almost inexorable, symbiotic relationship. Terrorism is capable of writing any drama—no matter how horrible—to compel the media's attention.... Terrorism, like an ill-mannered *enfant terrible,* is the media's stepchild, a stepchild which the media, unfortunately, can neither completely ignore nor deny.[1]

Though Miller was really describing a relationship between *news* media and terrorism, I would expand his claim and suggest that the same can be said about the relationship of all mass media with terrorism, including popular/entertainment media, as well as the emerging new media with computer-mediated communication (CMC).

In this chapter, we will examine the different ways by which we may frame the concept *mass media*, specifically thinking of it in terms of entertainment and news media, print and broadcast media, old and new media, and finally what is known as paid and free media. We will then briefly review the different rhetorical theories for media criticism, including those from semiotics, social psychology, and public opinion formation, before centering on what is called critical media theory and agenda setting and framing. Differentiating media and theory in this way will then lead to an application with terrorism in Chapter 9.

❖ UNDERSTANDING MASS MEDIA

Before we can explore how the relationship between terrorism and media works, we would be well served to define exactly what is meant by the term *mass media*. Richard Campbell, director of the School of Journalism at Middle Tennessee State University, has described mass media as "the cultural industries—the channels of communication—that produce and distribute songs, novels, newspapers, movies, Internet services, and other cultural products to large numbers of people."[2] Framed in this light, mass media can be seen as a conduit through which information about culture is transmitted to potentially sizable audiences. Campbell's definition is useful for our discussion because it references mass media from multiple perspectives: entertainment media and news media, print and broadcast media, and old and new media. The information about culture that is transmitted via this conduit includes all symbols of expression that individuals, groups, and societies use to make sense of their lives and articulate values and ideals.[3] Though all these channels of communication may be folded into our concept of mass media generally, they are all different and distinct from one another.

Entertainment Media and News Media

Entertainment media, which can include fiction books and short stories, cinema, and television programs, such as situation comedies, episodic and action dramas, and even televised sports contests, "real-life" programming, and game shows, are different from *news media*, which include newspapers and magazines, journals, Internet sites, and broadcast and cable news. How are they different?

To begin with, what I have described above as entertainment media function primarily to entertain or provide escape and recreation for their audiences. As it had always been with theater, literature, and popular fiction, and as it continues to be with television entertainment and cinema, these channels of media are not necessarily designed to be factual or literal in their interpretation of events or storytelling. Even when addressing real-world events and issues, as can be seen with reality-based television shows such as the still popular *Survivor* program or with movies based on real events such as director Wolfgang Peterson's *The Perfect Storm* (adapted from Sebastian Junger's book, which describes a real-life storm), it is implicitly understood that what is presented as reality will have been modified to package the broadcast or film as entertainment. For reality-based programs such as *Survivor*, this packaging begins with the careful selection of contestants as a cast, the fallacious presentation of what appears to be a remote and isolated location, the crafting of special contests for games, and the presence of cameras to record what seems like every thought and word and action by contestants. Even with these modifications, not all video shot for *Survivor* makes it into the broadcasting program. Editing choices are made about what to put in and what to leave out, and in what order, to make the story about the contest more entertaining.

Similarly, in films such as *The Perfect Storm*, which are said to be "based on" or "inspired by" real-life events—a certain amount of license is employed by the filmmaker to make the story more compelling.[4] Whether that takes the form of adding or deleting characters, changing timelines or locales, or even altering the focus of conflict in the story, it invariably makes the film a "story" in the fictional sense, not something to be taken literally.

News media, in contrast, operate under an admittedly risky assumption that what is presented as news is factual and can be trusted or taken literally. In contemporary America, journalism, the process by which news information is gathered and presented as stories for print or broadcast, has cast itself in the role of providing important information, facts, and ideas to assist citizens in making decisions about their lives and about participating in self-governance for democracy. Print news media (primarily newspapers and magazines and, to a lesser degree, online news sources) and broadcast news media (television news and, to a lesser extent, radio broadcast news) generally operate within the same context of providing necessary information for the public, but the peculiarities of each kind of medium (print vs. broadcast) make for important differences in the way news information is presented and packaged to the public.

Although print media, such as newspapers, must sell advertising to augment subscriptions and remain profitable, the articles and stories can generally be longer and more in depth than what is frequently presented in a televised or radio broadcast story. Of course, with televised news stories, the necessity for brevity in the actual number of words written and delivered can be compensated by the visual aspect of the medium: A news reporter's words can be augmented by video footage that communicates an amazing amount of detail to the viewer, even within the limited duration of a short televised news story.

It is also true for print media, such as newspapers and magazines, that what is reported often must trail what actually happens, simply because there must be time allowed to write, edit, and print a story in a publication that comes out late in the day, the following morning, or the following week. In this way, print news media provide a post facto coverage of news events and stories. In contrast, broadcast news (and to some extent, online news), especially since the advent of CNN and cable television, has the ability to broadcast and tell a story in real time as it is unfolding. Nowadays, this kind of news can be available to the viewing public on a constant 24-hour basis, every day of the year. From on-the-spot reporting to video footage broadcast as an event unfolds, this kind of news medium takes on a credibility similar to the account of an eyewitness to the news story. In fact, often this kind of coverage can make the viewer or listener an eyewitness. Of necessity, the ability to tell a story visually elevates the significance of the visual aspect of the medium. This in turn means that how and if a story may be told visually (with live video or file copy) plays a major role in determining when and if a story will be reported at all. Public relations experts and media consultants understand this aspect of broadcast news and often work to frame events that can be covered visually to help ensure that a story will be broadcast.[5]

Both print and broadcast news media follow another tradition of American journalism by framing stories about important issues in terms of *conflict*. Such conflict can be seen when ideas (e.g., Palestinian statehood vs. Israeli security and sovereignty), entities (e.g., the U.S. government vs. the government of Iraq), or individuals (candidates in an election campaign) in stories are pitted against one another, creating an illusion of balanced reporting but really generating conflict to make the story more compelling. In this way, news media take a cue from entertainment media.

The wonderful writer and thinker Ishmael Reed once told me that all "fiction is friction." By that he meant that the key to writing good fiction stories is in the friction or conflict that can be identified within. This much is true for literature, theater, or television and cinema. Conflict draws readers and viewers into a story and sustains their interest. And as it is for entertainment, so it becomes for news media. In truth, both fiction and nonfiction need friction.

Interestingly enough, though entertainment and news media differ in many ways, they also share points of *convergence*—both from within a media type (e.g., in entertainment media, when rap stars cross over to making television sitcoms or movies) and in between media types (e.g., when news media stories cross over and become entertainment media, such as books or movies). In this way, a series of newspaper stories in the *Washington Post* about the Watergate break-in can later become a best-selling nonfiction book (*All the President's Men*), which later crosses over and becomes an Oscar-winning movie with Dustin Hoffman, Robert Redford, and Jason Robards acting in the title roles. The focus of conflict that is common to both entertainment and news media allows for this convergence, as does the fact that being a high-profile story, author, or performer in one kind of medium can help generate popularity for a work that appears in a different medium.[6]

Old Media and New Media

A third possible reckoning of mass media can be found by looking at what is traditional (as we have done above in discussing entertainment, news or print, and broadcast media) and contrasting it with what technology has developed more recently. We may refer to this as a contrast between *old and new media*. In the category of old media (for mass media purposes), we would include print media in all its forms (e.g., books, magazines, journals, and newspapers), as well as broadcast/cable media (television and radio) and also film or cinema. In the category of new media, we might contrast these with innovations of the previous three decades' worth of technological development in CMC with the rapid explosion in the personal ownership of personal computers (or PCs); the development of software to create programs for communication, work productivity, and entertainment; and the development of the World Wide Web (WWW) and the Internet to link multiple computer users together. In a relatively short period of time, historically speaking, personal computers have become *de rigeur* for the majority of American households—as common (or maybe *more* common) as owning a television used to be[7]—and over the passage of time, they have become more common in other countries around the planet as well.

As a university professor, I occasionally ask my students how many computers they have had in their lives. Every year, the number they give grows larger. Ten years ago (in the mid-1990s), it was common for them to answer by saying that they were on their fourth computer by the time they had reached college age. Today, that answer is closer to six computers. The reason for that is a combination of the built-in obsolescence of computers[8] as well as a technological culture that has embraced or accepted the norm of replacing old equipment with new equipment on a fairly regular and consistent basis—perhaps not as often as one replaces running shoes but more often than one replaces something such as an automobile.

Initially, it appeared that most *personal use* of computers would be limited to educational activities (such as research or word processing for writing) or perhaps activities related to one's home (e.g., help with tax preparation or bill paying), or even for entertainment purposes (computer games, the ability to burn and record music or films, or applications for photography), but the advent of the aforementioned technology improving accessibility and speedy maneuvering of the Internet was what greatly altered the terrain. Today, millions of individuals and/or households in the United States are connected in one form or another to the Internet. Surfing the WWW has become commonplace for students seeking research, adults seeking news, individuals and businesses engaged in commerce, or people seeking to find, purchase, or share music, film, or movies—and even single people looking for potential mates! Because it is also largely unregulated by state or federal government entities, it is also a place where information about politics, campaigns, and governance can be posted, shared, and exchanged.

E-mail (personal messages sent from one individual to another or from one to many individuals), Web sites (sites created to post information), and Weblogs (or blogs, for short—Web sites set up by anyone, with personal narrative and links to other sites, and posted for all to see) have largely replaced the older versions of these (bulletin boards and listservs), and today it is common to find that most individual computer users have at least one e-mail account and regularly make use of at least one operating system and search engine to access the Internet.

In recent years, the drive for constantly improving and perfecting this kind of technology has led business to explore the possibilities of portability and wireless interconnectivity. Today, it is smaller and lighter laptops that demand top dollar in the computer market for individual use.[9] Software for connecting these laptops to the Internet via a wireless connection has created generations of users who carry their computers with them, able to use them almost anywhere. The desire to keep making these computers smaller has also led to the connection of this kind of media with another, personal cell phones—phones that also have basic computer features, such as the capacity to send or receive e-mail, surf the Web, or even download and play music or movies. Although unpractical for most word processing functions because of the small size of their keypads, these latter-day applications of traditional cell phone and computer functions have proved very popular with progressively younger generations of users, already groomed on text messaging and adept at video game hand controls, and thus able to easily control the cell phones for the purpose of maneuvering the Internet.

Free Media and Paid Media

A final way of dissecting mass media as they relate to terrorism is to divide them by comparing information that may be shared for no cost versus that which is carefully constructed and paid for. A simple way to reference this difference is to see this as *free media* as contrasted with *paid media.*

Free media here refer to print and broadcast news media, as referenced earlier, but with the understanding here that because *this is news media* it can be used to communicate a message to a larger audience if the communicator is skilled at attracting the interest of news reporters and in some fashion is able to influence or help shape how that message appears. When this occurs, the message is communicated by the news media in a manner that is almost free to the original messenger, hence the term *free media.* A simple example of this in a commercial context can be found with public relations efforts aimed at movie promotions. For example, by staging a premiere of a blockbuster Hollywood film, such as Steven Spielberg's *War of the Worlds*, and inviting many Hollywood celebrities and their families to a theater to watch the premiere, promoters of the film can likely attract the attention of numerous news outlets. When a news account reports on the stars and celebrities in attendance, it will also mention the premiere, which means that the movie itself will also be mentioned on the air. Broadcast reporters will likely get a sound bite from some of those in attendance who, as good guests (and as actors who want to work with Mr. Spielberg in the future), will be careful to say only laudatory things about the movie. The use of their words in the news account becomes both free advertising for the film *and* even acts to mute a little of the negative criticism the film might receive in a review.

A more subtle form of accessing this kind of free media can be found in more indirect approaches aimed at manipulating news. For example, while promoting the film *War of the Worlds*, the actor and star of the film Tom Cruise appeared on a number of talk shows (e.g., *The Oprah Winfrey Show* or *The Today Show*—with Matt Lauer) and at different points engaged in histrionic behavior, jumping up and down on the set as he declared his love for his then girlfriend and eventual fiancé, Katie Holmes. At other points, he delved into a serious and almost angry discussion about scientology, at one point arguing with *Today Show* host Lauer and accusing him of knowing neither the history of psychiatry nor any of the facts about an antidepressant such as Ritalin.[10] Later, while promoting the film overseas, he appeared with Holmes, posing for the cameras with dramatic kisses. For many, his behavior bordered on the bizarre but no doubt was newsworthy. Stories about the actor, his behavior, and his belief in scientology and speculation about his relationship with Holmes dominated media coverage for some time. While some wondered if this may have worried executives at Paramount, the studio behind *War of the Worlds*, the reality was that these stories kept the actor in the news, which also kept the film in the news, long past the need for advertising about it.

Free media contrasts with *paid media*, which for lack of a better term simply refers to advertising in any form, print or broadcast/cable—or even as it might appear in new media such as the Internet. Staying with the same example of Hollywood films, motion picture studios devote large budgets to the promotion of films, especially with the use of *trailers* (previews, shown at movie theaters) and advertisements shown on television. These, along with newspaper advertisements, billboards on well-traveled roads, signage used on the side of buses, or posters in areas of public transit and maximum human congestion are all designed to generate curiosity and build interest and enthusiasm for an upcoming motion picture. More recently, studios have shown additional interest in the creation of Web sites devoted to individual motion pictures, usually registered under the title name of the movie. In the previously used example, Spielberg's film had its own Web site at www.waroftheworlds.com. The expense for this kind of mass media can be considerable, but targeted carefully, it can greatly assist in placing filmgoers in a theater on opening night or the premiere weekend for a movie; from that point forward, of course, reviews and the all-critical *word of mouth* are key to a film's long-term prospects, but these too may be incorporated in future attempts at advertising. Newspaper ads, for example, typically trumpet (and often quote out of context) film reviewer's comments, while television ads may feature individual sound bites from audience members appearing to have just left the theater. Since these ads are paid for by the studios, the audience members' comments are naturally only laudatory and strongly supportive!

Understanding how mass media may be divided between entertainment and news media and how these may also be further segmented between print and broadcast news media, as well as old and new media and free and paid media, offers a useful place for continuing our discussion of the relationship between mass media and terrorism. To understand how that relationship affects the rhetoric of terrorism, it is first useful to review two of the theories of media-centered criticism alluded to in Chapter 2. In the following section, we will review the major components of such theories before focusing on those two parts most relevant to our discussion of media and terrorism.

❖ MEDIA-CENTERED CRITICISM

One aspect of the modern development of rhetorical theory and criticism has focused on the nature of media for communication and their ability to act as conduits for progressively larger or "mass" audiences. While this division of rhetoric can take many forms, including those from *semiotics* (dealing with the relationship between a sign, a referent, and the human mind),[11] *sociopsychology* (dealing with how individual audience members are believed to be affected by mass media),[12] and *public opinion* (dealing with how mass media and interpersonal communication may combine to develop public opinion, elevating the status of some issues and effectively silencing or never publicizing others),[13] the two areas most useful for our purposes in examining the relationship between mass media and terrorism concern what may be termed *critical media theory* (suggesting that mass media play an essential role in constructing cultural symbols and images that may be used to oppress marginalized communities)[14] and from a sociocultural perspective, *agenda-setting and framing theory* (dealing with the way in which mass media have the potential to establish the agenda of issues that are important for a society and additionally to determine which components of those issues are of the greatest value; the latter of these constitutes what will later be seen as media and public agendas, which may be used to influence public policy).[15] In the section below, we'll briefly examine the central tenets and assumptions underlying both critical media theory and agenda-setting and framing theory.

Critical Media Theory

Consistent with Campbell's perspective offered at the beginning of this chapter, critical media theory tends to assume that mass media can be seen as a conduit through which information about culture is transmitted to potentially sizable audiences. It also assumes that any of the ways in which mass media are conceptualized (e.g., print or broadcast, entertainment or news, new or old, free or paid) are potent texts from which this cultural information may be gleaned. Critical media theory operates from the premise that those who own mass media in their various forms (e.g., a newspaper chain, a movie studio, or a television network) purposely influence the content of the messages produced by mass media—and that this influence reflects their ideology, in a manner that allows them to dominate and marginalize others. This is often seen as promoting the interests of the owners of mass media, members of a dominant class or group, at the expense of all others.

Critical media theory has its origins in several different schools of thought, including a very early *Marxist perspective* that sees media as instruments of capitalism, promoting the interests of a dominant ruling class; *political-economic media*, which perceive media product as a commodity for consumption—with the result that only media content that appeals to the greatest number in the marketplace will actually become produced; perspectives from the so-called *Frankfurt School*, for which mass media were really used to help socially construct a meaning for culture, in a manner that allowed the ideological perspective of the elite class to dominate over all others; and *cultural criticism*, which looks at mass media and the dominant and oppositional manners in which media content may be constructed.

The latter of these, cultural criticism as a component of critical media theory, was in part discussed earlier in this text, when we examined the concept of *the other*, reflected in the arguments of theorists of ideological criticism like Edward Said. This kind of critical media theory is concerned with how some forms of mass media (e.g., print media such as a magazine article or a radio or television news broadcast) purport to be neutral, unbiased, objective, and autonomous of external controls when, in fact, they may be directly or indirectly exactly the opposite.[16]

A common complaint about critical media theory is that it does not acknowledge the positive effects of mass media on society, in the context of both their ability to provide information that may benefit or help people (e.g., stories about better nutrition or the symptoms of a contagious disease) and the role they may play in increasing participation in the democratic process (e.g., political news stories, documentaries, or Weblogs that offer counter viewpoints to official government propaganda or efforts at public relations over an issue such as the war in Iraq).[17] Equally so, critical media theory is also sometimes criticized for its failure to acknowledge that in the modern era there are many types of mass media available, representing a wide variety of perspectives and ideologies.[18] Particularly with the advent of the Internet and CMC, it may no longer be accurate to claim that elites of the ruling class dominate control over all mass media, especially when there are so many other ways to find oppositional points of view online;[19] indeed, the growing popularity of the Internet in its relatively unregulated form has threatened the business and profit viability of old traditional media such as newspapers, and even radio and television.

In Chapter 9, we will consider what a critical media perspective (particularly with cultural criticism) says about terrorism and mass media, specifically with respect to entertainment and news media.

Agenda-Setting and Framing Theory

The concept of agenda setting derives from the general observation that mass media are particularly adept at identifying issues for people. Almost 90 years ago, the noted journalist Walter Lippmann argued that ordinary life was too filled with competing information and priorities for the average person to know all the details and issues to think about. Said Lippmann,

> We are not equipped to deal with so much subtlety, so much variety, so many permutations and combinations. And all together we have to act in that environment, we have to reconstruct it on a simpler model before we can manage it.[20]

The result he suggested was that an entity—mass media as news media—was compelled to prioritize these issues for us, by selecting what issues would make compelling news stories for us to read, listen to, observe, and discuss. In 1972, Maxwell McCombs and Donald Shaw gave a name to this concept, labeling it as agenda setting;[21] the label took hold and became a common reference for understanding how news media tell the public "what to think about."[22]

Agenda setting occurs within news media because of the unique constraints that operate within this form of mass media, with a public consumption demand that requires a daily (now constant and in real time) refilling of news content but within formats limited by time and space, such as the number of minutes available to broadcast a news program or the page space and word count limits for a newspaper. Even with the addition of new media content on the Internet, there are still some limitations about how many stories or entries can be provided (with the expectation that they will be read) and how many words can be used. These kinds of constraints historically have forced reporters and editors in news media to make choices about what is newsworthy and what becomes a news story. The act of making a choice for one story means inevitably that other stories and issues do not receive coverage; it also means that those issues that are covered in news stories acquire a certain level of public importance and, inevitably, public focus.

Agenda setting is commonly thought to occur at two levels. The first level involves the choices referenced above, wherein reporters and editors (and those who influence them) decide what issues will become news stories. The second level focuses on the complexity of each issue as a news story and deals with the question of what part or attribute of an issue to emphasize and focus on in the telling of the story. When a decision is made to focus on a certain attribute of a story (e.g., discussing the general issue of President George W. Bush's decision to invade Iraq by focusing on his claim that Saddam Hussein had acquired weapons of mass destruction), the story implies that the featured attribution has a particular kind of significance or salience.

This second level of agenda setting is also what is referred to as framing.[23] According to Robert Entman, frames "select some aspects of a perceived reality and make them more salient in a communicating text, in such a way as to promote a particular problem definition, causal interpretation, moral evaluation, and/or treatment recommendation for the item described."[24] In practice, therefore, frames within news stories emphasize certain attributes of an issue by defining a problem, explaining its potential causes, exploring and making moral judgments, and suggesting potential remedies for problems or effects.

For example, in March 2009, a lone individual—an ex-convict and parolee named Lovelle Mixon—entered into a protracted gun battle with the Oakland (California) police, resulting in the deaths of four officers, three of whom were experienced veterans. It was not only a local story within the San Francisco/Oakland Bay Area;[25] it quickly evolved into a national and then an international news story.[26] Why? Understanding how the event was framed provides some insight. Initially, the story was framed with a focus on the number of police officers killed, as well as their veteran status. The event was repeatedly called in news accounts "the darkest day in the history of the Oakland

Police Department."[27] This frame defined the problem or conflict. The story lasted for many days. Later frames searched for causes, focusing on what the gunman's motive could have been, before settling on the fact that he was wanted for rape and feared being arrested and re-incarcerated when stopped initially by one of the officers at a routine traffic check. On each day of the coverage, there were repeated stories of moral outrage and public condemnation of the brutal event (the man used an AK-47 to shoot and kill two of the officers), and the state Attorney General and the Governor of California made visits to the police department and their families. Eventually, the coverage focused on the fact that a felon somehow had gained access to both a handgun and an AK-47 assault weapon, leading to more calls for strict gun control as a remedy.

This tragedy played out for many days in both television and newspaper accounts, often with multiple stories devoted to different frames of the event within the same broadcast or newspaper section. The inclusion of these naturally meant that on those days there was no time for other stories and, by their exclusion, their salience for the public was diminished.

When framing provides this second level for agenda setting, it is commonly agreed that news media's agenda of issues has had some powerful influence on what the public sees as important events and issues and that the public agenda (along with news media) then operates with public opinion to eventually influence and shape what the government's policy agenda will become.[28]

In Chapter 9, we will consider how terrorism and news media operate within the context of agenda setting and framing, especially with an eye to understanding how and why terrorism continued to dominate public discourse as a news issue for so many years after 9/11.

❖ SUMMARY

In this chapter, we have explored what mass media are and how entertainment media are different from news media. We then examined how broadcast media (television and radio) are different from print media (newspapers and magazines), new media (Internet and computer-mediated communication) are distinguished from old media (television, radio, newspapers, magazines), and paid media (advertising) are separate from free media (news coverage). We have also reviewed the different forms of media criticism generally, including semiotics, sociopsychology, and public opinion, before focusing on critical media theory and agenda-setting and framing theory. The latter two forms of media criticism will provide us a means for evaluating the relationship between terrorism and mass media (in all its forms) in Chapter 9.

❖ NOTES

1. Abraham H. Miller, *Terrorism, the Media and the Law* (New York: Transnational Publishers, 1982) at p. 1.

2. Richard Campbell, *Media and Culture: An Introduction to Mass Communication* (New York: Bedford–St. Martin's Press, 2003) at p. 6.

3. Ibid.

4. For example, in the movie, a helicopter rescues three people from the sailboat *Mistral,* 50 miles off Long Island, but later has to ditch in the Atlantic when traveling to another rescue. In reality, it was a helicopter attempting to rescue a lone Japanese sailor 250 miles offshore that ditched when returning to the mainland.

5. For example, demonstrators wishing to draw attention to animal rights and the fur trade might stage public relations events, such as a loud formal protest outside a department store hosting a fur fashion show, in the hope of drawing media attention. Make noise and possibly get arrested for disturbing the peace and you have a better chance of drawing media coverage.

6. For example, Howard Stern, who commands an audience in the millions for his syndicated radio program, also wrote two books, both of which were best-sellers based on his life. One of these books later became a movie—which did reasonably well at the box office and in video—starring Stern as himself. Though Stern is a funny writer and made a critically well-received acting debut, there is no doubt that the appeal and success of his books and movie owed in no small measure to his built-in audience and already established status as a celebrity in radio.

7. In the United States alone, sales of PCs in 2006 were put at 68.2 million. See "Vista Delay Seen Lowering 2006 PC Sales," with United Press International (UPI), March 27, 2006, at www.upi.com/Hi-Tech/viewphp?story ID=20060327-025456-6107r (accessed May 25, 2009).

8. That is, they are built to last only a certain number of years. Eventually, they either wear out—or because marketplace forces constantly drive technological innovations such as the speed of a processor chip, the computer you have today will be obsolete in two years—when compared with the new and improved and faster version of the same.

9. For example, in May 2005, laptop sales topped desktop PC sales for the first time that year. See Greg Sandoval, "Laptop Sales Outpace Desktop Sales for First Time," *Chicago Sun Times,* June 4, 2005, at p. B1.

10. For a full transcript of their interview and exchange, see http://msnbc .msn.com/id/8343367/page/3/ (accessed May, 29, 2009).

11. This approach focuses on the different ways signs are created by those who produce mass media and how these signs are interpreted by those audiences

who consume them. See, for example, Donald L. Fry and Virginia H. Fry, "A Semiotic Model for the Study of Mass Communication," in *Communication Yearbook 9*, ed. Margaret L. McLaughlin, 443–462 (Beverly Hills, CA: Sage, 1986) and for original theoretical perspectives, Jean Baudrillard, *Simulations*, trans. Paul Foss, Paul Patton, and Philip Beitchman (New York: Semiotext(e), 1983).

12. For an excellent overview of this and "effects-theory," see Tara M. Emmers-Sommer and Mike Allen, "Surveying the Effect of Media Effects: A Meta-Analytic Summary of the Media Effects Research," *Human Communication Research*, 25, 1999: 478–497.

13. Much of this stems from the work of Elisabeth Noelle-Neumann, *The Spiral of Silence: Public Opinion—Our Social Skin* (Chicago: University of Chicago Press, 1984).

14. For a broader exploration of this theory as an alternative paradigm, see Denis McQuail, *McQuail's Mass Communication Theory*, 5th ed. (Thousand Oaks, CA: Sage Press, 2005) at pp. 65–70.

15. For more on agenda setting, see Jian Hua Zhu and Deborah Blood, "Media Agenda-Setting Theory: Telling the Public What to Think About," in *Emerging Theories of Human Communication*, pp. 8–114, ed. Branislav Kovacic (Albany: SUNY Press, 1997) and Maxwell E. McCombs, "New Frontiers in Agenda-Setting: Agendas of Attributes and Frames," *Mass Communication Review*, 24, 1997: 4–24. For more on framing theory, see Todd Gitlin, *The Whole World Is Watching* (Berkeley: University of California Press, 1980) and Maxwell E. McCombs and Donald L. Shaw, "The Evolution of Agenda-Setting Research: Twenty-Five Years in the Marketplace of Ideas," *Journal of Communication*, 43, 1993: 58–67.

16. Linda Steet, *Veils and Daggers: A Century of National Geographic's Representation of the Arab World* (Philadelphia, PA: Temple University Press, 2000) at p. 26.

17. Pieter J. Fourie, *Media Studies: Institutions, Theories and Issues* (Cape Town, South Africa: Juta, 2004) at p. 247.

18. Ibid., p. 248.

19. For more on this, see Joseph S. Tuman, *Political Communication in American Campaigns* (Thousand Oaks, CA: Sage, 2008) at pp. 208–213.

20. Walter Lippmann, *Public Opinion* (New York: MacMillan, 1921) at p. 16.

21. Maxwell E. McCombs and Donald L. Shaw, "The Agenda-Setting Function of Mass Media," in *Public Opinion Quarterly*, 36, 1972: 176–187.

22. Donald L. West and Maxwell E. McCombs, *The Emergence of Political Issues* (St. Paul, MN: West, 1977) at p. 5.

23. For more on how framing works, see Erving Goffman, *Frame Analysis* (Boston: New England University Press, 1974); Robert M. Entman, "Framing U.S. Coverage of International News," *Journal of Communication*, 41(4), 1974: 6–28; Robert M. Entman, "Freezing out the Public: Elite and Media Framing of the U.S. Anti-Nuclear Movement,"*Political Communication*, 10(2), 1993: 155–173.

24. Robert M. Entman, "Framing: Towards Clarification of a Fractured Paradigm," *Journal of Communication*, 43(4), 1993: 51–58, at p. 52.

25. Jaxon VanDerbeken, Demian Bulwa, and Carolyn Jones, "3 Police Slain after Traffic Stop: Fourth Oakland Officer in Critical Condition," *San Francisco Chronicle*, March 22, 2009, p. A1.

26. See, for example, Jesse McKinley, "Seeking Answers to How a Traffic Stop of Parolee Set Off a Bloody Day in Oakland," *The New York Times*, March 23, 2009, p. A1.

27. See, for example, Kelly Rayburn, "Hundreds Attend Vigil for Slain Oakland Police Officers," *Oakland Tribune*, March 24, 2009, p. A1.

28. For more on this, see J. W., Dearing and E. M. Rogers, *Communication Concepts 6: Agenda-Setting* (Thousand Oaks, CA: Sage, 1996).

9

Mass-Mediated Images and Construction of Terrorism

❖　❖　❖

In this chapter, we will consider how mass media in the forms described previously interact with both top-down or state terrorism and bottom-up or dissent terrorism. In specific, we will examine how public perceptions about terrorism are primed by representations of terrorists in entertainment media, such as popular cinema and genre literature. In exploring the connection between news media and terrorism, we will consider how terrorists and news media share a symbiotic, mutually exploitative relationship; how public discourse about terrorism is also primed by mediated images of terrorists and terror violence in broadcast and (to a lesser degree) print news media; and how terrorists have learned to manipulate news media to ensure publication and distribution of their rhetoric to a global audience. Additionally, we will consider how *new* (not news) media create new possibilities for terrorists to communicate with target audiences, as well as to communicate with one another.

❖ TERRORISM FROM ABOVE AND MASS MEDIA

As suggested at the beginning of Chapter 8, terrorism and mass media share a symbiotic relationship of sorts, with each being dependent on the other for benefits and resources. The nature of this symbiosis depends in no small measure on whether the terrorism described is *from above* or *from below*. Most of the research documenting a relationship between terrorism and mass media has presumed a nonstate, dissent model, previously referenced as terrorism *from below*. Being allowed to communicate a message to a larger audience helps guarantee potentially greater significance and impression for the message. On occasion, this can legitimate the message or the messenger; at other times, it may lead to a lack of public sympathy for the terrorist or his or her cause. In contrast, the media benefit from this relationship, for terrorist activities also help generate viewer and reader interest, ensuring an even larger audience. In the remaining portion of this chapter, we will focus on some of this research and explore how rhetorical messages in terrorism are constructed via manipulation of and by mass media in the realm of both entertainment and news media.

For the time, however, it is important to also distinguish examples of terror *from above*, exploring how this kind of terrorism also has a symbiotic relationship of sorts with mass media, from which benefits and resources can be realized by the state. How these benefits are derived in turn depends on whether the state in question has eliminated or strictly controls mass media or operates a propaganda and public relations effort with a basically free mass media.

State Terror in the Absence of News Media

The Communist Khmer Rouge, which ruled the country of Cambodia from 1975 to 1979, practiced terrorism on its own people, including the use of mass murder, torture, starvation, forced relocation, forced labor, and destruction and/or confiscation of personal property. Estimates of the number of people killed by the Khmer Rouge have routinely been placed at 1.7 million out of a population of 8 million people, although these numbers may be as high as 2.2 to 2.5 million out of 8 million.[1] In such a repressive environment, there was no press or media as we understand it today, only the propaganda of the party. Unlike the example of other emerging Communist governments, which had made use of mass-mediated ideological persuasion to advance change in political and social mobilization, the Khmer Rouge preferred brute force to effect the change demanded by their leader Pol Pot. Karl Jackson has noted that

> the Khmer Rouge . . . did not expend much energy . . . on mass media
> to inculcate revolutionary values. Largely absent were the mass

rallies, heroic photos of the leader and blanket mass media coverage
. . . Instead there was a steady stream of executions.[2]

As such, it is difficult even to this day, nearly a quarter-century
later, to have accurate records and documentation about what happened. The absence of news media, which might have been critical of
the party or at least might have documented its activities, benefited the
Khmer Rouge by ensuring little or no opposition from within
Cambodia, only opposition from outside after the facts were known.

By way of example, in 1976, Pol Pot is believed to have delivered
an address now called the *Microbe Speech*, in which he complained of
certain elements within Cambodian society that needed control and
elimination. He said,

> There is a certain sickness inside the Party. . . . We cannot locate it
> precisely. . . . The illness must emerge to be examined . . . we search
> for the microbes without success. They are buried. As our socialist
> revolution advances, however, seeping more strongly into every
> corner of the Party, the Army and among the people, we can locate the
> ugly microbes.[3]

In a country with traditional mass media, even in one with state-
controlled mass media, this speech would have been disseminated
across a wide public audience. In this instance, however, the speech
was delivered to party leaders who generally viewed the speech as a
cue to begin a wide range of executions for those individuals who were
deemed the equivalent of a microbe or disease to the party. We only
know of this today because of the work of academicians who recon-
structed the events many years later.

Top-Down Terror and State Control of Media

In countries and societies allowing for different kinds of mass
media but exerting strict government control of either entertainment or
news, there are similar benefits in a lack of critique or opposition to
state terrorism and resources to be gained by the state from sponsor-
ship of propaganda. For example, the German National Socialist Party,
the Nazis, under Adolph Hitler as leader and Josef Goebbels as
Minister of Propaganda, ruthlessly subjugated its own people and
eventually terrorized the rest of Europe, resulting in the deaths of millions. Though the Nazis were not very successful in using mass media
to persuade countries outside Germany that conditions in Europe justified Nazi advances,[4] they were extremely successful in using the

same propaganda on their own people to all but eliminate opposition to the party and to introduce their own rationalization for the barbarity of their regime. As the semantics scholar and former U.S. Senator S. I. Hayakawa once noted,

> Anyone or anything that stood in the way of Hitler's wishes was "Jewish," "degenerate," "corrupt," "democratic," "internationalist," and as a crowning insult, "non-Aryan." On the other hand, everything that Hitler chose to call "Aryan" was by definition noble, virtuous, heroic, and altogether glorious.[5]

The same may be said of the former Soviet Union, which under Josef Stalin aggressively used state-sponsored propaganda to justify the existence of the Soviet Communist Party[6] while also muting any mention or criticism of the fact that Stalin was responsible for the deaths, torture, persecution, and forced relocation of millions of his own people. The Soviet Union that survived Stalin, though perhaps not as openly repressive, nevertheless pursued an equally directive relationship with the state news agency, Tass, which presented the official Soviet view of news, while also muting and avoiding any criticism of the state's actions.

This was a pattern also followed (and continued to this day) in Communist China, which strictly controls the news media and regulates what kind of entertainment media may be produced from within or imported from outside the country. For decades, China's former leader, Mao Tse-tung, used the state news media to try and knit a cohesive message about the glories of the Communist Party while also being openly critical of anything outside China. The same medium historically did not allow for internal coverage or commentary of anything that might be critical of the government or the party, including any stories about arrests or executions of dissenters. Years after Mao's rule, the state continues to control mass media in China, with some success in events such as the uprising at Tiananmen Square in 1989. Many student demonstrators were killed or injured during this uprising, a fact transmitted widely on television outside China but described very differently, if at all, within China. In modern times, however, though the state continues to try to regulate mass media in China, the realities of marketplace competition have meant that more and more quasi-independent news media and entertainment media have begun to challenge the state's control.[7] This competition, along with the advent and spread of the Internet, has provided the opportunity for some reduction in the strength of the state's grip on mass media in China.

A similar result may be observed in Rwanda, where an orchestrated mass media campaign by the Hutu majority to eliminate any Hutu political opponents and the Tutsi minority population resulted in a horrendous genocide. In this case, the mass media, including journals such as *Kangura* or a radio and television station called *Radio Television Libres des Milles Colline*,[8] were not operated directly by the government but rather were influenced by the same; in the latter case, they were owned by relatives former President Habyarimana and employed to distribute messages that encouraged the oppression of disloyal Hutus and the mass slaughter of Tutsis. In what became a case of state terrorism that led to genocide, the Tutsis were labeled as *ibyitso* (traitors) and *inyenzi* (cockroaches).[9] Precise numbers of the dead are not known, but the estimate is that between 800,000 and 1 million people were killed in this genocide.

Top-Down Terror and News Media in Democratic States

For countries that see themselves as open societies with free and democratic governments and little or no restriction of mass media, there are still benefits and resources to be gained from manipulation (if not strict control) of media. Even a democracy may be observed to engage, either by accident or by design, in what some may consider as state terrorism. The United States's historical treatment of Native Americans might fall under such a heading, as might its involvement in My Lai during the Vietnam War or in any military conflict where innocent civilians were killed or injured, such as the episode with the Soviet military in Afghanistan, mentioned in Chapter 3. Likewise, a democratic country such as Israel may have its own actions questioned in dealing with a Palestinian uprising, when, in cases such as the military response to a rash of suicide bombings in 2002, the Israeli military adopted a policy of using Palestinian neighbors in housing complexes and apartment buildings to identify where terrorists were hiding by having them go (in the place of Israeli soldiers) and knock on the doors of suspected terrorists, on the assumption that the terrorists would not kill their own people. This policy, which resulted in the deaths and injuries of some Palestinians, raised a hue and cry in both Palestine and Israel, including criticism in the Israeli news media. In this case, as has been the pattern with the U.S. government when dealing with similar criticism, the response has not been to censor the media or to limit what can be said. Rather, democratic countries manipulate their messages by practicing public relations (a more politically acceptable term for *propaganda*) by providing their own version of "the facts" for news media, replete with their own briefing sessions, their own supply of experts and authorities to quote, and the time-honored tradition of *spin*. As to the latter of these, media-savvy governments are quick to get their version of a controversial story out in front of the media early in order to try and influence what the story will be rather than being forced to react to what it has become. Though this kind of response pales in comparison with elimination of all media or strict control of state media, it is nevertheless a method of manipulating how mass media present and report messages about terrorism, and it again allows the state to benefit from diminished or little lasting criticism.

❖ TERRORISM FROM BELOW AND MASS MEDIA

As mentioned earlier in this chapter, the traditional approach to studying and identifying a relationship between terrorism and mass media has usually focused on nonstate, dissent terrorism *from below* and its relationship to mass media—really in the form of news media. In the last part of the chapter, I will discuss this relationship for terrorism *from below*, although I will expand the treatment of how this relationship works by also including entertainment media, along with news media. To that end, I will address how terrorist stereotypes are engendered by representations in popular entertainment, such as movies and books; how mythologizing of specific terrorists can occur in both news and entertainment media; and generally how terrorists can manipulate—and become manipulated by—news media.

Terrorist Stereotypes and Entertainment Media

As suggested in Chapter 8, cultural criticism as a component of critical media theory suggests that media content may be shaped to reflect and perpetuate the perspective of a dominant class or culture while rarely, if ever, giving way to oppositional perspectives or worldviews. Media content, which identifies and demonizes individuals or populations as "the other," represents them as the opposite (or a deviation) from the norm. One way this can happen is with perpetuation of stereotypical beliefs as to what actions and behavior constitute a sense of the other. While there are many examples of this in news media, it is equally, if not more, prevalent in entertainment media, especially with respect to depiction of dissent or bottom-up terrorism.

It should come as no surprise to the reader that if Ishmael Reed's words about fiction and friction are accurate, terrorism as subject matter and terrorists as character studies should prove an undeniable attraction for storytellers, novelists, and later for filmmakers. Examples of terrorism and terrorists can be found in any number of writings by prominent authors, including Joseph Conrad's *Secret Agent*[10] (dealing with a theme of betrayal within a group of anarchist terrorists), Robert Louis Stevenson and Fanny van de Grift Stevenson's *The Dynamiter*[11] (dealing with a crazed bomber who ends up blowing up an innocent woman's home in the hope that it will terrorize all of England[12]), Fyodor Dostoyevsky's *Besy*[13] (translated as *The Devils* or *The Possessed*, which deals with themes of murder and destruction for their own sake), Liam O'Flaherty's *The Informer*[14] (dealing with themes of betrayal and martyrdom for the terrorist), and, in more recent times, John LeCarre's *The Little Drummer Girl*[15] (also dealing with a portrait of terrorists, a theme of betrayal, and how law enforcement must use people to catch and kill terrorists).

Though these works of literature have contributed to a growing image of terrorists in different historical contexts, they have not been as widely influential[16] in more modern times as the books of so-called thriller writers, who have mixed genres of crime novels and spy and espionage to develop their newer variation, featuring terrorism as the focus of conflict and terrorists as the new villains to be stopped at all costs. Although the collapse of the Soviet Union and the Iron Curtain created a greater temptation for West-based thriller writers to look to other sources (besides the Soviets or their henchmen in the Eastern Bloc countries) for villains, books featuring terrorists were popular and slowly beginning to affect public perceptions about terrorists and terrorism decades before the breakup of the U.S.S.R. Many of these earlier works focused specifically on Middle Eastern terrorism, usually featuring Palestinian terrorists or their Arab allies in the roles of terrorist villains. Fresh with the real-life examples of Middle East terror violence at the 1972 Munich Olympics, or the years of ensuing airline hijackings, terrorist bombings, kidnappings, and assassinations, writers found that thriller books on the same subject could appeal to a wide audience but only if the premise of the book was in some way more audacious than reality as presented in news media. Bookstore shelves quickly filled with the commercial works of thriller writers focusing on Middle Eastern terrorism. One audacious and successful example of this was a 1975 book by the thriller writer Thomas Harris (the same person who would later write *The Silence of the Lambs*), *Black Sunday*,[17] an extremely popular story about Palestinian terrorists who attempt to detonate a bomb carried in the Goodyear blimp as it passes over America's sacred ritual—the Super Bowl. Although today (in a post-9/11 world) the premise for such a book may not appear so outlandish, at the time it did appear that way, and that made for a large part of its commercial success and crossover convergence to the Hollywood movie, with the late Robert Shaw in the role of an Israeli intelligence agent who . . . (sorry, you'll have to read the book or rent the video to find out what happens).

In works such as Harris's thriller and the film adaptation of the same, however, a disturbing stereotype of the terrorist as Arab began to emerge. This individual was a fanatic, fiercely anti-Semitic, passionate about his or her cause but without empathy for the humans who become sacrificed, a cold-blooded killer, and, in the end, something less than a human being. Unlike LeCarre's complex characters or the morally ambiguous individuals presented by Conrad or Dostoyevsky, these characters were mostly one-dimensional stereotypes, from their wooden dialogue to the clichéd descriptions of their appearance or personal habits.

Similar depictions, even if less significant by their numbers, began to appear of other terrorist groups—most prominently Irish terrorists and Latin or South American terrorists. Books such as William Granger's *November Man*[18] (dealing with the real-life murder of Louis Mountbatten by Irish terrorists) and later work by the techno-thriller writer Tom Clancy in *Patriot Games*[19] (dealing with IRA plots for assassination and revenge against British and, later, American targets) suggested more one-dimensional views of the terrorist as an Irish fanatic, a quasi alcoholic, and a cold-blooded killer—whether male or female. A later Clancy book, *Clear and Present Danger*,[20] dealt with the relationship of terrorist violence and narcotics trade in Colombia. In this second book, Clancy suggested an image of the modern narco-terrorist as a cross between zealous fanatic, ardent nationalist, and stereotypical drug lord/thug.

Though these books have had some impact on large commercial audiences in preconditioning (or reinforcing) stereotypes about terrorists and terrorism, a more prominent source of stereotyping has been the movie versions and adaptations of these same stories or original screenplays (is there such a thing as an original screenplay?) for action/thriller movies. The following are some more contemporary examples of films that, like the books discussed above, stereotype individuals as terrorists and simplify terrorist causes.

In 1994, the Hollywood director James Cameron wrote and directed Arnold Schwarzenegger in *True Lies*, a story about international intrigue, Middle East terrorism, a plot to detonate a nuclear device in Florida, and (of all things!) marital infidelity—the latter of which explains the film's title. A huge hit at the box office, *True Lies* also created considerable controversy for its stereotyping of Arabs as terrorists.[21] Fearing just such a backlash, Cameron pointed to the inclusion of a sympathetic and humorous Arab sidekick character for Schwarzenegger. As played by the actor Grant Heslov, the sympathetic or good Arab character is Schwarzenegger's "computer nerd," named Faisal. Critics, however, weren't swayed. Faisal's role is minor and plays like a token character when contrasted against the villainous bad Arab terrorists. The main terrorist villain in *True Lies* is Salim Abu Aziz, also nicknamed the "Sand Spider" to make him appear more ominous. As played by the veteran actor Art Malik (who also appears forever type-cast), he leads a large army of Arab terrorists of nondescript origin, linked together by what the movie calls the "Crimson Jihaad." Ironically, in many of the early scenes of the film, the actors playing Faisal, the good Arab, and Aziz, the bad Arab, actually physically resemble one another, although as the film progresses, Aziz's character slides into the more typical stereotype of Arab terrorists. As presented, Aziz and his men are sexist, violent brutes, and religious fanatics; they have more money than they know what to do with, and they are fiercely anti-American. Most possess exaggerated Arab features—dark skin, oily hair, and thick beards or unshaven faces—and they dress in para-military clothing baggy enough to barely conceal large automatic weapons, even when casually strolling the streets of Washington, D.C. To make the stereotype complete, they are also extremely incompetent.

True Lies compares with another film, released in 1996, called *Executive Decision*. As produced by the veteran action filmmaker Joel Silver, *Executive Decision* featured Kurt Russell as a think tank expert named Dr. Grant (a role perilously close to Tom Clancy's Jack Ryan character), who teams with Steven Seagal to stop a group of fanatical Arab terrorists who have seized a commercial airline jet en route to Washington, D.C. The terrorists are led by a character called Nagi Hassan, and early in the film we see him reading from the *Koran* and praying, so that there can be no doubt that he is Muslim. As played by actor David Suchet, Hassan's character pretends to want to exchange hostages on the plane for an imprisoned terrorist colleague, but in real-ity, he has packed the airline with nerve toxin bought in the black mar-ket from the former Soviet Union, and he intends to crash it into the nation's capital, using the jet as the delivery vehicle. Like the characters in *True Lies*, the terrorists in *Executive Decision* are portrayed as religious fanatics, misogynists, and brutal thugs who have plenty of money to finance their operations (presumably because oil-rich Arab states have financed their activity). Again, the cast of Arabs possess exaggerated physical features, such as dark skin, thick beards or unshaven faces, shaggy clothing, and poor grooming. Once more, they are also presented as hugely incompetent. These stereotypes are really no different, however, from those of countless other depictions of Arabs in films stretching back more than a century.[22]

These stereotypes of Arab terrorists can also be compared with Hollywood depictions of other groups, most prominently, Irish and South American terrorists. For example, in the 1992 film *Patriot Games*, adapted from the Tom Clancy book of the same name, Harrison Ford plays Dr. Jack Ryan, a scholar and a CIA analyst, who inadvertently foils a ULA (Ulster Liberation Army) plot to assassinate members of Great Britain's royal family. Ryan's success in foiling their assassination attempt triggers a campaign of revenge against Ryan's family (his wife and daughter) on American soil and later, once more, against the same royal family member, played by Edward Fox. The Irish terrorists, Sean Miller and Kevin (played by Sean Bean and Patrick Bergin), are presented as one-dimensional stereotypes of Irish people generally and Irish terrorists specifically. They are portrayed as radical zealots, myopic in their views about the British, hard drinkers, ruthless killers, and only marginally more competent than the Arab terrorists of the films mentioned above. Bean's character, Sean Miller, is so ruthless that it is mentioned that he once murdered a priest! They are also as willing to kill their fellow terrorists, when it suits their purposes, as they are committed to killing Ryan or the royal family. The latter point is also intended to suggest that they are really committed to nothing except mindless violence. Their physical appearance exaggerates the stereotype: They have pale skin, shaggy, unkempt hair and unshaven beards, and baggy clothing, and they keep alcohol always close at hand. Their image is contrasted in the film with that of another Irishman, played by the veteran actor Richard Harris, who appears to have no conscience about Irish terrorist violence but who helps Ryan avoid the negative publicity that may come from extending this terrorism to America. His character assumes that such bad publicity will hurt Irish American fund-raising to assist the IRA or other groups in Ireland. Thus, Harris's character does the right thing but for the wrong reasons.

These films can also be contrasted with another film vehicle for the action star Schwarzenegger, the movie *Collateral Damage*, released in 2002 to no small share of controversy. This film had been scheduled for release in the fall of 2001, but the release was delayed because of fear of a public backlash given its subject matter. In this film, Schwarzenegger stars as a Los Angeles–based firefighter whose wife and young son are killed by a terrorist bombing. Though not the primary target, his family was nevertheless caught in the same violent explosion. In the words of a character in the movie (mouthing the oft-repeated euphemism used by terrorists and even our own military spokespeople), these innocent victims were so much "collateral damage." Engaging in more than a bit of fantasy, even by Hollywood standards, Schwarzenegger's character departs on a journey of revenge, taking him into the heart of Colombia in search of the drug-trafficking Colombian terrorist leader Claudio Perrini, played by the actor Cliff Curtis. Claudio, who is initially suggested to be the nefarious El Lobo ("The Wolf"),[23] and his fellow narco-terrorists are depicted slightly differently from Arab and Irish terrorists in other Hollywood films. Here, they are given uniforms and natty berets, suggesting some kind of army, but again they have dark skin, long oily hair, and beards, and they live in general squalor as they protect their drug trade and plan their next terror mission. El Lobo's reason for bombing a building in America is to pay back the United States for military assistance to the Colombian government in the war on drugs. Again, a stereotype of the South American, and specifically Colombian, terrorist emerges. Terrorists there are also drug traffickers. Their uniforms suggest a past connection to revolution, most likely sponsored once upon a time by Cuba or the Soviet Union. They are also bloodthirsty killers without a conscience. In one scene of violence, ostensibly placed for no other purpose than to emphasize how psychopathic Claudio is, Perrini tortures one of his own men, forcing a poisonous snake down his throat and watching as the man suffers a slow and agonizing death. Claudio's treachery pales, however, next to that of his wife, the real El Lobo, who connives to use a child to carry a second bomb into a federal building to kill more Central Intelligence Agency (CIA) and State Department officials.

The forcefulness of the stereotypes employed in these films can be better appreciated when they are all, in turn, compared with another Hollywood blockbuster, starring Bruce Willis and dealing with the taking of hostages in a building in Los Angeles. The 1988 film *Die Hard*, itself a mix of disaster genre films such as *Towering Inferno* and the police/action films of previous decades, served up a template for many films that would follow, depicting terrorism and lone heroes.[24] In this film by director John McTiernan, Willis plays a New York police officer on vacation to visit his estranged wife at Christmas. As he reaches her place of business in Los Angeles, a monolithic building called the Nakatomi Tower, a group of armed men take the building, claiming all inhabitants as hostages. Willis spends the balance of the movie without shoes, running through broken glass, smoking cigarettes, making wisecracks, and shooting villains. These men are led by Hans Gruber, played by Alan Rickman, who initially makes pronouncements about the "greed" of the company whose building he has taken and makes other passing references to "Arafat" or the need to "teach a lesson," suggesting that he and his men are what they appear to be: terrorists. Shortly thereafter, however, they remove one of the hostages and isolate him, demanding that he give up a security code to allow them access to their real objective: a company vault containing $600 million in negotiable bearer bonds. The hostage exclaims in surprise, "You want money? *What kind of terrorists are you?*" Gruber laughs and replies, "Who said we were terrorists?" Although this was the director McTiernan's nod to the audience that not all things are what they appear, Gruber's rhetorical question is not as surprising as it sounds. From the moment these men appear on screen, they do some of the things we associate with terrorism, but their appearance and dialogue and ultimate actions have already cued the audience that something is amiss here. They do not fit the stereotype of the terrorists in other films mentioned above. These men are handsome, tall, strong, focused, articulate, well educated, and (with two exceptions) distinctly German. With long, carefully brushed hair, a fashionable wardrobe that includes rock star leather pants for some and Savile Row suits for another, they could as easily have fit in at a trendy restaurant in Santa Monica or Beverly Hills. Although the promotional literature for *Die Hard* describes Gruber and his men as terrorists, the audience (already preconditioned to see terrorists as something and someone different) knows them for what they are: elegant criminals.

When considered in this light, the impact of stereotyping specific groups as terrorists by their inclusion in literature, popular fiction, and, most significantly, Hollywood movies helps precondition a belief or expectation in any audience member that certain kinds of people and terrorists are indeed one and the same. In this way, they very forcefully contribute to a sense of *the Other*. Can there be any mystery about the fact that Middle East terrorists were initially suspected in the Oklahoma City bombing, well before anyone in the law enforcement community connected the act of terrorism to Timothy McVeigh?[25] This is not to suggest that books and movies alone are responsible for such preconceptions. But this kind of mass media representation of terrorism exerts a powerful influence on how we see and understand terrorists. This influence, however, must itself be contextualized in the ways mass media mythologize, or are used to mythologize, terrorism and how terrorists interact with news media.

Mythologizing Terrorism in News and Entertainment Media

One of the reasons why stereotypes about terrorists have influence on our discourse about terrorism is the presence of mass-mediated myths about terrorist groups and individuals.[26] Myths are fabrications crafted from analysis and ideas of half or partial truths. As fabrications, they become exaggerations or morph into claims that have little basis in fact. When employed in popular culture, however, they can have a lasting impact on public beliefs and discourse. In the context of terrorism, simple yet damaging myths support stereotypes such as those referenced above for Arabs, the Irish, and South Americans. For example, there is a myth that all Arabs are Muslim. In truth, many Arabs may be Muslim, but many are also Christian. Moreover, Islam as a religion reaches nearly half the world's population, including people around the planet. There is also a myth about Arabs suggesting that they are rich with oil money, although the reality is that only some countries with Arab populations have oil resources, and even within these countries, the wealth generated by the sale of oil is not shared by all in the population. Nevertheless, these myths about Arabs support the stereotypes of Arab terrorists as always being Muslim and having their activities always financed with oil money.

Some myths also contain the potential to become stories, reinforcing the same stereotypes but also with the capacity to make something, or someone, larger than life. In the context of terrorism, two examples of mythology constructed within news and entertainment media suffice to illustrate this point.

Earlier, in Chapter 4, I discussed the historical origins of the American Ku Klux Klan, emphasizing that what we understand as the Klan today is actually the product of three different incarnations of this group, the second of which occurred at the beginning of the past century. It was in this period that a book by Thomas Dixon appeared, recasting the history of Reconstruction in the South as told from the perspective of heroic Southerners. Dixon himself had been born in North Carolina and educated at Wake Forest College before graduate school at Johns Hopkins. As a young man, he had lived through the Reconstruction era he would later depict, first in *The Leopard's Spots*, published in 1902, and then in *The Clansman: An Historic Romance of the Ku Klux Klan*, published in 1905. Though the first of these books had been well received, the latter book (referred to as *The Clansman* for brevity) was a strong commercial success. *The Clansman* tells the story of a young ex-Confederate colonel named Ben Cameron, who is taken care of in a prison hospital by Elsie Stoneman, who turns out to be the sister of Cameron's captor, and chief foil, Phil Stoneman. Ben and Elsie fall in love. Phil Stoneman, in turn, falls in love with Cameron's sister, but much of this love story/metaphor for reconciliation of North and South is thwarted when Phil and Elsie's father, Congressman Stoneman, enters the story, determined to force Reconstruction on the

South and use Negroes as his tools. The Negroes of Dixon's story are not sympathetic characters; they are ignorant, savage, brutish, and degenerate. It is up to Cameron, as the Grand Dragon of the Ku Klux Klan, to save the South from Negroes and Reconstruction, in a way suggesting the Klan as a noble group of honor-bound men protecting tradition and civilization. Naturally, Dixon's historical revision takes great license with the facts. As suggested in Chapter 4, the origins of the Klan did include the membership of ex-Confederate officers who fancied themselves as honorable gentlemen. The historical record of the original Klan also documents that any nobility of purpose in the Klan quickly dissipated as its members became more openly violent and vigilante-like.

Here, popular fiction helped create a mythology of the Klan, a terrorist organization, promoting it as something more noble and acceptable. This representation of the terrorist group then went through a kind of media convergence, as D. W. Griffith purchased the rights to the story and set out to make a historic epic film that would later be retitled *The Birth of a Nation*. While keeping the roots of Dixon's story intact, Griffith added new and untried cinematic advances, including sweeping panoramic shots, different forms of close-up shots for contrast, and a huge and rich orchestral score that emotionally charged the epic historical/love story. Though *The Birth of a Nation* was not without its detractors, it did enjoy immense commercial success. Full-house audiences were willing to pay as much as a whopping $2 to see the film, and it grossed nearly $18 million in box office revenue before moving on to art house theaters.

It was in no small measure the result of the success of the book and later the film (which reached an admittedly larger audience) that the myth of the old Klan grew, transforming its reputation from one of racist and vicious thugs to one of noble and responsible gentlemen who only wanted to preserve what was best about the old South. When the Klan thus went through its aforementioned second incarnation under the guidance of Colonel Simmons, it was the existence of this myth, as developed through the mass-mediated convergence of book and cinema, that allowed the new group to be seen as nothing more than a service club and a fraternal organization, devoted to civic service. Such a myth allowed the membership ranks of the new Klan to swell well into the millions. Only the reporting of years of savage and violent activity by the Klan, now directed against unionists, immigrants, Catholics, and Jews, as well as blacks, along with reporting of financial improprieties, would again restore the public perception of the Klan as a group of racist and bigoted vigilantes/terrorists.

In this first example of mythology and terrorism, a mass-mediated mythology was developed outside the direction of the terrorist group, although the same group was quick to derive benefits and resources from this interaction. In a second example, I will now discuss how the individual terrorist known as Carlos the Jackal enjoyed similar benefits from the mythology constructed around his identity, although in his case, it is clear that he had a direct hand in developing the myth.

Ilich Ramirez Sanchez was the son of a well-to-do lawyer from Venezuela named Jose Altagracia Ramirez Navas. His father, an ardent Marxist, had named his son Ilich in honor of his favorite Bolshevik, Vladimir Ilich Ulynov, also known as Vladimir Ilich Lenin. As the first child and eldest son of Ramirez Navas, Ilich was raised in a relatively pampered environment (compared with his countrymen), yet he also learned much of the Marxist doctrine his father believed in, along with the history of the South American revolution. As a teenager, his father sent him abroad, first to study in London and later to attend the Patrice Lumumba University, a Soviet university designed for children of the ruling class in many of the Soviet Union's Third World client states. Here, Ramirez Sanchez met and interacted with Palestinian students, some of whom were connected to the Popular Front for the Liberation of Palestine (PFLP). Some of them introduced him to Wadi Haddad, who, along with George Habash, had been instrumental in helping start Palestinian terrorism against Israel. Ramirez Sanchez became smitten with their cause, or perhaps romanticized the idea of being a revolutionary, and decided to attend a military training camp for foreign students interested in helping the PFLP.

Thus began his transformation from the pampered and spoiled, slightly lazy university student to the terrorist who would remain in the headlines and on the most-wanted lists of international law enforcement agencies for decades. In that period of time, Sanchez would become known by his *nom de guerre*, Carlos, and would become involved in a series of high-profile bombings, assassinations, hostage takings, and hijackings. These episodes of terror violence included the bombing of several French newspaper offices, the tossing of hand grenades into a crowded area at the Drug Store St. Germain in Paris, rocket attacks on Israeli airliners, the murders of a fellow-terrorist-turned-informer, along with his two French DST (Directorate of Territorial Security) agents, and the kidnapping for ransom of several OPEC (Organization of the Petroleum Exporting Countries) ministers at the OPEC offices in Vienna. It was at the last of these that Carlos communicated to the press through a mediator, "Tell them I'm from Venezuela and my name is Carlos. Tell them I'm the famous Carlos.

They know me."[27] By this, Carlos meant to convey that because of his reputation for ruthlessness, the authorities should expect that he would kill hostages if he said he would kill hostages. But it was at this time that Carlos also discovered how much he enjoyed being notorious as well as noteworthy. Communicating to the authorities in a public way (with the assistance of the media), Carlos would eventually demand and receive a jet to fly both himself and his colleagues and hostages throughout the Middle East before collecting a ransom and eventually escaping from Dar Al Beida Airport, outside Algiers. While still in the bus to the airport in Vienna, Carlos waved at reporters and their cameras, behaving like someone who felt comfortable in the limelight. On the flight, he reportedly handed out autographs, trying to present himself as a modern Robin Hood.[28]

The OPEC terror operation gave Carlos an international reputation and demonstrated how the news media (covering every aspect of the hostage drama) could be manipulated to project his act of terror while also beginning the process of mythologizing his identity as an outrageous but successful terrorist. Media coverage also took note of hostage descriptions of him as well dressed and groomed, multilingual, and seemingly well educated. To this were added reports of his fondness for the opposite sex.

Over time, media reports would be quick to claim that Carlos was responsible for any terror attack, directly or indirectly. Carlos was now also called by an additional name, *the Jackal*, because a reporter from the London-based *Guardian* newspaper had found, among other things in a London flat rented by Carlos, a copy of the thriller writer Frederick Forsyth's novel *The Day of the Jackal*.[29] The news media would openly speculate about whether Carlos had been reading the book and had perhaps left it behind to intentionally influence the news coverage of him. That this would later prove false (the book reportedly belonged to the owner of the flat) did not matter; from that point forward, another mass-mediated convergence took place. Between news accounts of the legendary Carlos and news accounts labeling him with the title character of a best-selling thriller novel, Carlos became *the Jackal*.

The following years led to more media convergence as Carlos the Jackal became the focus of numerous fiction books. For example, Robert Ludlum, whose thriller books reached more than a 100 million copies worldwide before his recent death, wrote what became one of his biggest best-sellers, *The Bourne* Identity,[30] in 1980. Here, Ludlum fictionalized a story of Jason Bourne, an American agent with a constructed identity as the world's top assassin, designed to lure out the legendary Carlos the Jackal in an effort to capture or kill him. To make the media convergence all the more complete (if not confusing!), Ludlum even opened his book by reprinting actual articles from the *New York Times* and the Associated Press, dealing with the exploits of Carlos and helping to bring his now mythic reputation as a well-dressed ladies' man, ruthless killer, and master of disguise to a full boil. Carlos was James Bond as a terrorist. Ludlum did not allow Carlos to be caught or killed in *The Bourne Identity* and brought him back again in a sequel.[31] A made-for-television miniseries of *The Bourne Identity* helped complete the media convergence, and Hollywood movie treatments followed suit, though not using Carlos's name. One example of the latter, a 1981 film called *Nighthawks*, starring Sylvester Stallone and Billy Dee Williams as New York cops on an antiterrorist task force, dealt with their efforts to stop a notorious terrorist named Wulfgar, played by Rutger Hauer. Hauer's character, obviously modeled on Carlos, was in New York to kidnap and hold hostage representatives from the United Nations. The plot line was derivative of Carlos and the hostage taking at the OPEC headquarters in Vienna.

These acts of mass-mediated convergence and mythologizing helped Carlos enjoy a global reputation while also putting fear into the public. That many of his later years were spent actually on the run and in hiding, or that he would be captured in 1994 as a pudgy, middle-aged man, in humiliating fashion by French DST agents working in Sudan, seemed to matter little when these facts were placed against his myth. Carlos derived bravado from his mythology during his very public trial in Paris for the murder of the fellow terrorist/informant and the two DST agents. Although assisted by the counsel, he defended himself before ultimately being convicted. The release of the movie version of the *Bourne Identity*, in the summer of 2002, featured an adaptation of Ludlum's story, minus Carlos the Jackal. With the real middle-aged, pudgy Carlos languishing in prison, featuring and mythologizing him on screen no longer made sense.

Manipulation of and by News Media

Though mass-mediated stereotypes precondition public assumptions about terrorism, and these stereotypes in turn can be reinforced by terrorist mythology, the most effective opportunity for terrorists themselves to really control and manipulate mediated coverage of their messages resides in the interaction they have with news media. Paradoxically, this is also the place where news media have the ability to manipulate how and if terrorists communicate their message. To understand this paradox, I will first reexamine how news media are attracted to stories they consider newsworthy and how terrorism has been influenced by a desire for media coverage. I will then consider how a modern terrorist interacts with the news media in much the same fashion as a political candidate, with interviews and press conferences, as well as the selective use of videotaped messages for broadcast.

As suggested at the beginning of this chapter, mass media in the form of news media are often drawn (like entertainment media in books or movies) to stories that suggest conflict and the potential for what is shocking and sensational. Mainstream news media, of course, filter these requirements of conflict and the sensational through an initial requirement that a story also be of public interest. Stories describing terror violence almost always meet these requirements, for the violence first and foremost threatens public safety (thereby making it of public interest) and showcases conflict between terrorists and their target audience(s) in a manner that is increasingly dramatic and sensational.

As M. Cherif Bassioni, a recognized expert on international criminal law, has argued, this paradox has created a situation in which terrorists are drawn to news media coverage because they desire maximum publicity for their messages, while media coverage of terrorism magnifies the threat and resulting fear of terrorism to the public.[32] The desire for maximum publicity, in turn, creates a tendency in terrorist violence to select targets and engage in types of symbolic action that translate well visually in coverage and broadcast. *Translating well* means that the violence is a dramatic form of spectacle—something engaging enough to make a viewer stop and take notice.

Though terrorists may feel they are manipulating media in selecting targets for this purpose and engaging in sensational violence to ensure coverage, the opposite is actually true. In a world with media saturation, and news stories already devoted to coverage of so many issues relating to violence, death, and tragedy, guaranteeing coverage of a terrorism story requires visually compelling, dramatic, and therefore devastating violence on a larger and larger scale; sadly, this also means that with each act of terror the threshold for what is dramatic and truly terrifying must be raised. To put the case plainly, if you kidnap three missionaries in the Philippines and demand that the government release rebel leaders, you might get a print news story and some local coverage. If you detonate a bomb at an embassy or in a public market, killing hundreds and injuring more, you will get more attention from print and broadcast news media.

Palestinian terrorists learned this lesson in the early 1970s. Though they had not been the first to hijack planes as a means of terrorism to draw media attention, they did learn that media coverage would be acute if several planes were hijacked and subsequently blown up. This they did at Dawson's Field in Jordan, in September 1970, while holding a press conference and in the full view of journalists and with cameras running. The resulting spectacle, which was watched by people around the world, only served to raise the bar or standard for what would be considered sensationalized, violent terrorism.

Terrorist groups also learned that manipulation of media could be achieved if they approached news reporters acting less like terrorists and more like politicians or public relations experts. To that end, some terrorists discovered the advantages of selective access to information— a regular tactic of political candidates seeking favorable media coverage. By granting interviews to some but not all reporters as individuals, or newspapers or television networks as entities, terrorists could hold out the promise of a competitive scoop while also guaranteeing coverage and possibly more favorable treatment in a story.[33]

In a similar vein, Ted Kaczynski, the so-called Unabomber, left a trail of murders, attacks, and bombings over 17 years (from 1978 to 1995), killing three people and injuring 29 others, creating a sense of national hysteria, and making many university professors uneasy about receiving and opening their mail. Kaczynski once offered certain news organizations unlimited access to what he called his "manifesto," a complete statement of his political philosophy, but only if they agreed to publish it in its entirety. The *New York Times* and the *Washington Post* took him up on his offer, sparking a national debate about journalist ethics and manipulation by terrorists.

❖ AGENDA SETTING AND THE FRAMING OF TERRORISM IN NEWS MEDIA

As described in this text, terrorism is seen as a discursive process, provoking and affecting the discourse of multiple target audiences who negotiate the meaning (among other questions) of what terrorism is, who is a terrorist, and how these target audiences should respond to a terrorist act or threat. Precisely because dissent terrorists understand how news media frame stories about terrorism (e.g., conflict, sensational violence, powerful visual imagery, alarming threats to public safety, and moral allusions to good vs. evil), they not only help shape what stories will be told but they also influence what attributes of a story (e.g., extreme violence with the beheading of kidnap victims in Iraq) will be emphasized. In this way, they help influence the media agenda, which primes a public agenda about the exigency of the terrorist act or threat. The media agenda, however, is also influenced by government sources and decision makers—all of whom may also be part of the target audiences for a terrorist act or threat. Without question, they too help influence what the news media decides is newsworthy.

For example, consider how effectively the Bush administration influenced not only domestic news media but also global news media coverage after September 11. The acts of terrorism on that day created an obvious agenda, and the administration skillfully, and almost artfully, gilded the mass media lily to create appropriate frames for focusing public attention. These included the thematic emphases of *good versus evil*; *us versus them*; *you are either for us or against us*; *fear, self defense*, and *defense of freedom*; *international unity*; the *axis of evil*; and, of course, the all-purpose *war on terror*, to name but a few. For six years after the event—really up to 2007 and the run-up to the 2008 presidential election—the terrorism agenda remained front forward in media coverage. It was so dominant an agenda, and so effectively framed, that it not only necessitated the selection of a particular kind of Democrat (Senator John Kerry, *a decorated war hero*) to run against President Bush, but it also informed the way the Bush campaign would negatively argue against Kerry's candidacy (questioning his patriotism and whether he was "fit to lead"), as well as determining where Republicans would choose to hold their convention—in New York City, only a few weeks before the anniversary of the 9/11 attacks. There was no way to mention the campaign without invoking the 9/11 terrorism agenda and seeing it through any of the various frames suggested by the White House. As described in a previous chapter, Osama bin Laden's videotaped speech to America, only days before the final vote, provided the extra reminder of this agency and the saliency of the frames of *us versus them* and *good versus evil*.

Agenda setting and framing of terrorism was not unique to news media in this country. Indeed, in Great Britain, for example, the same agenda and many of the same frames featured prominently in news media stories. One study of newspapers in the United Kingdom covering the period between 2001 and 2004 found that several prominent British newspapers, including *The Daily Telegraph/The Sunday Telegraph* and *The Times/Sunday Times*, had coverage of the frames *war on terror*, along with *good versus evil*, *us versus them*, and *international unity*, in amounts that resembled U.S. coverage for the identical period.[34]

A different study of German news media in a similar time period observed that German newspapers made use of many of the same frames in their coverage while enjoying robust increases in readership.[35] Of several German papers studied, including the *Frankfurter Allgemeine*

Zeitung, the *Suddeutsche Zeitung*, the *Tageszeitung*, and *Die Zeit*, between September 12 and December 20, 2001, it was observed that the terrorism agenda trafficked in frames, such as *good versus evil*, and later shifted to *geopolitics* and *world order* once the Bush administration set a course for the military invasion of Afghanistan.[36]

The White House also effectively continued to influence news framing by later inviting journalists to become embedded with coalition troops in Iraq. This was in contrast to what had been allowed in the first Gulf War, when journalists and reporters were forbidden access to theaters of combat and restricted to pool reporting and press briefings by Department of Defense officials at encampments a safe distance away in Qatar. In this new invasion of Iraq, the administration claimed they would welcome transparency, and they allowed 700 journalists and reporters to travel with U.S. and British troops as they moved into Iraq—all covered and reported within the frame *war on terror*.[37] Transparency was a noble goal, or a subtle ruse. The reality of embedding journalists with troops (on patrol, in combat, eating meals together, etc.) was that eventually and inevitably relationships were formed that affected the objectivity of the reporting.[38] One significant study on embedding, objectivity, and media frames compared coverage from embedded and nonembedded reporters in Iraq and found that "news coverage from embedded reporters during the invasion and occupation were significantly more positive toward the military than those of nonembedded reporters."[39]

❖ TERRORISM AND NEW MEDIA

While broadcast and print media undoubtedly reach a substantial portion of the world's population, they are in many respects media in decline. Indeed, what television did to newspapers and magazines in terms of attracting consumers, the Internet is now doing to television. Both broadcasting and print media are dependent on advertising revenue to supplement subscription rates or viewing/listening audiences; unfortunately for both, however, their readership and audience shares have declined. For that reason, they have been steadily migrating toward the Internet for several years. It is not at all uncommon today to find Web sites for television, for radio (network or affiliate), or for the vast majority of newspapers—all of which offer their media content online. As of 2009, one study of Internet usage placed the global number of users at just over 20% of the world's population, or roughly 1.5 billion users.[40] While most of this occurs in more developed and affluent parts of the world, such as the United States, Europe, and parts of Asia, the fastest and largest growth in usage has occurred in Africa and the Middle East.[41] In the years since 9/11, dissent terrorist groups have turned increasingly to new media technology and computer-mediated communication. The appeal of this new media for dissent terrorists is not difficult to fathom. The Internet, which originates from the original research projects involving the U.S. government, defense industries, libraries, and academic researchers (with both ARPANET and DARPANET), is generally understood as a network of networks. Like a spider's web, constructed with redundant connections, it is (and has been since its earliest days) decentralized and relatively unregulated or censored. It allows both asynchronous (communicator and audience(s) do not all have to be present at the same time) and synchronous (individuals can chat or text with one another at the same time) communication in virtual spaces, with virtual identities, or even total anonymity. Equally significant, with the advent of newer and more affordable technology, it is easily accessible and navigable for even the most novice users. Even though these groups will easily disseminate information through a variety of Web sites, according to Gabriel Weiman, "e-mail, chat rooms, e-groups, forums, online magazines, and virtual message boards—are used more and more by terrorists."[42]

While numerous strategic purposes can be served by new media for terrorism (e.g., recruitment of new volunteers, fund-raising to support operations, sharing of logistical information, instruction for tactics such as bomb making and the like), the single objective most relevant for our discussion concerns the manner in which terrorists increasingly have come to rely on the Internet as a means of communicating with their target audiences. Sometimes this is done as sheer propaganda, other times as a means of claiming credit (real or false) for an attack, and still others for the purpose of communicating a threat—as with the rash of communiqués from the *al Qaeda in Iraq* fighters, concerning the fate of the kidnap victims, some of whom were later beheaded on camera and online.

In all these respects, dissent terrorist groups have come to resemble American political operatives. In America, candidates who want to run increasingly negative campaign attacks against their opponents (especially in a general election) sometimes face hostile public and media scrutiny for particularly nasty attacks, usually in the form of advertisements. In recent elections, this has created a situation in which individuals and political interest groups become *surrogates*, also known as 527s,[43] who do the dirty work for the candidate they support by creating negative political advertisements against another candidate and launching these ads on their Web sites. A typical example of this in the 2004 election could be seen with the group known as the *Swiftboat Veterans*, whose negative attacks on John Kerry helped derail his campaign for the presidency. In 2008, there were more of these kinds of groups and, indeed, even individuals who found ways to participate in the election by launching homemade advertisements online at Youtube.com.

Of relevance for our discussion of terrorism is that these ads were launched on the Internet and then eventually experienced media convergence—crossing from the Internet to television news media—once reporters discovered their existence and decided to use them in framing a story about the election. The key point here is that when these stories were shown on television news, they inevitably had to replay the ad as part of the story, thus extending the shelf life of the original online appearance.

❖ TERRORISM AND PAID MEDIA

In a manner similar to that described above, modern dissent terrorist groups have become sophisticated about controlling messages for broadcast and distribution. Like political candidates who use *paid media*, as in political advertising, to guarantee that a message gets out to the public, some terrorists have resorted to producing their own videos for selective release, either through the Internet or directly to news entities, in the understanding that such material will be broadcast to a larger audience. The use of this video can have different effects for the multiple audiences it reaches.

For example, in early October 2001, only weeks after the September 11 attacks on the United States, Al Jazeera television, a small and increasingly influential news channel operating in the tiny nation of Qatar, broadcast the first of what would become several exclusive videotapes of Osama bin Laden. Al Jazeera's exclusive prize scooped all other news media entities, forcing them to rebroadcast what had already been broadcast with credit to the small news station. Many would complain that Al Jazeera was becoming a pawn for bin Laden and his al Qaeda organization,[44] but others correctly observed that the very same video was being broadcast intact by all major Western television news media[45] feeding off the initial broadcast from Al Jazeera. Indeed, CNN was eventually compelled to make an interim arrangement with Al Jazeera, offering to exchange resources for news stories for a chance to get the same exclusives the small station was getting.

Over time, numerous videos were released, and most were aired. The bin Laden tapes, although shot in a style suggesting an amateur working with a simple video camera, were actually fairly sophisticated rhetorical artifacts. Intended not only for his Arab audience in the Middle East—a fact suggested by his speeches in Arabic and his choice of Al Jazeera as the news station for broadcast—these tapes also targeted a larger global audience, including the United States, her allies, and those neutral countries President Bush had warned in his speeches.

The imagery within each tape was compelling. In one tape, as shown in Photo 9.1a, bin Laden is shown at what appears to be a meal, perhaps at a wedding reception of a family member. For Western audiences, the tape at first glance appears to depict a normal meal and celebration. But a slower frame-by-frame analysis, as shown in Photo 9.1b, shows that bin Laden is acutely aware of where the camera is and how he appears in it. The event is clearly staged to depict normalcy in his life, as well as a seeming indifference to the threats of imminent military action from President Bush in response to the attacks of 9/11.

Photo 9.1a   This still, taken from a video and later broadcast on all news outlets around the world, begins by showing bin Laden in a normal meeting, with an aide and a friend, getting ready to be seated for a meal. The approach looks like a home video.

In another tape, bin Laden is shown standing with his close collaborator, Al-Zawahri, in what appears to be a training camp for al Qaeda fighters. Of note here is the way bin Laden and Al-Zawahri are dressed in white, with open robes, and standing comfortably among so many armed men, whose own faces are concealed beneath wrapped scarves.

The image created by their appearance suggests an attitude of open indifference and defiance of the United States. It is also here that a certain gentleness in bin Laden's demeanor comes across. He does not appear angry or visually fanatical—both characteristics that a viewer would expect given his reputation, history, and rhetoric in other videos. But here, as in later videos, he exudes a sense of calm that communicates either inner strength or a false sense of confidence. Both possibilities make the video in some way more frightening for a global audience, while perhaps giving solace to the Arab audience he wants to inspire.

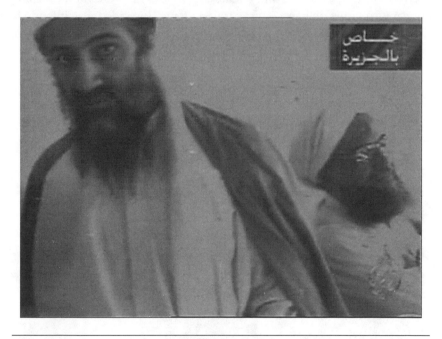

Photo 9.1b   A frame-by-frame analysis of the same video, however, reveals that bin Laden knows exactly where the camera is.

In a later, now famous video, he appears before what seems to be a cave entrance with a gun at his side, holding a microphone as he delivers a vitriolic speech in a relatively calm voice. A partial translation of his words, warning of an apocalyptic religious conflict between Muslims and non-Muslims, shows him to say,

These events have split the world into two camps: the camp of the believers and the camp of the infidels. It is the duty of every Muslim to make sure that his religion prevails. The winds of faith and the winds of change are blowing against the infidels who occupy the land of the Prophet Mohammed, may peace and God's blessing be upon him.

Then to the American audience he adds,

To America and its people I say a few words: I swear to God, who raised the sky without pillars, that America and those who live in it will not be able to dream of security until we live it on the ground in Palestine, and before all of the infidel armies leave the land of the Prophet, may peace and God's blessings be upon him.

Again, his voice is soft and yet confident. There is a disconnect between the harsh rhetoric and threatening tone of his words and the calm appearance of his delivery. This is no accident. This video was intended, like the others, to assert his leadership in the challenge against the United States and Israel, while also continuing to threaten Americans by reminding them of September 11, with veiled references to a lack of "security."

Photo 9.2   This still, lifted from another video shown by news outlets around the world, depicts bin Laden and an aide visiting an al Qaeda training facility. Note how the men are dressed and how this compares with the al Qaeda fighters around them.

Because of his decision to give exclusive access to the tape to Al Jazeera, bin Laden ensured its broadcast in the Middle East and its rebroadcast in other parts of the world. His words were frightening for an American audience already on edge, and the calmness of his demeanor, along with the presence of his gun, suggested that more of a struggle was coming.

Photo 9.3   In this still, taken from another video played on news outlets, bin Laden speaks directly into the camera and to his various audiences, including viewers in the United States.

Terrorism, Codes, and Cues

On occasion, terrorist video messages may more clearly parallel political advertising techniques. In American political advertising, we have often witnessed the use of what Kathleen Hall Jamieson, Dean of the Annenberg School for Communication at the University of Pennsylvania, calls "codes" and "veiled visual cueing." Found in many kinds of political advertising but especially effective in television advertising, codes are the double meanings of words or other signs and symbols: those meanings that are literal and obvious and those that amount to subtext, the meaning between the lines. Jamieson writes,

> Persuaders often leave clues in the form of otherwise inexplicable details, small lapses in generic propriety, minute blunders—all designed to whisper and gently prompt the sensitive susceptible audience to

divine subtextual meaning. In swayable audiences, these cues invite code switching—a shift from the explicit to the implicit text.[46]

On occasion, this code switching is cued by something visual in the video of the political advertisement. For example, during the 1990 U.S. Senate race in North Carolina, Democratic candidate and former Charlotte Mayor Harvey Gantt faced off against incumbent Senator Jesse Helms and actually led in the polls with 10 days to go in the campaign. Helms then released a series of television ads targeting Gantt for what appeared to be normal campaign issues concerning abortion and affirmative action. In each of these ads, however, were visual cues to subtextual messages about *race*. Gantt was African American, and each of Helms's ads was used to prime the audience about race and the need to avoid electing a black man to the Senate. Naturally, these cues were subtle (in Jamieson's language, a "whisper"), but whether through slowing down a video of Gantt, replaying something he had said but in the process exaggerating the slurred sound of his voice, or using black-and-white photos of Gantt, with his skin color altered to make him appear very dark, the cue to race was unmistakable. For those white voters with the unspoken potential for racial prejudice, the ads primed the issue and raised it as a campaign litmus test. After the 10-day period, Helms won the reelection, taking back 62% of the white vote in his state.

Photo 9.4a In this still, taken from a video released to and broadcast by worldwide media outlets, a man charges dramatically toward the camera and the viewer on horseback.

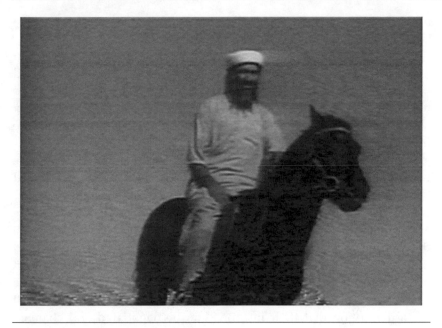

Photo 9.4b   A second still from the same video shows the rider to be Osama bin Laden. Note that he never conceals his identity, and in this picture he does not appear to be armed.

The same technique may be seen in a final bin Laden video (Photos 9.4a, 9.4b). This video shows bin Laden on horseback, at first galloping toward the camera as if he is charging it and later casually riding his horse. Here, we may see a more careful form of visual cueing to the subtextual message. The image here suggests a warrior, although in this piece, he does not appear armed. He does, however, appear purposeful and determined.

For Western audiences, unfamiliar with the history of Islam or the more specific controversy in modern Jerusalem over the status of the so-called Wailing Wall, the sight of bin Laden on horseback conveys only a strong, determined individual and, in our uniquely American way of seeing things, the image of a cowboy. But for audiences in the Middle East conversant with such history and controversy, the symbolism of this imagery is altogether different. Here, we find the subtextual message in this video. Many Jews regard the Wailing Wall (HaKotel HaMa'aravi in Hebrew, or just the "Kotel") as a deeply sacred site for Judaism. It is considered to be the only surviving remnant of the Second Temple, and a chance to pray before it has great symbolic meaning for Jews used to being in a historical state of Diaspora, without a homeland. Controlling access to this wall is one of the reasons, if not the most important reason, that makes Jerusalem a nonnegotiable issue for Israel when negotiating with Palestinians.

Conversely, many Muslims also see this wall today as a significant holy place. It is claimed that at this spot Prophet Mohammed tethered his winged stallion, called al-Burak, shortly before he ascended to heaven. This story is also called the *Night Journey and Ascension of Mohammed* and has been retold many times, inspiring more literature than even that addressing the miracles of his birth.[47]

Many Israelis today complain that the Muslim connection to the wall is only contrived to complicate negotiations over Jerusalem and legitimize Palestinian claims to the area. They observe that in earlier times, Muslims recognized the al-Aqsa Mosque as the holy site where Mohammed ascended to heaven. Muslims reply that what Jews call the Wailing Wall was never part of the original Second Temple, and they cite archeological evidence suggesting that the wall is only part of a retaining structure built to support the mount above. The response and reaction of both sides speak about the power of symbols, as well as to the notion that their meaning can be negotiated and changed over time.

This bin Laden tape shows the al Qaeda leader on a stallion. The horse and rider supply the visual cue, leading bin Laden's Middle Eastern audience to the subtextual message. Given his own rhetoric about the United States and Israel, there is little doubt that bin Laden means to suggest a connection to the symbolism of Muhammad and al-Barak, as well as reminding the audience about the Wall and Jerusalem.

❖ SUMMARY

In this chapter, we considered how public perceptions about terrorism are primed by representations of terrorists in entertainment media, such as popular cinema and genre literature. These allowed us to generalize about how terrorists and news media share a symbiotic, mutually exploitative relationship. We also considered from a perspective of cultural criticism how public discourse about terrorism is primed by mediated stereotypical images of terrorists and terror violence and how these stereotypes are supported by mythology about terrorism, as well as by the news media's relationship with terrorism. Additionally, we have reviewed the different ways in which terrorists and governments engage in agenda setting and framing of terrorism and, in turn, how dissent terrorists make use of new media on the Internet and have become increasingly sophisticated about creating the equivalent of political advertisements to communicate with and sometimes threaten target audiences, with little more than the carefully timed appearance of words and images.

In the end, all these factors regarding mass media combine with the official rhetoric of our leaders, ideas about terror as rhetorical symbols, and the rhetorical choices that are made in defining an event as terrorism or an individual as a terrorist. The combination allows us to see how terrorism truly is best understood as a communication process between terrorist and audience(s), the meaning of which is socially constructed in the public discourse and dialogue we have about the subject. Although this understanding may not shield us from the physical dangers of terror violence and destruction, it can help us understand *why* we feel threatened by this violence and how it operates rhetorically. The violence of the tragedy on September 11 was visited physically only on those in New York, Washington, and Pennsylvania, but the psychological and emotional damage that came from the fear of these acts was shared by people in all corners of the world. Knowing how and why we feel threatened by what is, in the end, a communicative, rhetorical process is a starting place for considering how we should process the meaning of terrorism and, in the future, how we might respond.

❖ NOTES

1. Seth Mydans, "Researchers Put Together the Story of the Khmer Rouge," *New York Times*, September 15, 2002, p. 10.

2. Karl Jackson, *Cambodia 1975–1978: Rendezvous With Death* (Princeton, NJ: Princeton University Press, 1992) at pp. 243–244.

3. David Chandler, Ben Kiernan, and Chanthou Boua, *Pol Pot Plans the Future: Confidential Leadership Documents From Democratic Kampuchea, 1976–1977* (New Haven, CT: Yale Center for International and Area Studies, 1989) at p. 183.

4. For example, Germany's radio broadcasts during World War II often employed British and American defectors such as William Joyce or Mildred Gillars (referred to as "Lord Hee Haw" and "Axis Sally") in an attempt to draw the sympathies of Britain and the United States to the Nazi cause—or, at the very least, to undermine the morale of British and American troops in the European theater. However, these radio broadcasts, operating in a larger marketplace of radio media, had to compete with many other programs and entertainment—ultimately unsuccessfully.

5. S. I. Hayakawa, *Language in Thought and Action*, 2nd ed. (New York: Harcourt, Brace & World, 1964) at p. 233.

6. For example, early internal propaganda references to the party described communists as "peace loving, progressive and scientific," while describing outsiders as "war-mongering, bourgeois, reactionary, idealist and imperialist." Ibid., p. 236.

7. See, for example, Elisabeth Rosenthal, "Beijing in a Rear-Guard Battle Against a Newly Spirited Press," *New York Times*, September 15, 2002, p. 1.

8. For more, see Jonathan Glover, *Humanity: A Moral History in the Twentieth Century* (New Haven, CA: Yale University Press, 1999) at p. 121.

9. Robert Gellately and Ben Kiernan, *The Specter of Genocide: Mass Murder in Historical Perspective* (Cambridge, New York: Cambridge University Press, 2003) at p. 333.

10. Joseph Conrad, *The Secret Agent*, rev. ed. (1907; New York: Oxford University Press, 1998).

11. Robert Louis Stevenson and Fanny van de Grift Stevenson, *The Dynamiter* (New York: Longmans Green, 1903).

12. Indeed, in *The Dynamiter*, the main protagonist is a terrorist named M'Guire—no doubt, a nod to the Molly Maguires mentioned earlier in this book when discussing symbolism. For more on this, see Barbara Arnett Melchiori, *Terrorism in the Late Victorian Novel* (Oxford, UK: Taylor & Francis, 1985) at p. 67.

13. Fyodor Dostoyevsky, *The Devils*, trans. David Magarshack (New York: Penguin Books, 1953); originally published as *Besy* (1871).

14. Liam O'Flaherty, *The Informer* (New York: Random House, 1925).

15. John LeCarre, *The Little Drummer Girl* (New York: Alfred A. Knopf, 1983).

16. I make this point based on the gross number of books sold and their ultimate media convergence from books to screenplays for cinema or television. Of the authors mentioned, some (like Conrad) have had their works translated to the silver screen, and others (such as LeCarre) enjoy similar convergence and lasting commercial success today. These authors are, nevertheless, considered to have produced works of literature—which makes their work less appealing to a mass audience.

17. Thomas Harris, *Black Sunday* (1975; New York: E. P. Dutton, 2000).

18. William Granger, *November Man* (New York: Warner Books, 1993).

19. Tom Clancy, *Patriot Games* (New York: G. P. Putnam's Sons, 1987).

20. Tom Clancy, *Clear and Present Danger* (1989; New York: Berkeley Publishing, 1990).

21. See, for example, Narmeen El-Farra, "Arabs and the Media," *Journal of Media Psychology*, 1(2), 1996: 1–7. El-Farra notes, "When it was released, this movie created anger among Arab Americans. The Arab community felt that the negative portrayal of Arabs, namely as terrorists, encouraged existing stereotypical views. Not only were the Arabs in the film religious fanatics bent on destroying the world, they were also sexist, racist and idiotic" (p. 4).

22. See, for example, Jack Shaheen, *Reel Bad Arabs: How Hollywood Vilifies a People* (Northampton, MA: Interlink Books, 2001). In this work, Shaheen traces back some 1,000 films that stereotype Arabs as terrorists, oil-hoarding sheikhs, American-hating Muslim fanatics, brute murderers, sleazy fanatics, and abusers of women.

23. Perhaps this is intended as a homage (or more likely, a time-honored Hollywood tradition of plagiarism) to the real-life terrorist Carlos the Jackal.

24. If imitation is the sincerest form of flattery, this movie was amazingly flattered by the copycat films that followed, including 1992's *Under Siege* (*Die Hard* on a battleship), 1995's *Sudden Death* (*Die Hard* on the hockey rink), and 1997's *Air Force One* (*Die Hard* on the president's personal plane).

25. Jonathan Alter, "Jumping to Conclusions," *Newsweek*, May 1, 1995, p. 55.

26. El-Farra, "Arabs and the Media," *Journal of Media Psychology*, 1(2), 1996: 4.

27. Carlos, as quoted in John Follain, *Jackal: The Complete Story of the Legendary Terrorist, Carlos the Jackal* (New York: Arcade, 1998) at p. 77.

28. Ibid., citing the memoirs of Iran's OPEC Minister Jamshid Amouzegar. Amouzegar was one of the hostages taken by Carlos.

29. Frederick Forsyth, *The Day of the Jackal* (New York: Viking Press, 1971).

30. Robert Ludlum, *The Bourne Identity* (New York: Marek Books, 1980).

31. Robert Ludlum, *The Bourne Ultimatum* (New York: Random House, 1990).

32. M. Cherif Bassioni, "Terrorism and the Media," *Journal of Criminal Law and Criminology*, 72, 1981: 1–55.

33. This was one of the ways CNN and later Al Jazeera television gained a competitive advantage over other networks.

34. Anmol Kalsi, "A Content Analysis of UK and US Newspaper Coverage of the War on Terrorism 2001–2004," *Knowledge Politics Quarterly*, 1(2), 2008: 2–60, at p. 33.

35. Anke Struver, "Spatializing Terrorist Networks: Geopolitical Narratives and their Representations in German Print Media after 9/11," *Journal of Economic and Social Geography*, 99(1), 2008: 125–130, at p. 127.

36. Ibid.

37. For an excellent treatment of this, see Frank Rich, *The Greatest Story Ever Sold: The Decline and Fall of Truth* (London: Penguin Group, 2006) at p. 74.

38. Lisa Finnegan and Norman Solomon, *No Questions Asked: News Coverage Since 9/11* (Santa Barbara, CA: Greenwood, 2006) at p. 89.

39. Michel Haigh, Michael Pfau, Jamie Danesi, Robert Tallmon, Tracy Bunko, Shannon Nyberg, Bertha Thompson, Chance Babin, Sal Cardella, Michael Mink, and Brian Temple, "A Comparison of Embedded and Nonembedded Print Coverage of the U.S. Invasion and Occupation of Iraq," *The Harvard Journal of Press/Politics*, 11(2), 2006: 139–153, at p. 149.

40. See report by Miniwatts Marketing Group at http://www.internet-worldstats.com/stats.htm. Accessed as of 6/9/2009.

41. David Gray and Albon Head, "The Importance of the Internet to the Post Modern Terrorist and its Role as a Safe Haven," *European Journal of Scientific Research*, 25(3), 2009: 396–404, at p. 397.

42. Gabriel Weimann, "The Psychology of Mass Mediated Terrorism," *American Behaviorial Scientist*, 52(1), 2008: 69–86, at p. 76.

43. This refers to the portion of the Income Tax Code, which defines these entities as nonprofit organizations.

44. Fouad Ajami, "What the Muslim World Is Watching," *New York Times Magazine*, November 18, 2001.

45. Mohammed El Nawaway and Adel Iskandar, *Al-Jazeera: How the Free Arab News Network Scooped the World and Changed the Middle East* (Cambridge, MA: Westview Press, 2002) at p. 173.

46. Kathleen Hall Jamieson, *Dirty Politics: Deception, Distraction, and Democracy* (New York: Oxford University Press, 1992) at p. 85.

47. See, for example, Annemarie Schimmel, *And Muhammad Is the Messenger: The Veneration of the Prophet in Islamic Piety* (Chapel Hill: University of North Carolina Press, 1985) at p. 159.

Index

About the Author

Joseph S. Tuman is Professor of Political and Legal Communications at San Francisco State University, where he regularly teaches upper-division courses in rhetoric and terrorism, political and legal communication, argumentation and advocacy, and technology and human communication. A past recipient of the Jacobus tenBroek Society Award for Teaching Excellence, he has also taught at the University of California, St. Mary's College, the New School for Social Research, and Paris II, the top law school in France. He is the author of *Political Communication in American Campaigns* and the coauthor of numerous books, including *Freedom of Speech in the Marketplace of Ideas*, and *The Bedford St. Martin's Guide to Public Speaking*. He has also been the journal editor of *Contemporary Argumentation & Debate: The Journal of the Cross Examination Debate Association*. His work has been featured in news publications, such as the *New York Times, Los Angeles Times*, and the *San Francisco Chronicle*, and he has served as a network analyst for news programs on ABC, NBC, CNN and CNN International, FOX, and the BBC. In 2009, he received an Emmy nomination for his political analysis and currently appears as a regular political commentator for CBS in the western United States.